IMAGES
of America

WINFIELD

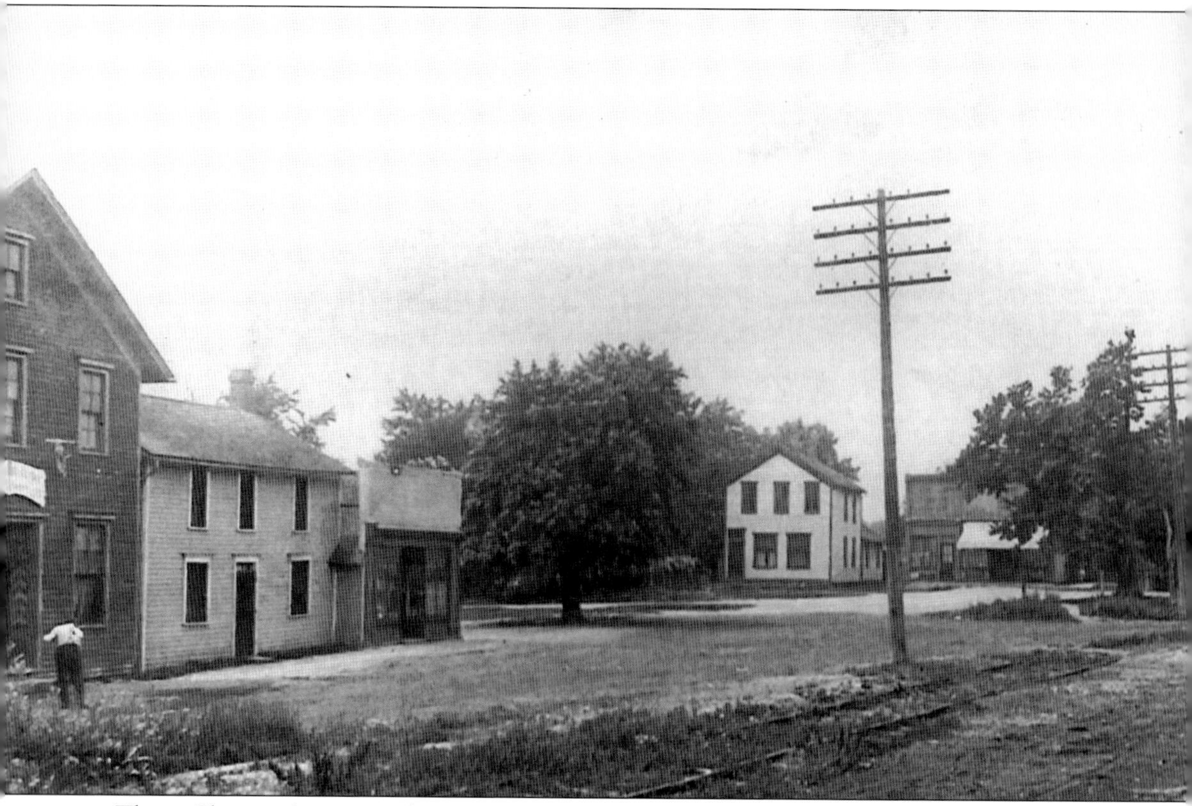

This is Chicago Avenue in the center of Winfield around 1919. Paul C. Sehnem is shown standing outside in front of Sehnem Hall, formerly Hamm's tavern, on the far left. Peter Schmidt's home and meat market are to the right of Sehnem Hall, while the old Mueller home and Baum store that was run by Katherine Baum Enders is in the background, across what is now Winfield Road. Chicago Avenue was the commercial hub of early Winfield. (Courtesy of the Winfield Historical Society.)

On the Cover: Members of the Caecilia Mannerchor are onstage at Forester Hall in 1905. Among the members standing in the photograph are, from left to right, Paul Sehnem, Matt Tinnes, Joseph Baum, Aloysius Wolff, and Michael Tinnes. The director of the group, Jacob Baum, is seated in the foreground. The group performed at the opening of Forester Hall in 1902. (Courtesy of the Winfield Historical Society.)

IMAGES
of America

WINFIELD

James R. McGuire

ARCADIA
PUBLISHING

ISBN 978-1-4671-2728-8

Published by Arcadia Publishing
Charleston, South Carolina

Printed in the United States of America

Library of Congress Control Number: 2017953090

For all general information, please contact Arcadia Publishing:
Telephone 843-853-2070
Fax 843-853-0044
E-mail sales@arcadiapublishing.com
For customer service and orders:
Toll-Free 1-888-313-2665

Visit us on the Internet at www.arcadiapublishing.com

To my late mother, Nadine McGuire, who always believed in me. She was not only my mother but also my trusted friend and confidante.

Contents

Acknowledgments

I would like to recognize the hard work and dedication of the Winfield Historical Society not only in restoring Hedges Station, the oldest standing depot in Illinois, as a local history museum but also in collecting, maintaining, and presenting the history of this unique community. Each member of this organization, which first started in 1978, has been extremely helpful in educating me about Winfield's past and present. They have all been generous in their support of my work for them at Hedges Station and are to be commended greatly. I would also like to recognize the prior work of Louise Spanke in her book *Winfield's Good Old Days: A History*. Spanke's book is a fascinating read about all that was early Winfield, and the information that appears in this book was first shared in hers. She presents a great deal of information that I additionally relied upon in learning the history of Winfield. Much of the information that she presents in her book is shared in the captions for this book and credit goes to her work. My thanks go to the people of Winfield, especially those who have shared their own photographs and who have allowed the historical society to copy for its collection. David "Skip" Higgins, Alice Besch, Michael Klein, JoAnne Pins, John Karwoski, Fritz Karwoski, and Kevin Davis are among the many people whose time and contributions are greatly appreciated. I would also like to thank all visitors to Hedges Station. Your interest and sharing of stories always are welcome and fascinate me. Additionally, my thanks go to the entire staff at the DuPage County History Museum in Wheaton for assisting me in searching for additional photographs. They were all extremely generous and very helpful. Finally, I would like to thank my title manager, Stacia Bannerman, for her guidance and tremendous patience in helping me with this project. This was a new endeavor for me, one which was trying yet fun, but Stacia was there every step of the way.

Introduction

It could have be LeRoy or Greenwood,
Both proposed as the village name
But Winfield it became,
And Winfield it remains.

Spawned by the choice of a rail route
Connecting Chicago and Galena
A stop midway between Wheaton and Junction
The first village building, the depot.

In '84 the name might have become Frederick Park
But incorporation failed
And the original appelation held fast.

Many were the early occupations:
Butcher, blacksmith, wagonmaster, seamstress,
Schoolteacher, saloon keeper, cooper, carpenter,
Shoemaker, mason, physician, postmaster.

At the turn of the century,
A single wooden sidewalk on Church Street
From the railroad to St. John's,
Higgins's store, Schmidt's ice house, the Baum store,
The Forester Hall, Hamm's Tavern.

And there was the river . . .
Digging turtles from the mud
Searching for clams
Skating in winter, skinny-dipping in summer,
Diving from the top of the CA&E bridge.

Surviving the depression and World War II
Winfield pressed on in the 50's.
The '54 census put the village population at 862
And though growth has steadily increased
We still have a pleasant ambiance.

We who live here now
Owe a debt to the early ones
The pioneers and planners
Who started, then persevered.
It could have been LeRoy or Greenwood
But thankfully it's friendly, inviting,
Winfield!

This is a poem that is currently part of the collection of the Winfield Historical Society at Hedges Station. The poem came mounted with a small drawing. Who wrote this poem and the year that it was written are both not known, though the name inscribed on the drawing is W. Atkinson. Nonetheless, this poem represents the ideal start to an introduction to what this book covers.

Welcome to Winfield! With the town officially incorporating in 1921, Winfield's roots go back much farther. One could go back to the end of the Black Hawk War. Louise Spanke, in her book *Winfield's Good Old Days: A History* writes that the Black Hawk War ended on September 26, 1833, after the Treaty of Chicago was signed by the United States and 77 chiefs. The federal government assumed possession of lands all throughout northern Illinois, including land in what would eventually become DuPage County. Land was open and available and settlers would soon come. Early settlers included the Gary brothers, Erastus, Jude, and Reverend Charles, who started an early settlement in the area that featured a sawmill, schoolhouse, blacksmith shop, and post office. Better known as the Gary's Mill settlement, this was the start of what would become a vibrant community. Other settlers to the area included Caspar Kline, John Murray, Proctor Cooley, Elias Jewell, and Peter Burr Curtis. Col. Julius Warren, who would start the town of Warrenville just to the south and west of the Gary's Mill settlement, was the largest landholder in the greater Winfield area for over 30 years.

DuPage County was created on February 9, 1839. It was one of the first counties in Illinois to adopt a township form of government within its first decade of existence. What to call this particular new township was up for debate. Charles Gary chaired a meeting in Warrenville, where votes were split on the names LeRoy and Greenwood. Why those names were considered is anyone's guess, but to break the deadlock, county commissioners settled on the name *Winfield*, a nod to Gen. Winfield Scott, a hero in the Black Hawk War who was believed to have come through the area, though nothing was ever definitively confirmed.

The new township attracted more settlers, especially with its proximity to the DuPage River. Sanders Howarth and his wife moved into the area, as did James Prescott Doe and Edwin C. Beggs. Doe's land holdings had extra significance for another "resident" in the area, that being the railroad. The railroad came in thanks to the charter received by the Galena & Chicago Union Railroad Company. The Wheaton brothers, Jesse and Warren, were quick to offer the railroad company right-of-way through their land if they could be guaranteed a station. Their offer was readily accepted, though there was still the matter of creating a stop halfway between their land and the Junction lands, which would later become West Chicago. The ideal locale settled upon for this midway stop was the land owned by James P. Doe.

Doe did not immediately seize this new opportunity. After construction of the railroad was completed in 1849, the township sought to create a road that would connect this new stop with its neighbors to the south in Warrenville. Locals took action beginning in 1850, while Doe would not formally file his plat of land with the DuPage County recorder until 1853, under the name Fredericksburg. However, because of this delay, the railroad did not recognize this name. Rather, it chose the name Winfield, most likely after the township and it honoring Gen. Winfield Scott. Doe began to sell off his land, and among his first sales was to John Hedges, who immediately set about to construct a station for the railroad. Hedges Station, as this building came to be known, was the first building in what would become Winfield. Though it was only a depot for five years, Hedges Station has remained an important part of Winfield's history—not only for being the home for Michael and Eva Besch's family but also as the home for the Winfield Historical Society's local history museum today.

Winfield's early ethnic heritage was predominantly German. Many of its early residents had come over from German lands during the 1850s. There was Nicholas Dieter, merchant Caspar Voll, and brewer Paul Warner, and Seiber brothers Michael, Bartel, and Donatius, who had come over from southern German lands. Nicholas Enders and George Wolff brought their families over from the Alsace-Lorraine region, while the Klein, Steils, Tinnes, Welter, Hamm, Schmidt, Huels, and Mueller families came over from Ernsen in the Bitburg region of the German lands.

Jacob Mueller was quick to purchase Paul Warner's brewery business, while Mathias Huels was proprietor of a general store.

Winfield's early residents were quick to answer President Lincoln's call for troops to fight in the Civil War. Among those residents eager to serve was John Klein, who had left the German lands because he did not want to be forced to serve in their military. He was quick to enlist in Company I of the 105th Illinois Infantry Regiment because he fell in love with his new home here.

Post–Civil War Winfield still welcomed settlers. Henry Germann came over from the German lands, and he built a saloon and general store that he would sell to George Fehrman and his son, William, in 1879. Gilbert Higgins came to the area via Ohio, bringing with him his farming and coal enterprises. One of Gilbert's sons, Sanders Moses, eventually leased the general store that George Fehrman had purchased, and Higgins Store was born. While Sanders passed away suddenly at the young age of 42, his devoted wife, Barbara, ran the store operations and raised their family. Higgins Store served the Winfield area from 1894 to 1956.

While Higgins Store would become the community's complete store, this was not the only enterprise in the community. There was the Winfield Cooperative Creamery that was managed by Maurice Dooley and John Wilcox. Nicholas Berkes worked as a tailor, Anton Schmitt produced boots and shoes, John Hamm operated his tavern, and William Hastert constructed coffins and furniture.

The young community still did not have a formal name, though. Sure, it was recognized as Winfield by the railroad, but that was not is official incorporated name. An attempt at incorporating under the name Frederick Park looked like it would succeed at first, but injunctions filed against such a move prevented this. Colonel Warren was among the parties to file an injunction to prohibit Frederick Park's incorporation, as he claimed that there was not a sufficient population to make that move. While incorporation failed initially, the community continued to grow and thrive.

Peter Schmidt set up his home and business along Chicago Avenue, which was rapidly becoming the commercial hub for the community. Schmidt not only had his meat business, which was quite popular with residents, but he also constructed his own pond that he would use to cut ice blocks to use for his shop and also for residents. Jacob Baum purchased Mathias Huels's general store, and his wife would carry on the business after his death, just as Barbara Higgins did for Higgins Store after Sanders's death. John Heinz, Milton Player, J.C. Schramer, John Klein, and John Besch worked as dairy farmers.

It was not always all work in the community. Residents did engage in many social activities. For many years, social gatherings revolved around John Hamm's popular tavern. His death in 1895 changed that. Hamm's widow, Magdalene, married Paul Sehnem, and the tavern was converted into Sehnem Hall, with its special significance being that it was the site of the first village board meeting after Winfield's official incorporation. Baseball was quite popular, but it was the DuPage River that brought out additional activities including ice-skating, skinny-dipping, clam digging, and hunting for frogs and turtles for those in the community, both young and old. Picnics and friendly gatherings often could be found at the old lime kiln that was north of what would become Gary's Mill Road. Skiing and sledding were often found at Boie's Hill. Perhaps no other place brought people together more than Forester Hall, widely regarded as the social gathering center for the community.

Forester Hall opened in 1902 as the preeminent meeting place for the Winfield Social Club and Catholic Order of Foresters, both of whom had the same membership of most of the adult men in town. The Madonna Court consisted of most of the adult women in town, and during gatherings for dances, Jacob Baum's Caecilia Mannerchor would entertain the guests.

Many of the residents in the community would attend mass at St. John the Baptist Church, which started on February 21, 1867, with a warranty deed that conveyed the plot of land held by Colonel Warren to Rt. Rev. James Duggan, bishop of the Chicago Diocese, for the use of constructing a church, rectory, and school. The hard work put forth among the community's early residents, including Michael Besch, Nicholas Fuchsen, Nicholas Schramer, Jacob Berkes, and others, made this vision a reality. Fr. John Wiederhold may have been its longest-serving pastor, but it was Father Corbinian who presided over the first wedding to be held at the church, as well as its first baptism. The hard work that went into bring the church to Winfield was needed once again after a lightning strike on August 16, 1906, started a blaze that burned down the church. The church and community banded together once again to rebuild the structure, and rebuild it they did, as the new church was dedicated just over one year later.

Most of the children who grew up in the community would often attend both schools that called Winfield home. The Catholic school was a dream realized by Sisters Paula, Euphemia, and Michaela. The first school that was located across from the church doubled as the first rectory. Classes in the morning were taught in English, while German was the language for afternoon classes, a practice that continued until World War I. Students who planned to continue their education in high school would often attend the public school for their last couple of years to get the proper certification to move on.

Today's Winfield is most often thought of in conjunction with Central DuPage Hospital. The hospital was not always here though. Just as the village had its humble beginnings, so too did hospital facilities in the community. Jesse Forsythe found Winfield an ideal locale for her new rest home that she planned in November 1897. The two-story structure was known more for its practice of getting its patients rest, often through massages. Jesse and her sister Christine presided over the institution until the latter's death in 1907. The following year, Jesse sold her farm and intended to retire to Wheaton, a plan that was cut short by her death in 1909. Forsythe's property quickly was given to three charitable organizations, chief among them being the Jewish Consumption Relief Society, to start a new institution for those suffering from tuberculosis. For the better part of the next half-decade, the Chicago-Winfield Tuberculosis Sanitarium was a fixture in Winfield. By the end of this period, with a declining list of patients staying at the facility, the sanitarium passed to the ownership of the Central DuPage Hospital Association. The rest, as they say, is history.

It is this history that makes this community unique. It is this history that is revealed in the following pages, to give the reader a sense of what it was like coming to Winfield, growing up in Winfield, and ultimately, living in Winfield. As the last verse of the poem says, the community owes a lot to its early pioneers and planners. This could have been LeRoy or Greenwood. This could have been Fredericksburg or Frederick Park. At the end of the day, though, simply put—it's Winfield!

One

Meet Winfield's Many Early People

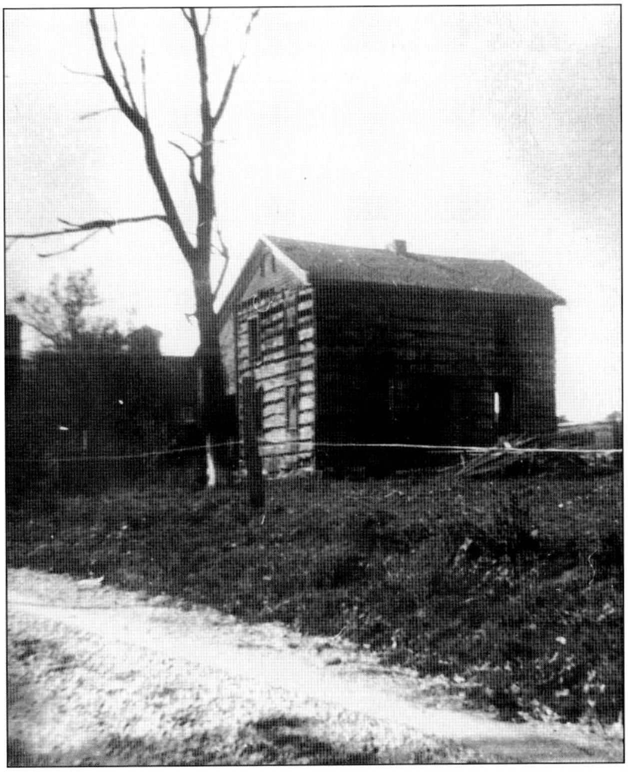

This is a photograph of the two-story log home that Casper and Lettisha Kline raised their family in. This home would remain with the Kline family from 1835 until 1969, when the DuPage County Forest Preserve District acquired it. The land today is now Kline Creek Farm, a living history museum located just north of Winfield in West Chicago. (Courtesy of the Winfield Historical Society.)

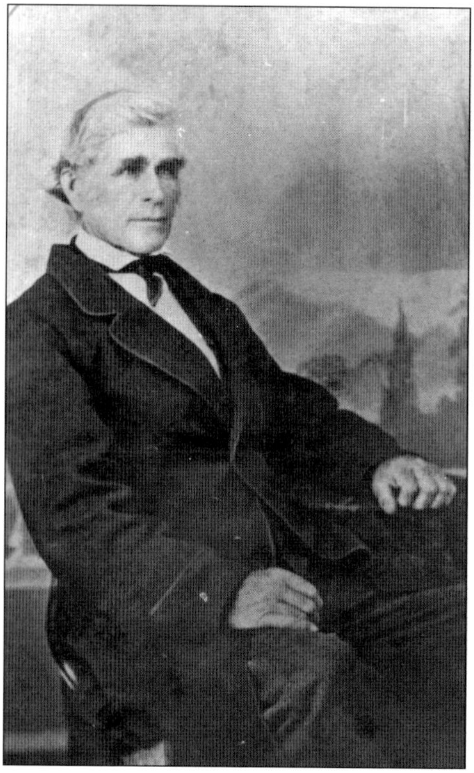

These are photographs of Casper Kline, who staked a claim in the area in 1835 and constructed a two-story log dwelling for his family, and his wife, Louisa (Krebell) Kline. Casper, born in Holland, described himself as a farmer. He served as a supervisor, of sorts, along with James Woodward and John Grant, to oversee the early developments of roads in the area. Casper and Louisa settled in the area just north of the original Gary's Mill Settlement in 1835. They brought with them the first four of their eventual six children. One son, John, would serve as DuPage County sheriff for three terms during the 1870s. (Both, courtesy of the Winfield Historical Society.)

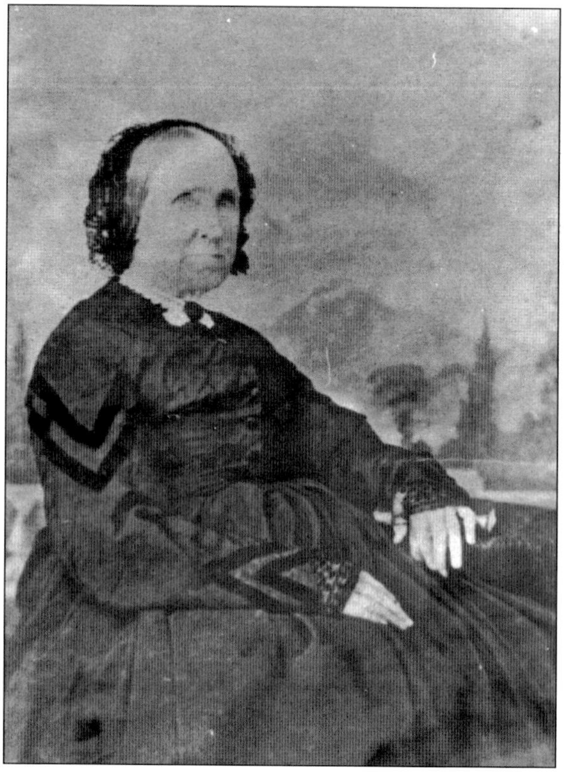

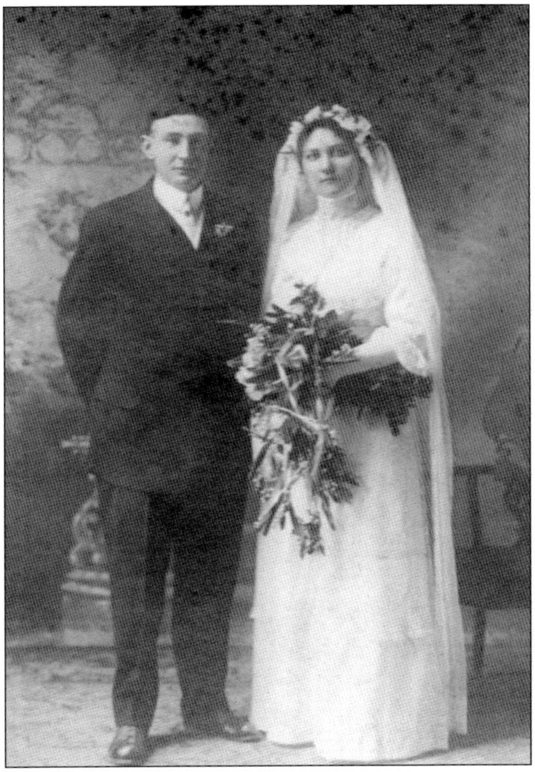

Joseph and Anna (Fortman) Kline are pictured on their wedding day in April 1912. Joseph and Anna owned the family farm before it was acquired by the DuPage County Forest Preserve District in 1969. They raised their three sons John, Robert, and George here on the family farm. John, George, and their mother were the final occupants of the farm before relinquishing it. Robert served in the Coast Guard during World War II and was briefly stationed in Greenland as well as on the American mainland. Many of Robert's letters and postcards to his family while he was in the service are a part of the Winfield Historical Society's ongoing collection. (Both, courtesy of the Winfield Historical Society.)

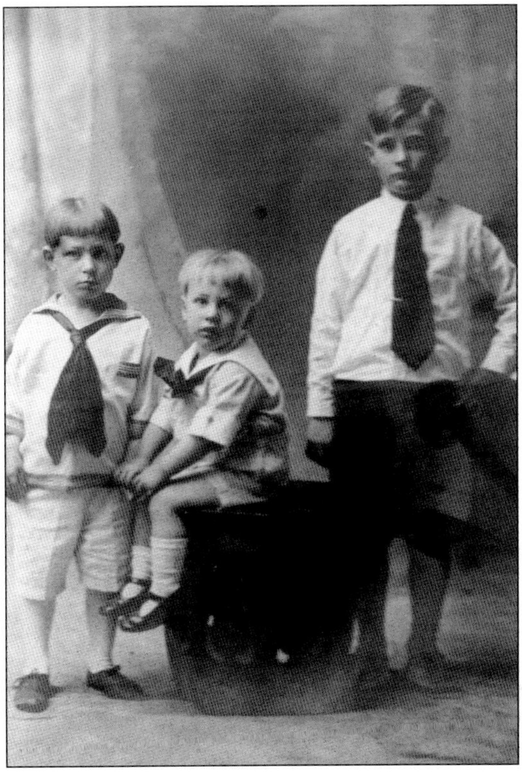

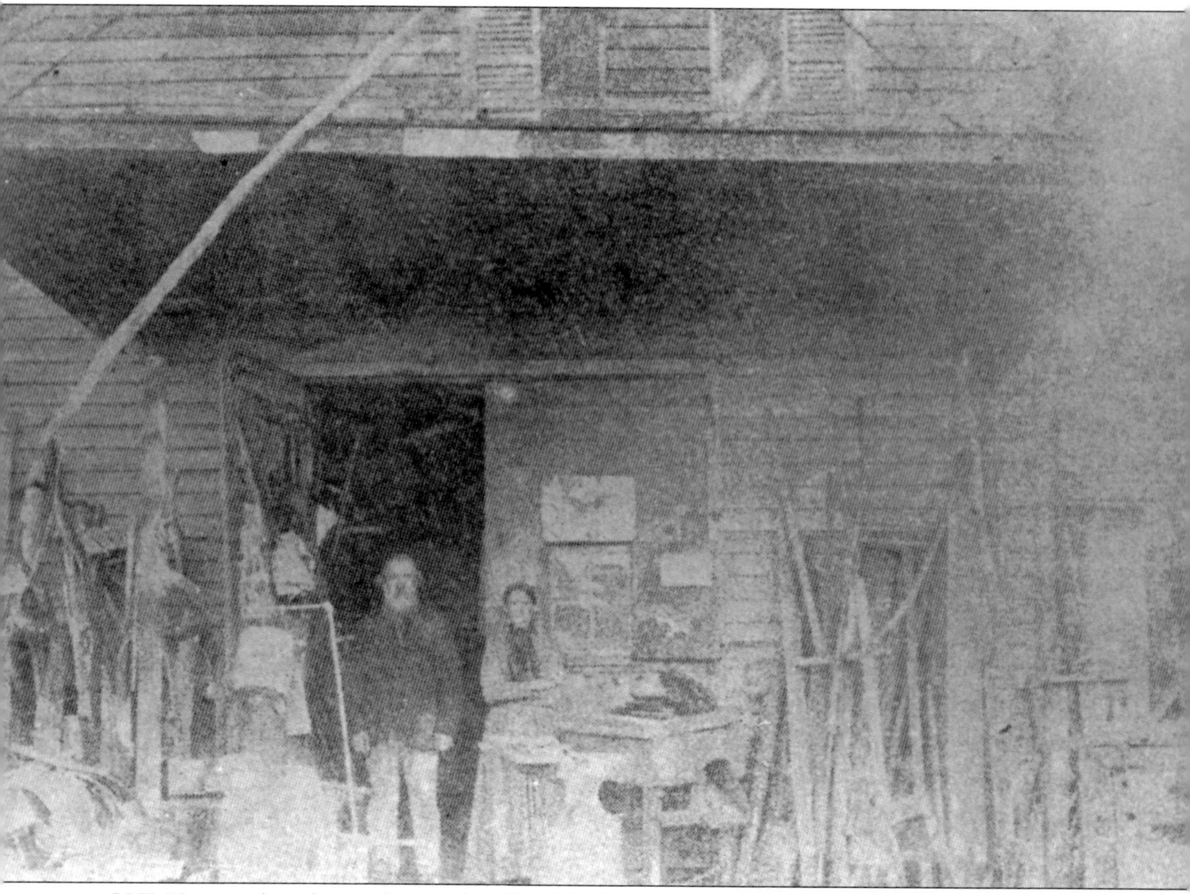

H.T. Hammschmidt stands outside of his blacksmith shop in early Winfield. Hammschmidt had set up shop during the 1860s. Louise Spanke notes that this was according to the census that had been done by Col. Julius Warren. Hammschmidt's blacksmith shop was one of many set up by new merchants in the area, including Alphonso Hale's butcher shop and Herman Hammschmidt's wagon shop. Whether or not H.T. Hammschmidt and Herman Hammschmidt were related is not known. This photograph is most likely from the 1860s or 1870s. (Courtesy of the Winfield Historical Society.)

Edwin C. and Lettisha (Higgins) Beggs are pictured in 1890. Edwin came to the United States from Great Britain in 1845. Shortly after applying for citizenship in New York in September of that year, Edwin came to DuPage County. He fell in love and married Philona Cooley in October 1849. Philona was the daughter of Proctor Cooley, another early settler to the area. Edwin did settle in Winfield, but not before seeking fortune in California during the Gold Rush. This was quite common among settlers in DuPage County. Philona died after giving birth to their third child. Edwin married Lettisha in October 1869, and together they resided on the family farm that later became part of Winfield Heights. Lettisha is seen sitting outside in the undated image below. (Both, courtesy of the Winfield Historical Society.)

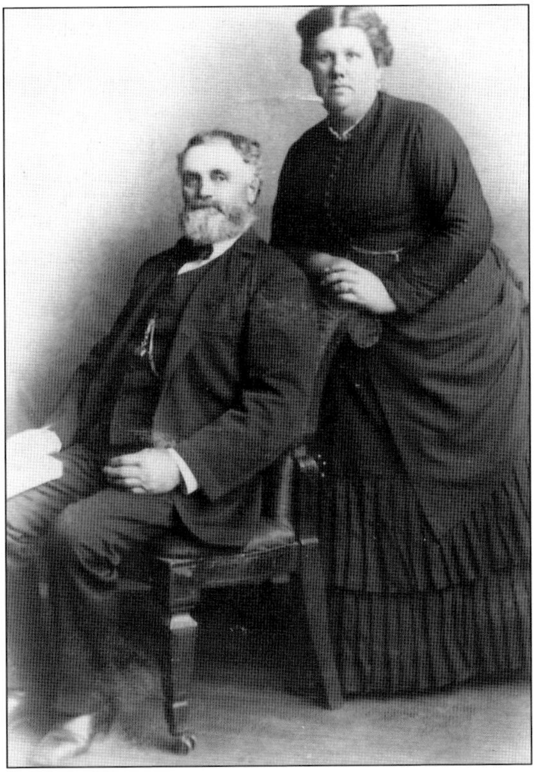

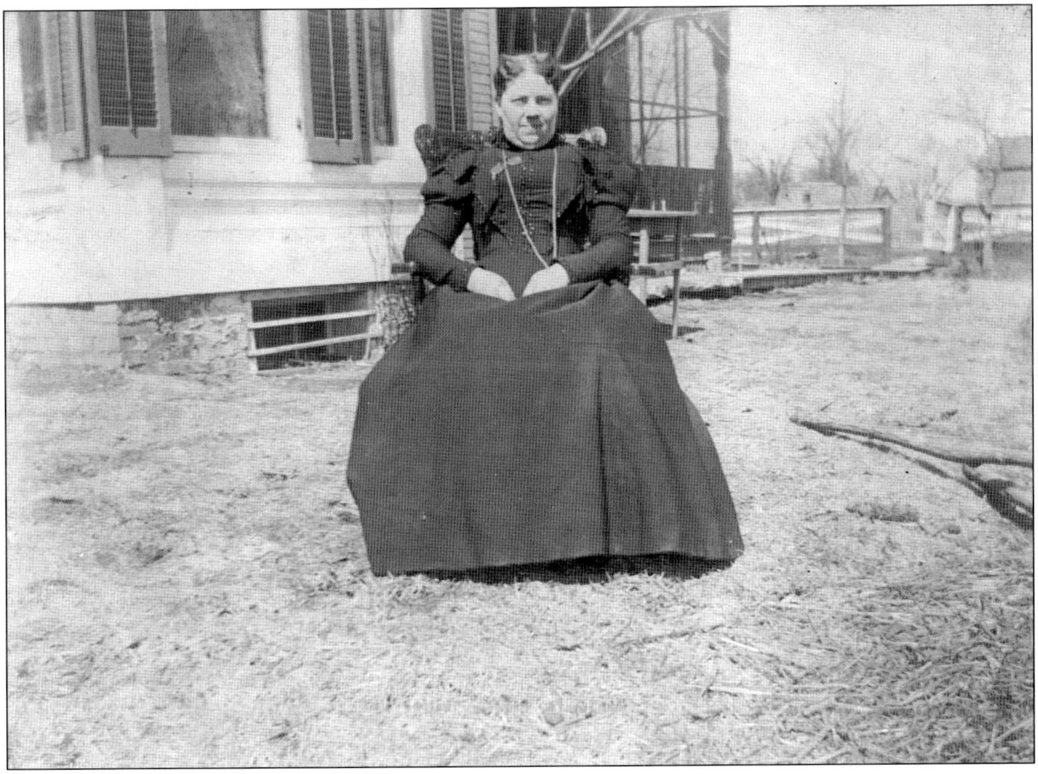

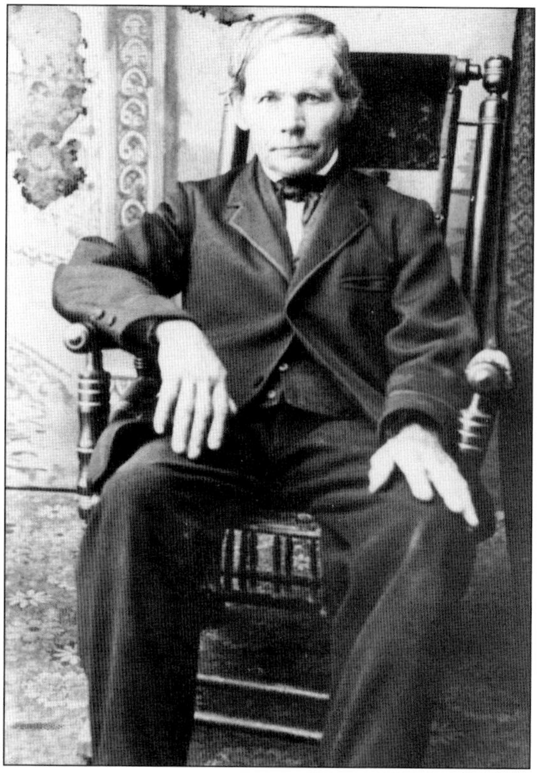

Donatius and Margaret (Griebel) Sieber are pictured in 1885. The Siebers, along with other early settlers Paul Warner, Casper Voll, and Nicholas Dieter, were known as South Germans. Michael Sieber originally settled in St. Charles in 1850 before moving to a new settlement in the area on Geneva Road in 1852. Louise Spanke notes that shortly after settling here, he summoned his brothers Donatius and Bartel to join him. The brothers sailed from Hamburg to New York before finally arriving in the area to join Michael. Donatius later fell in love and married Margaret Griebel. (Both, courtesy of the Winfield Historical Society.)

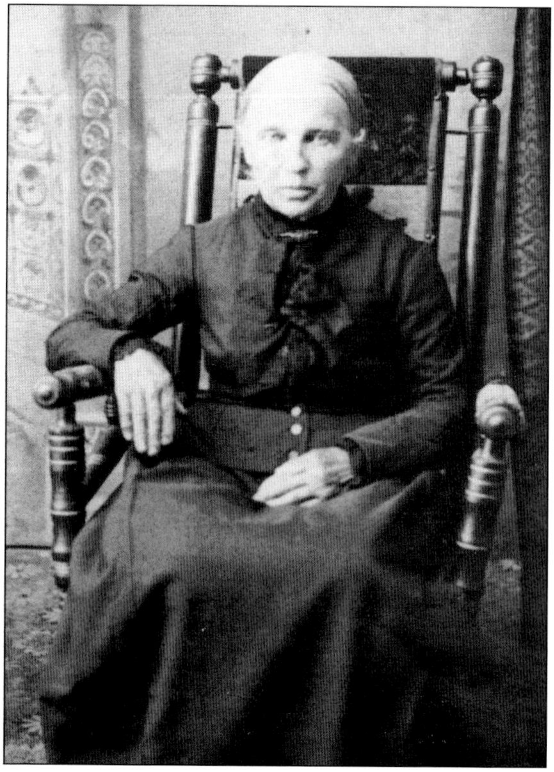

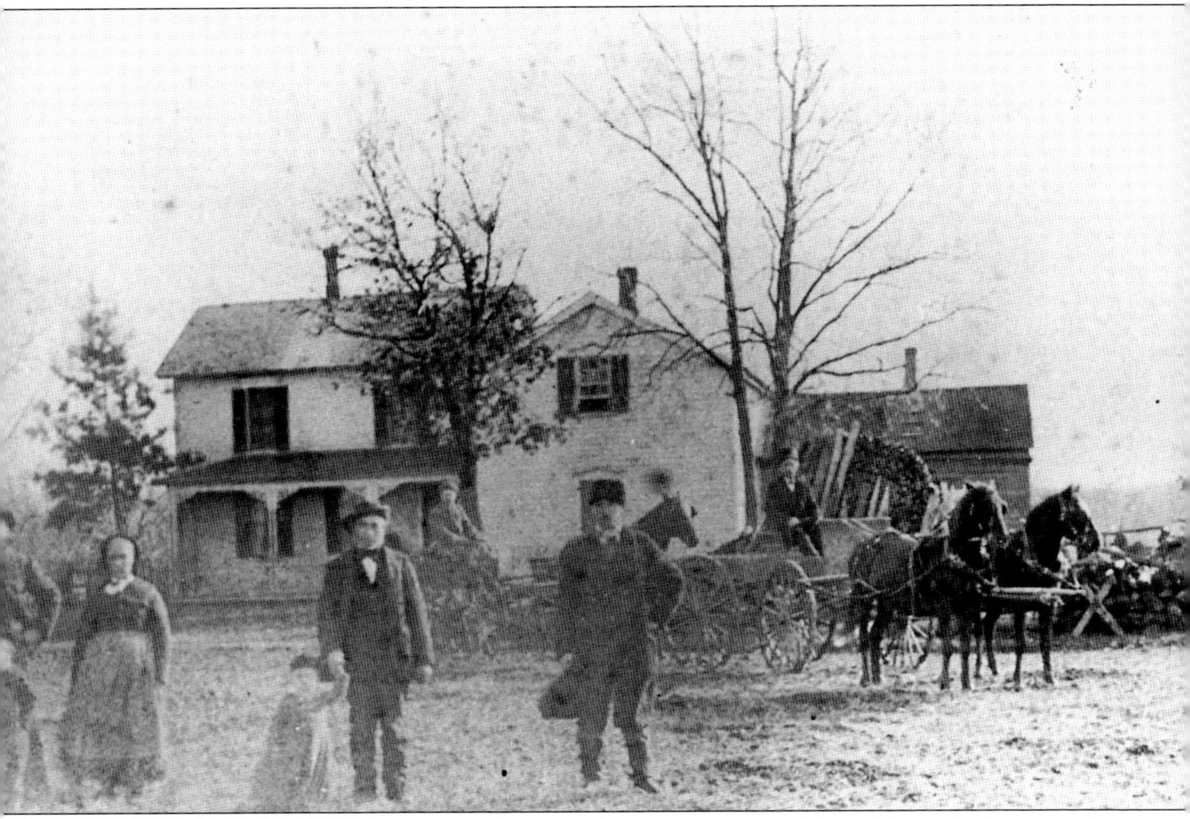

John and Margaret Schramer's family is shown at their home in 1890. The adults in the foreground are, from left to right, Mathias, Margaret, John Sr., and John Jr. Michael and Nicholas appear in the background. The children are John Jr.'s sons John (left) and Nicholas. The family residence that is set to the back was the second to have been built on the Schramer farm. John joined Schneider Berkes and three other area residents to urge the bishop of Chicago, Rt. Rev. James Duggan, to bring a church to the community. The home pictured here later became the residence of Richard and Vivian Blossfield. (Courtesy of the Winfield Historical Society.)

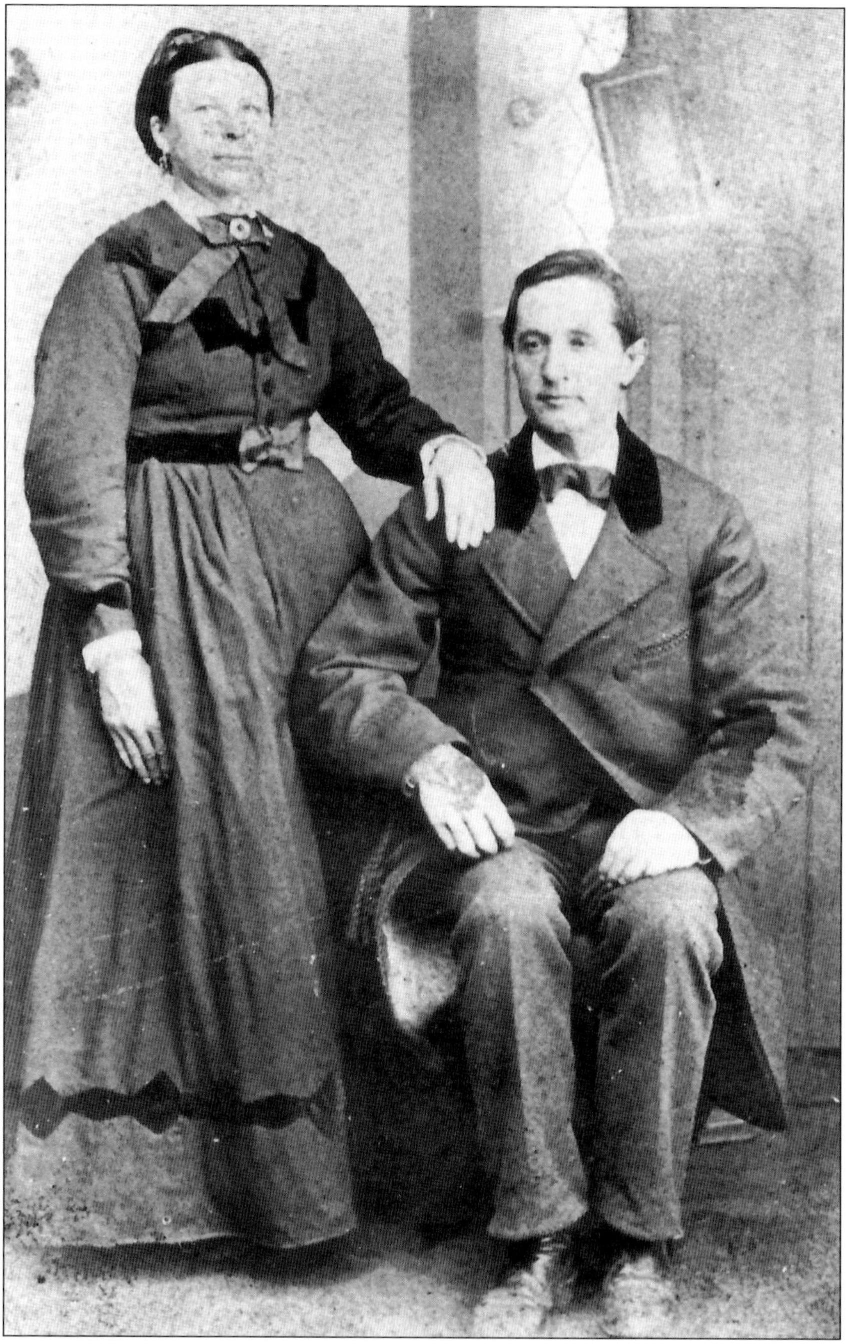

Nicholas Schneider and Barbara Berkes are shown in 1865. Louise Spanke notes that Nicholas had come to the area from the Bitburg region in Prussia (later Germany) in 1854. Nicholas was a tailor. He worked out of his home across from Henry Germann's store on Church Street, south of the railroad tracks. Nicholas was one of five residents in the community, along with John Schramer, Anton Schmitt, John Hix, and Nicholas Geras, to personally urge Rt. Rev. James Duggan, the bishop of Chicago, to start a church in Winfield. Nicholas also served as postmaster in the young village for one month in 1876. (Courtesy of the Winfield Historical Society.)

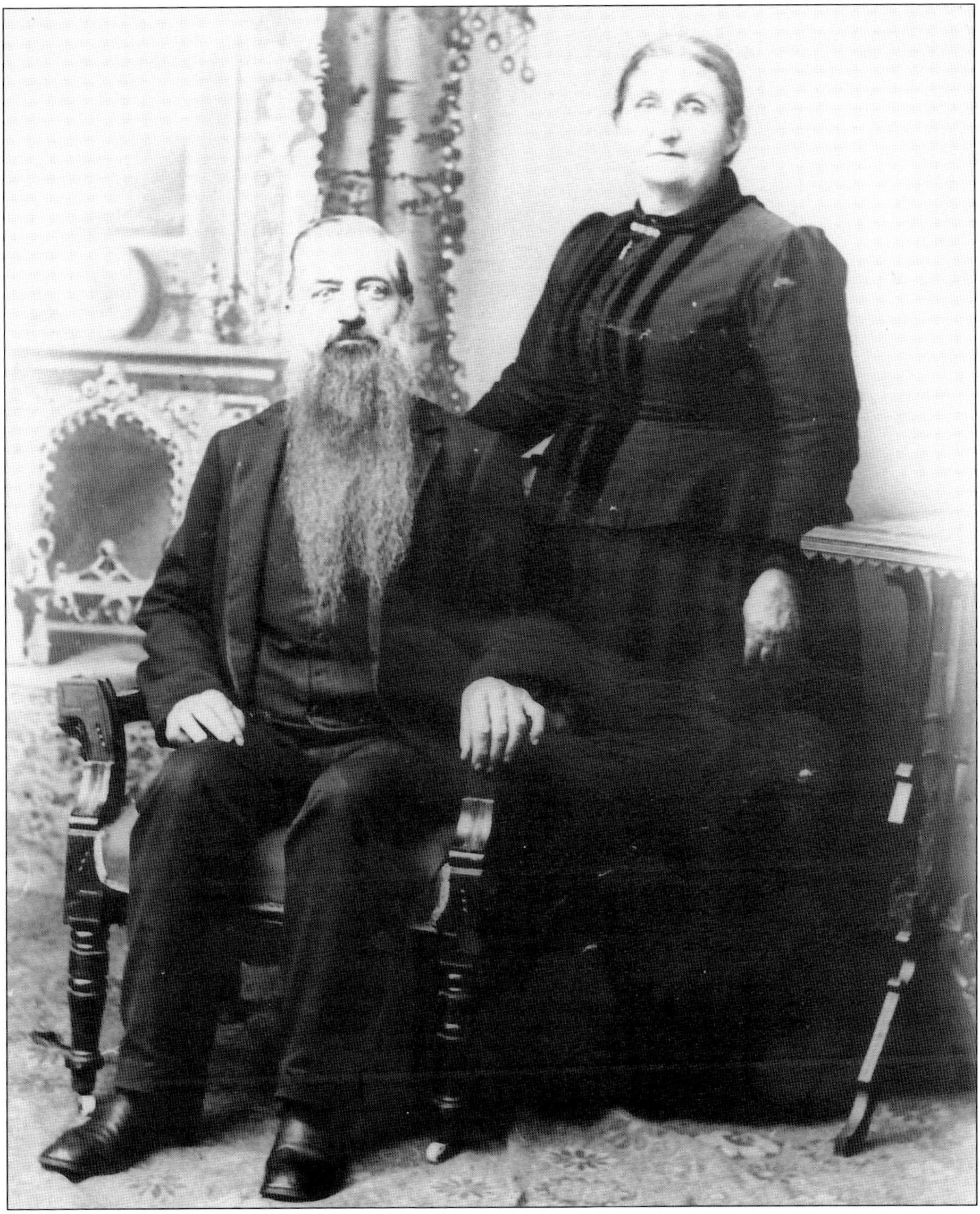

Jacob C. and Anna K. (Hentges) Mueller were among the next wave of early settlers. Jacob came from the Bitburg region in Prussia and arrived in Wayne Township in 1852. He married Anna Katherine Hentges before coming to Winfield. In 1868, Jacob bought Paul Warner's brewery that was west of Winfield Road, south of the railroad tracks. Besides being a brewer, Jacob sold limestone and gravel. This other venture came in handy for Jacob after his brewery burned in 1870. Additionally, Jacob served as the village notary and later became township highway commissioner. Jacob was often remembered for his beard that he ceased to shave after 1877. The beard eventually went from chin to toe. Jacob turned down a financial offer of $15 a week from Ringling Bros. to travel with the circus. (Courtesy of the Winfield Historical Society.)

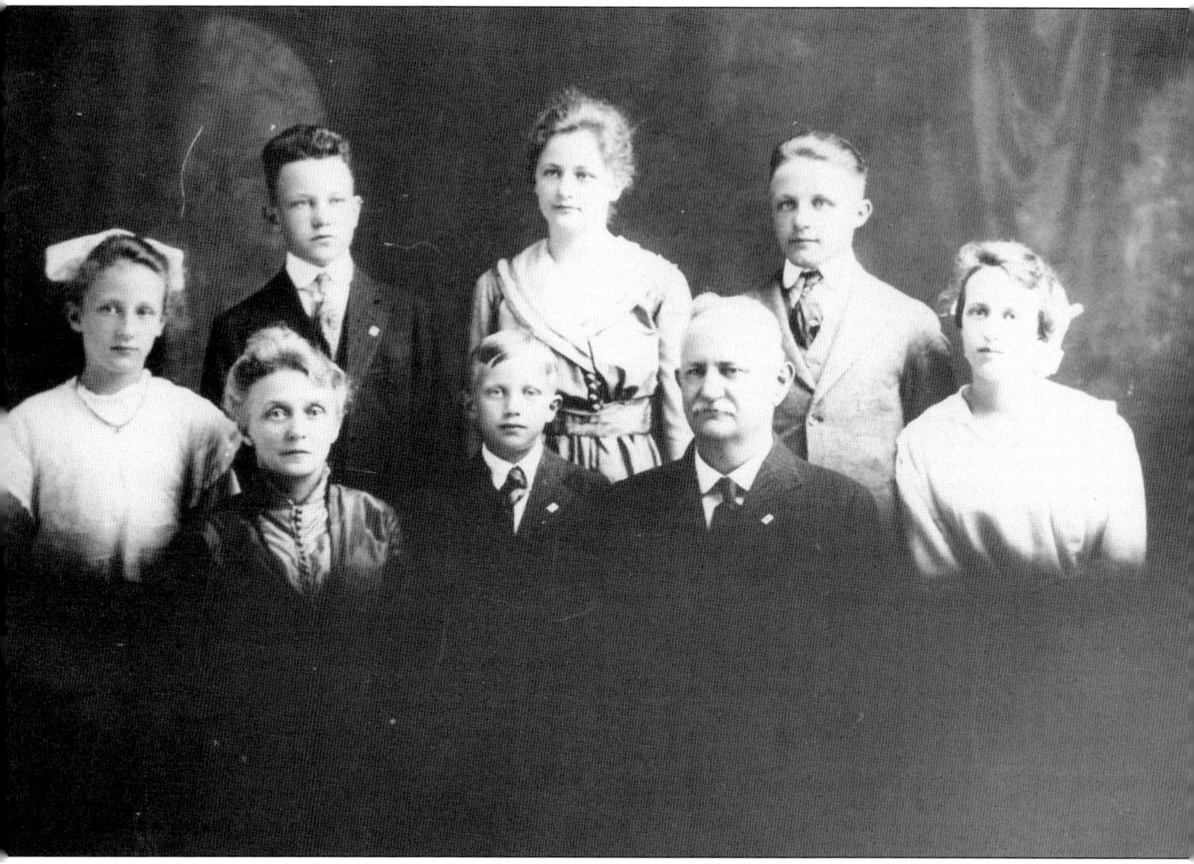

Clem Mueller poses with his family in this undated photograph. Jacob Mueller had a grandson, Clement, and available information regarding this photograph does not specify if this is Jacob's grandson. Clem and his wife are seated in the foreground with their children standing behind them; they are, from left to right, Tessy, Clem Jr., Nicholas, unidentified, Arthur, and Clara. Arthur, in particular, would go on to serve a variety of roles in the community, from village clerk to the fire department to postmaster. (Courtesy of the Winfield Historical Society.)

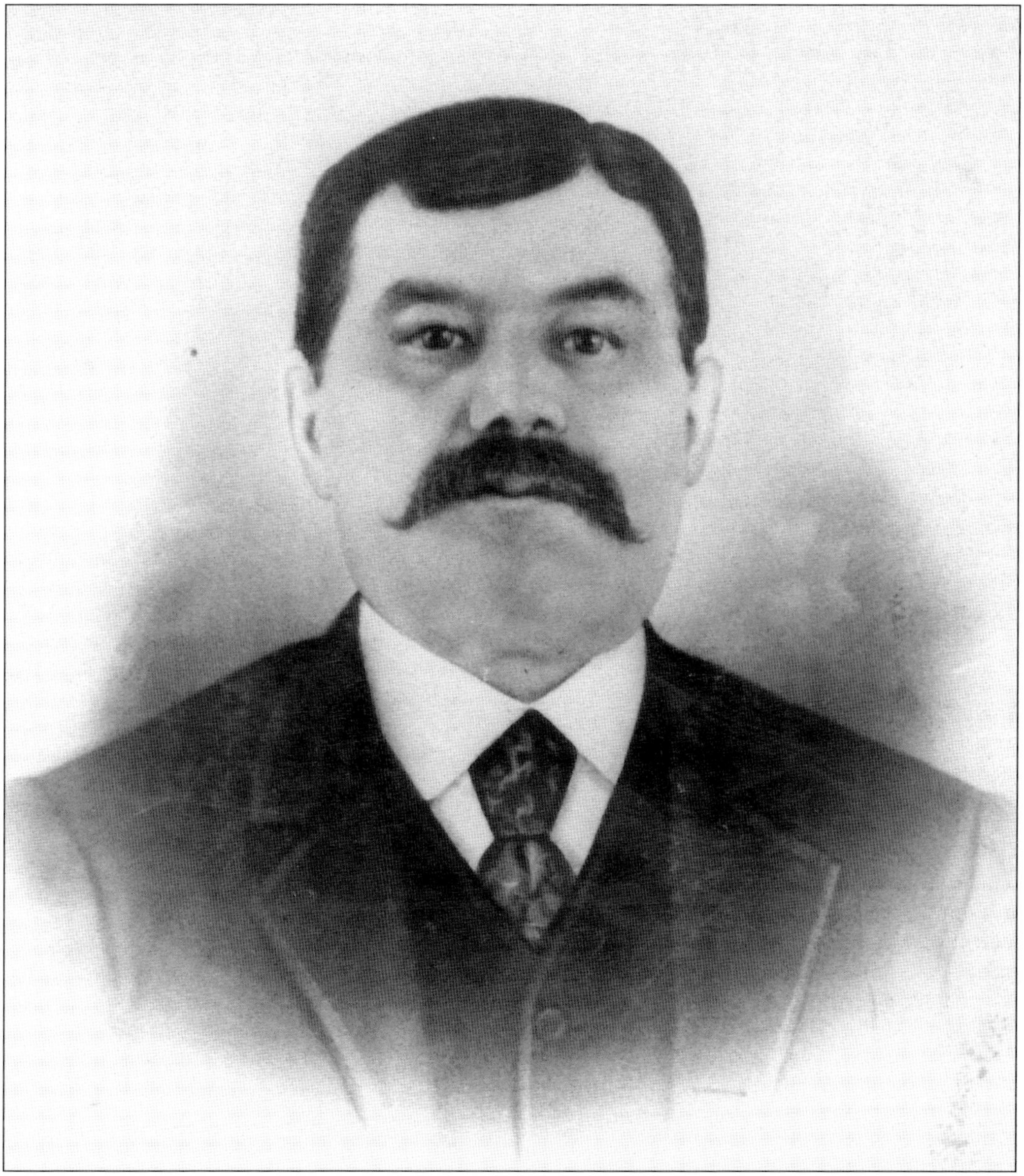

This is a sketch rendering of Johann "John" Hamm. John operated a popular local tavern for many years. He originally ran his tavern operations out of the first freight depot that John Hedges had built on Church Street. However, as the community began to grow and a second depot was constructed along Chicago Avenue, John relocated his tavern to that locale, the commercial hub of the burgeoning community. Hamm's tavern was a frequent and popular gathering spot for local activities in the community prior to the start of the 1900s. John and his wife, Magdalena Wolff, had six children. He passed away in 1895. (Courtesy of Roger Higgins and the Winfield Historical Society.)

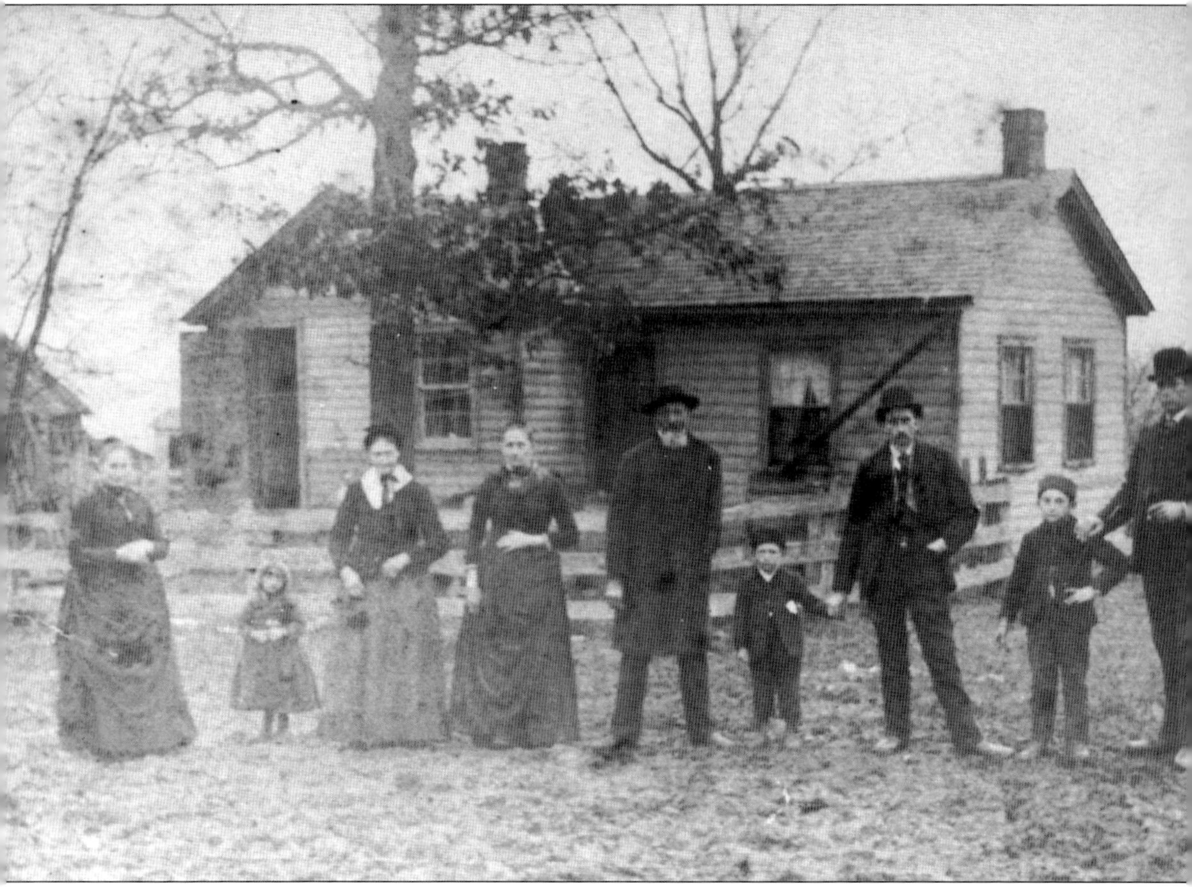

Magdalene "Lena" Wolff Hamm is pictured at far left in this photograph. Magdalene was married to John Hamm until his death in 1895. Other members of her family pictured here are Mary Schohn Wolff (third from the left), Mary Wolff Keil, George Wolff Sr., Anthony Hamm, Al Wolff, and George Wolff Jr. Anthony, fourth from the right, is just a boy in this picture. He later perished in a fire at the Paul Sehnem property in 1931. (Courtesy of the Winfield Historical Society.)

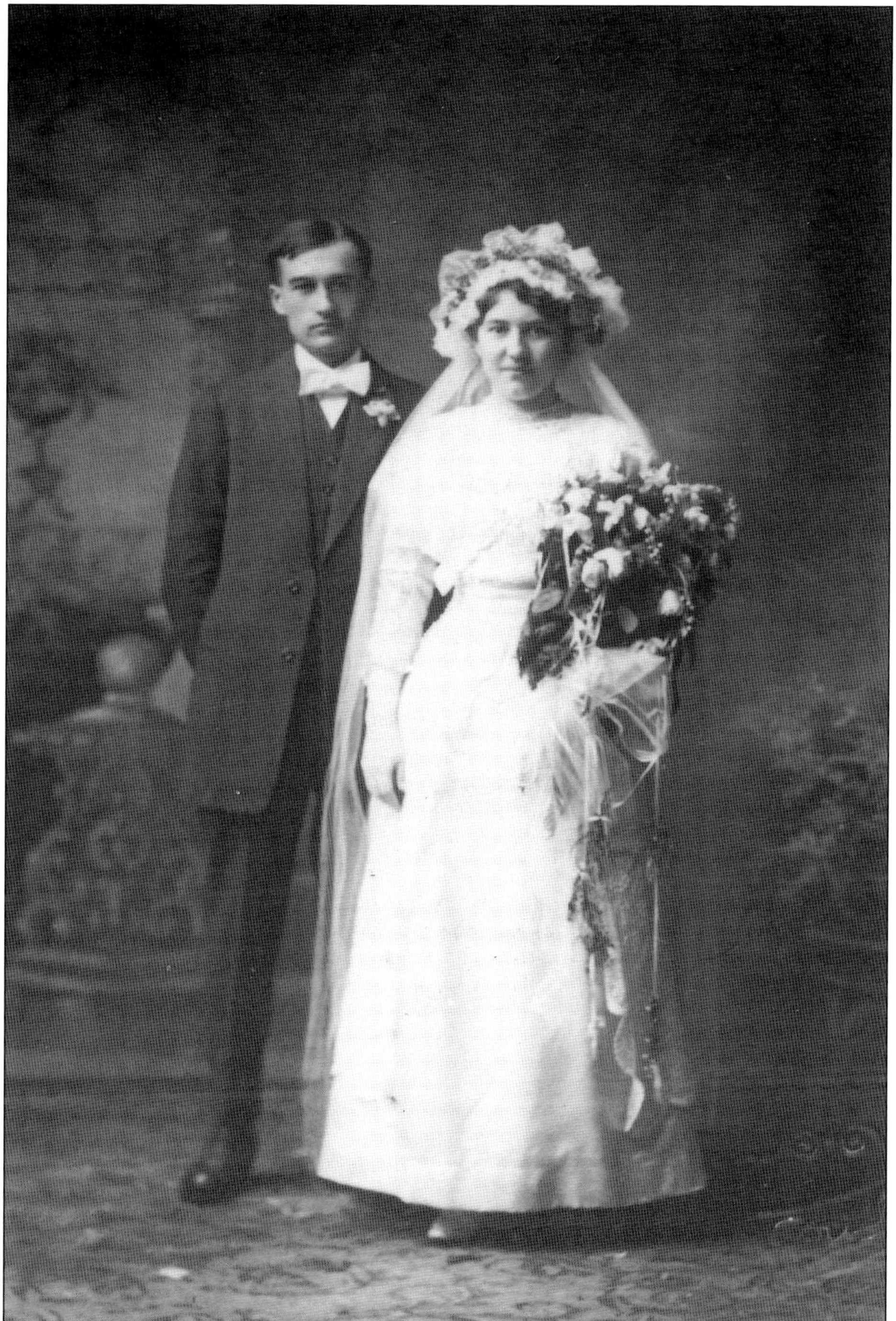

John Berkes is shown here with his wife, Lena Hamm, daughter of John Hamm, on their wedding day, October 15, 1912. John and Lena had three children. Louise Spanke writes that Lena had fond memories of her father's tavern—from the Junques beer that was brought in from Chicago, to the tavern's private icehouse, to different organizations that met there. (Courtesy of the Winfield Historical Society.)

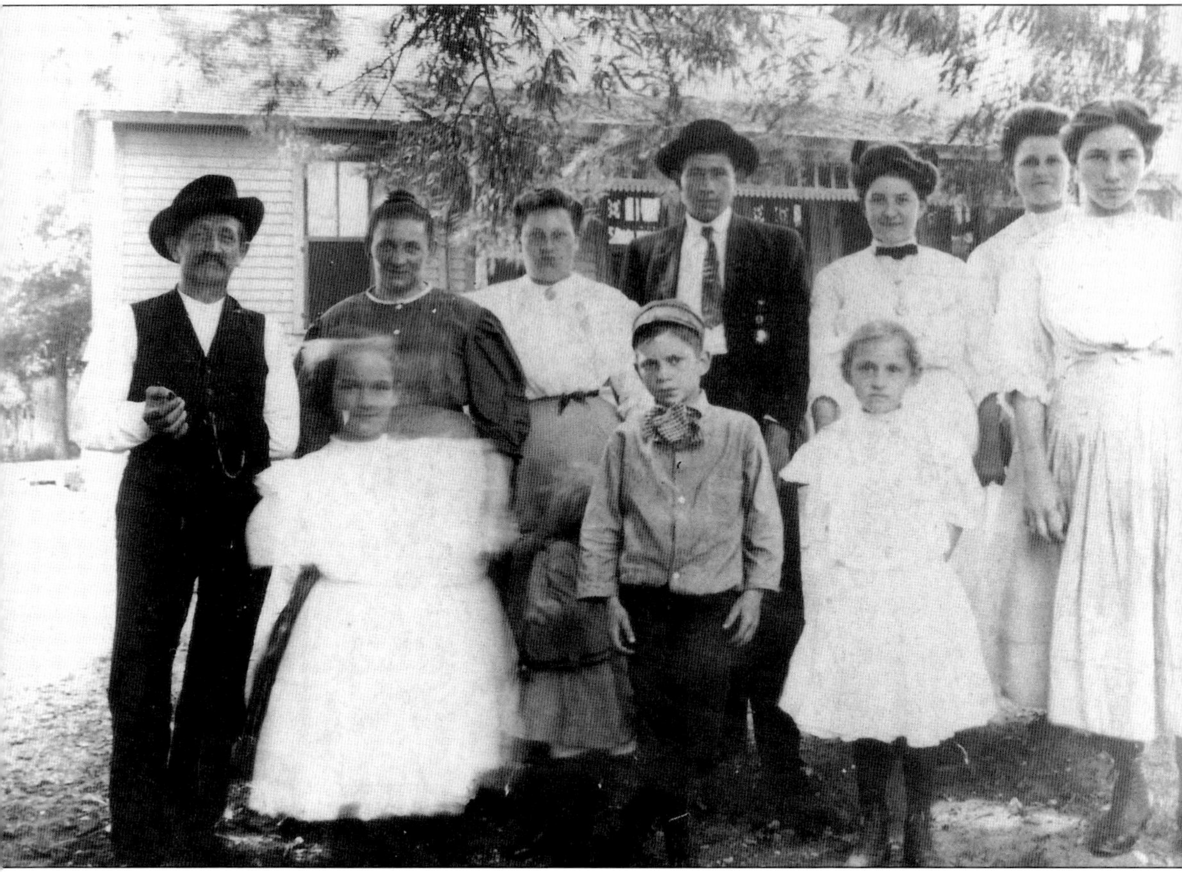

A gathering of friends and family of Paul C. Sehnem is shown here. From left to right are (first row) Elsie Weniger, Helen Baum, Paul N. Sehnem, Elsie Sehnem, and Jeanette Hamm; (second row) Paul C. Sehnem, Magdalene (Hamm) Sehnem, Katie Hamm, John Hamm, Lena Hamm, and Mary Hamm. Paul C. Sehnem's home is in the background. The Sehnem home was located just around the corner of Chicago Avenue, just passed Sehnem Hall and the home and meat market of Peter Schmidt's family. (Courtesy of the Winfield Historical Society.)

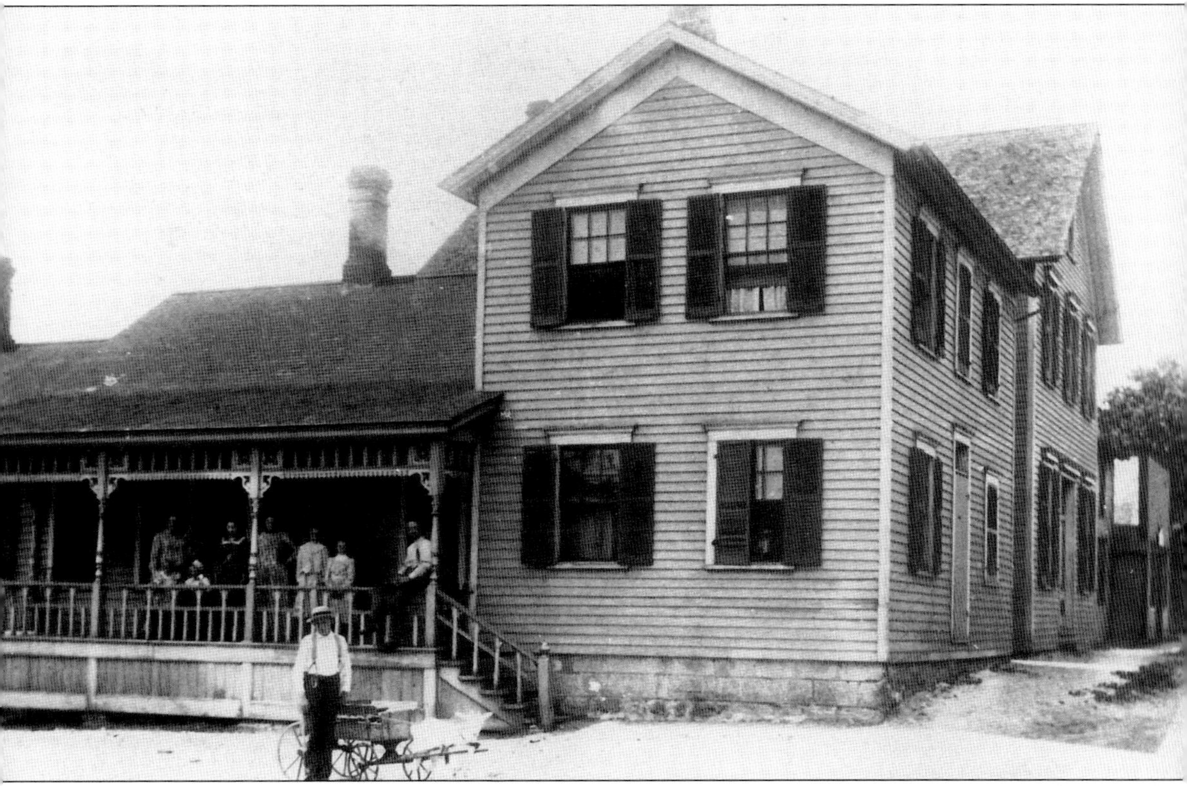

The Hamm and Sehnem families gathered for this photograph of Paul Sehnem's home in the early 1900s. Magdalene Hamm married Paul Sehnem after John Hamm's passing in 1895. They resided at this home, next door to Hamm's tavern, which was later converted in Sehnem Hall, this first meeting locale for the incorporated Winfield village government in 1921. Magdalene is shown standing at the porch rail, with, from left to right, Elsie Sehnem, Paul N. Sehnem, Lena Hamm, Katherine Hamm, Mary Hamm, Jeanette Hamm, and Paul C. Sehnem. John Hamm, named for his father, stands with the goat cart in the foreground. (Courtesy of the Winfield Historical Society.)

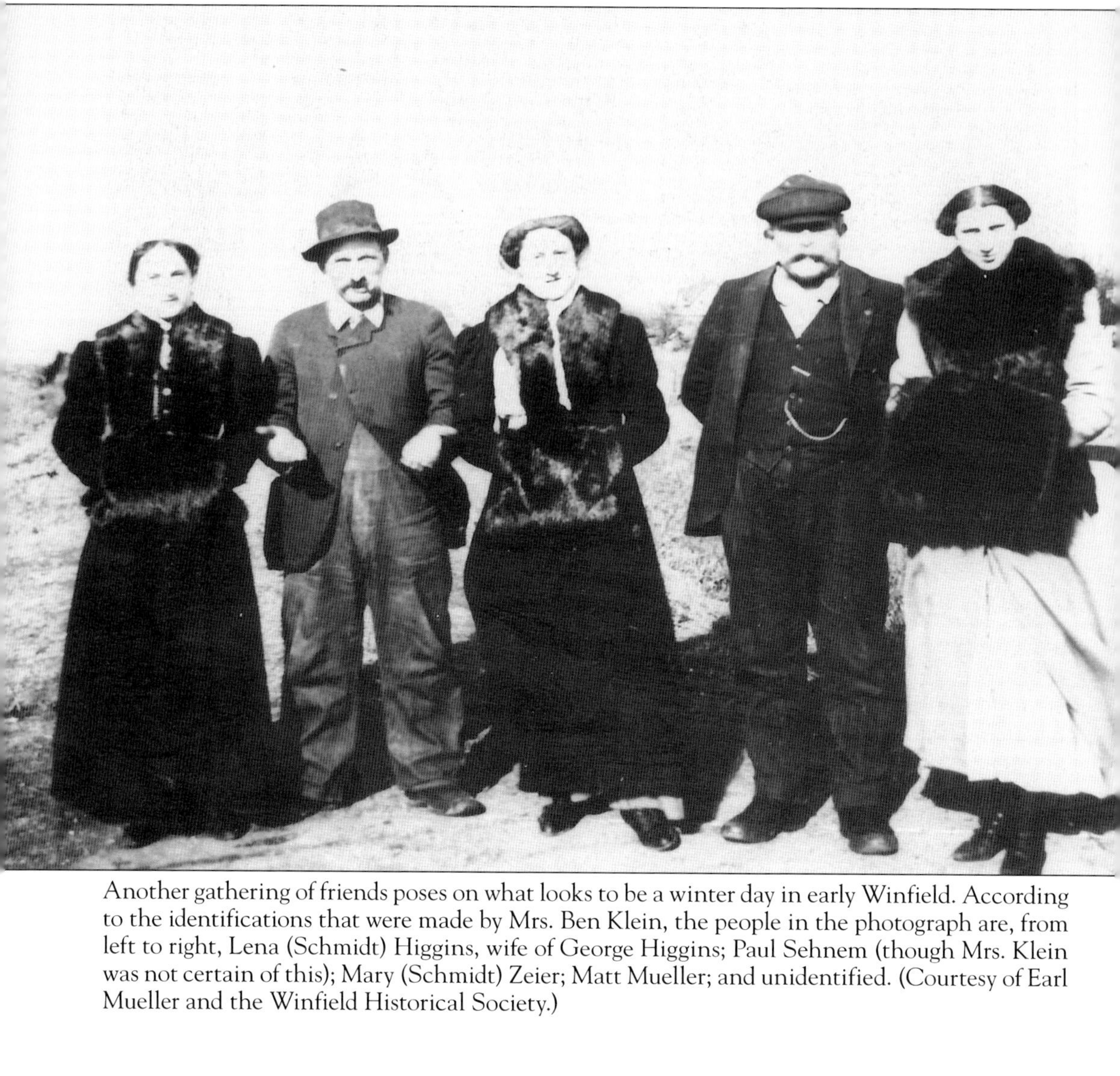

Another gathering of friends poses on what looks to be a winter day in early Winfield. According to the identifications that were made by Mrs. Ben Klein, the people in the photograph are, from left to right, Lena (Schmidt) Higgins, wife of George Higgins; Paul Sehnem (though Mrs. Klein was not certain of this); Mary (Schmidt) Zeier; Matt Mueller; and unidentified. (Courtesy of Earl Mueller and the Winfield Historical Society.)

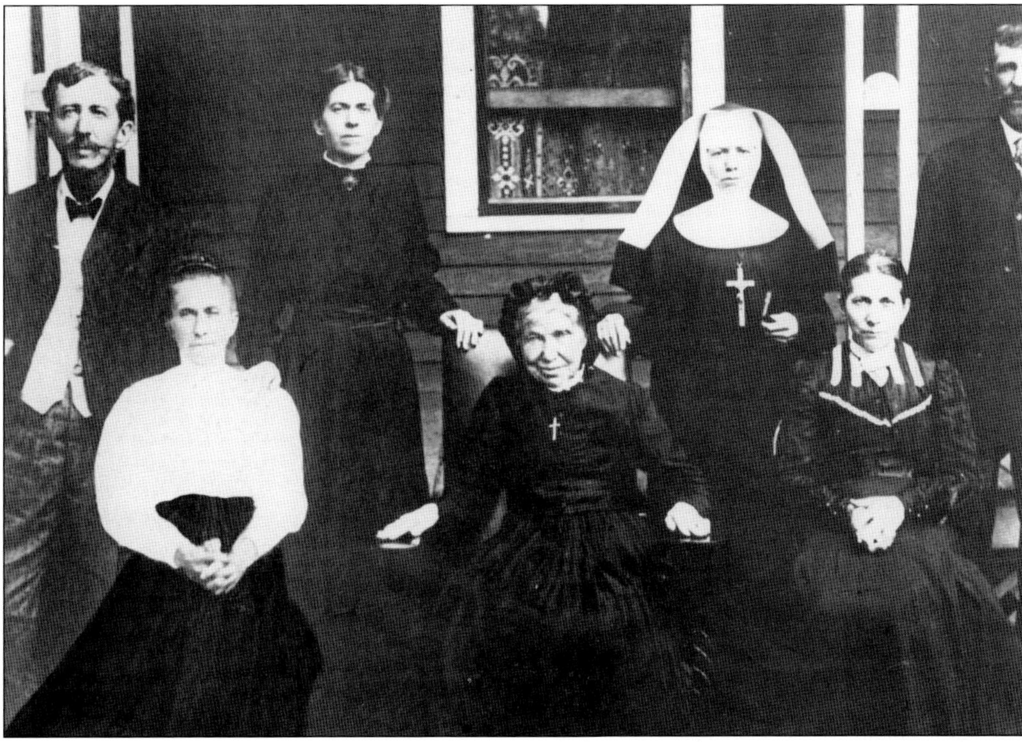

Among other families in Winfield was that of Stephen Elsen. Above, the family is posing for a portrait in 1912. From left to right are (first row, seated) are Anna (Bollweg), Christina (Ewen) Elsen, and Catherine; (second row, standing) Michael, Susan (Daleiden), Helena (Sister Frieda), and Matthias. In the image at right, Susan appears with her husband, William Daleiden, on their wedding day. William and Susan had eight children—Christine, John, William, Catherine, Anthony, Edward, Mary, and George. (Both, courtesy of the Winfield Historical Society.)

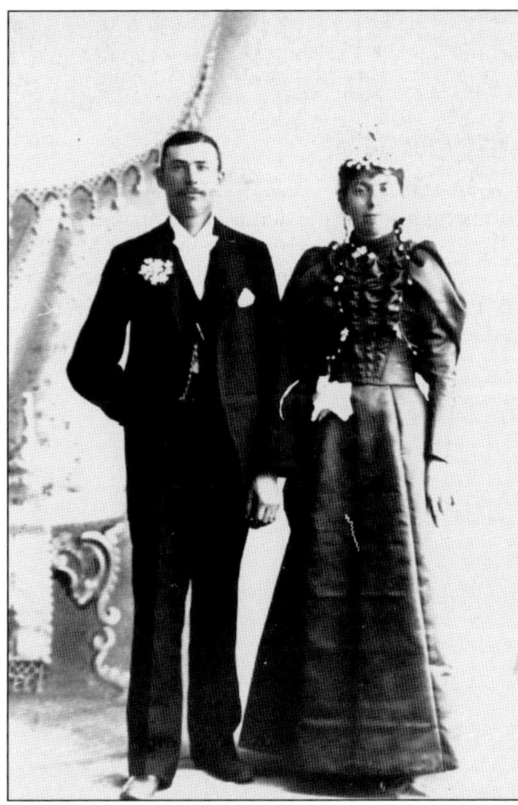

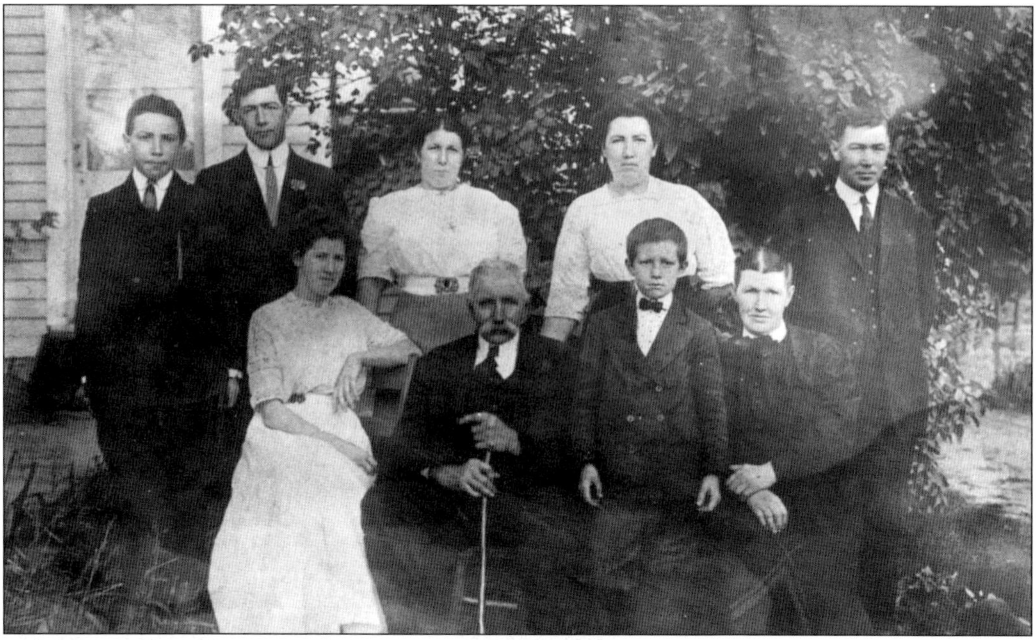

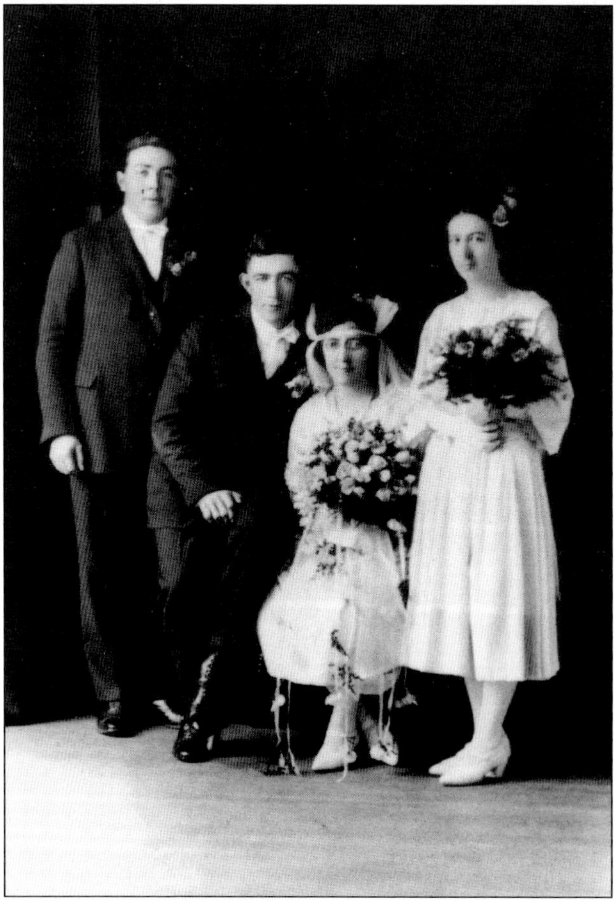

John Zeier and his family are shown above posing for a portrait in 1908. From left to right are (first row, seated) Katherine, John, Herbert, and Lucy (Higgins) Zeier; (second row, standing) Jacob, Frank, Barbara (Rinehart), Lulu (Beggs), and William Zeier. John was one of the charter members of St. Aloysius Court No. 148, Catholic Order of Foresters. At left are Mr. and Mrs. Frank Zeier on their wedding day. Frank's brother Jake served as his best man for the ceremony. (Both, courtesy of the Winfield Historical Society.)

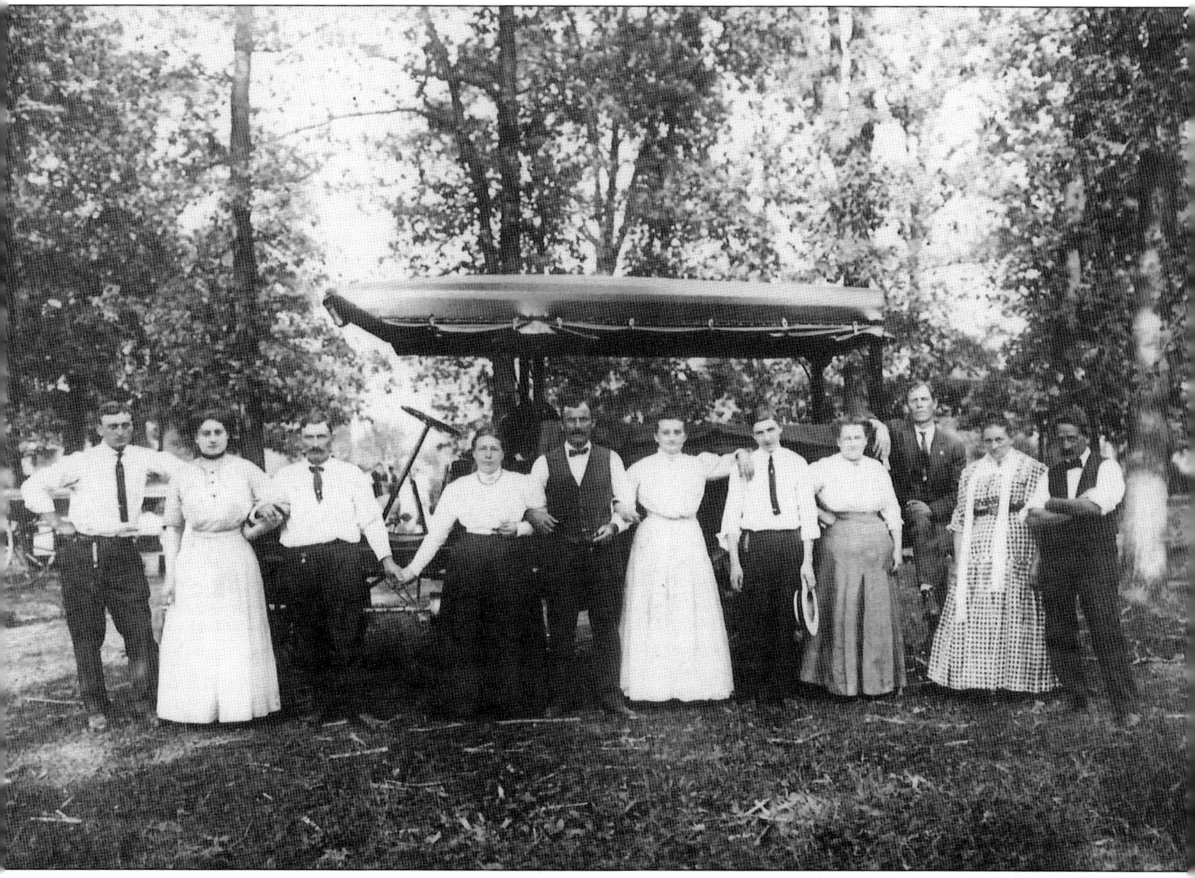

Early Winfield was a small and close-knit community. Families knew and genuinely enjoyed spending time with one another. Here, Peter Schmidt is seen standing with family and friends at a picnic in Roselle. The gathering was to celebrate Peter's purchase of a brand-new 1911 McIntyre truck, the first such vehicle in the village. Standing from left to right are Al Schmidt, Mary (Zeier) Schmidt, Nicholas and Anna Schramer, Peter and Mary Schmidt, George Higgins, Katherine and Peter Baum, Magdalene (Wolff) (Hamm) Sehnem, and Paul Sehnem. (Courtesy of the Winfield Historical Society.)

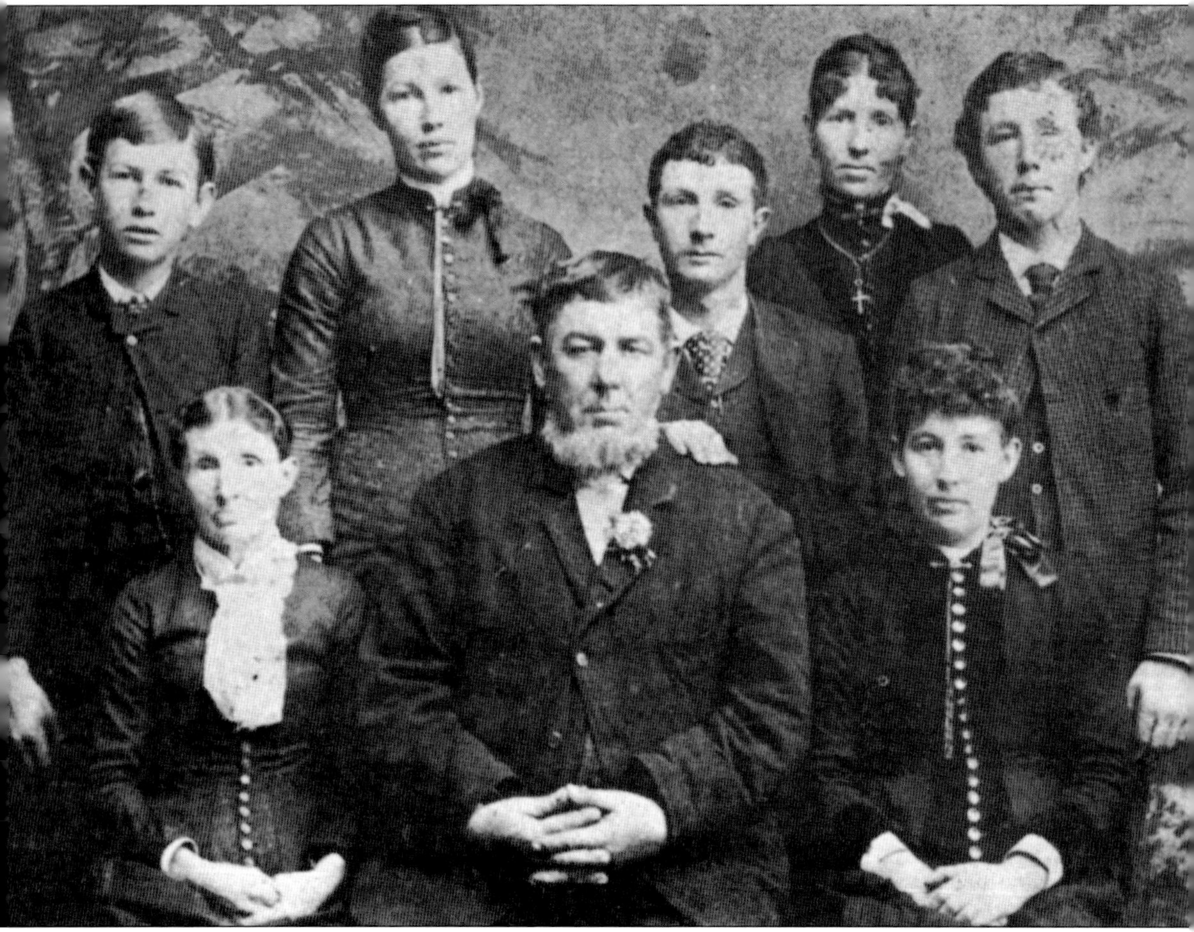

This is the Gilbert Higgins family in 1879. Pictured from left to right are (seated) Cornelia, Gilbert, and Mary Higgins; (second row) Oscar, Lucy, Sanders, Eliza, and William. Gilbert had come to the area in the mid-1850s from Ohio. He was quite active in the young community, and he had a fine reputation as a mechanic. Gilbert worked on a boiler for the Mueller Creamery, maintained his farm's threshing machines, and sold coal for these machines to other local farmers. He also hauled gravel and other materials around town. Additionally, he served as a local judge, along with Mathias Huels and Jacob Mueller, in the 1884 election attempt to incorporate the young village under the name of Frederick Park. Gilbert died in 1890 and is buried in Pleasant Hill Cemetery in Winfield. (Courtesy of the Winfield Historical Society.)

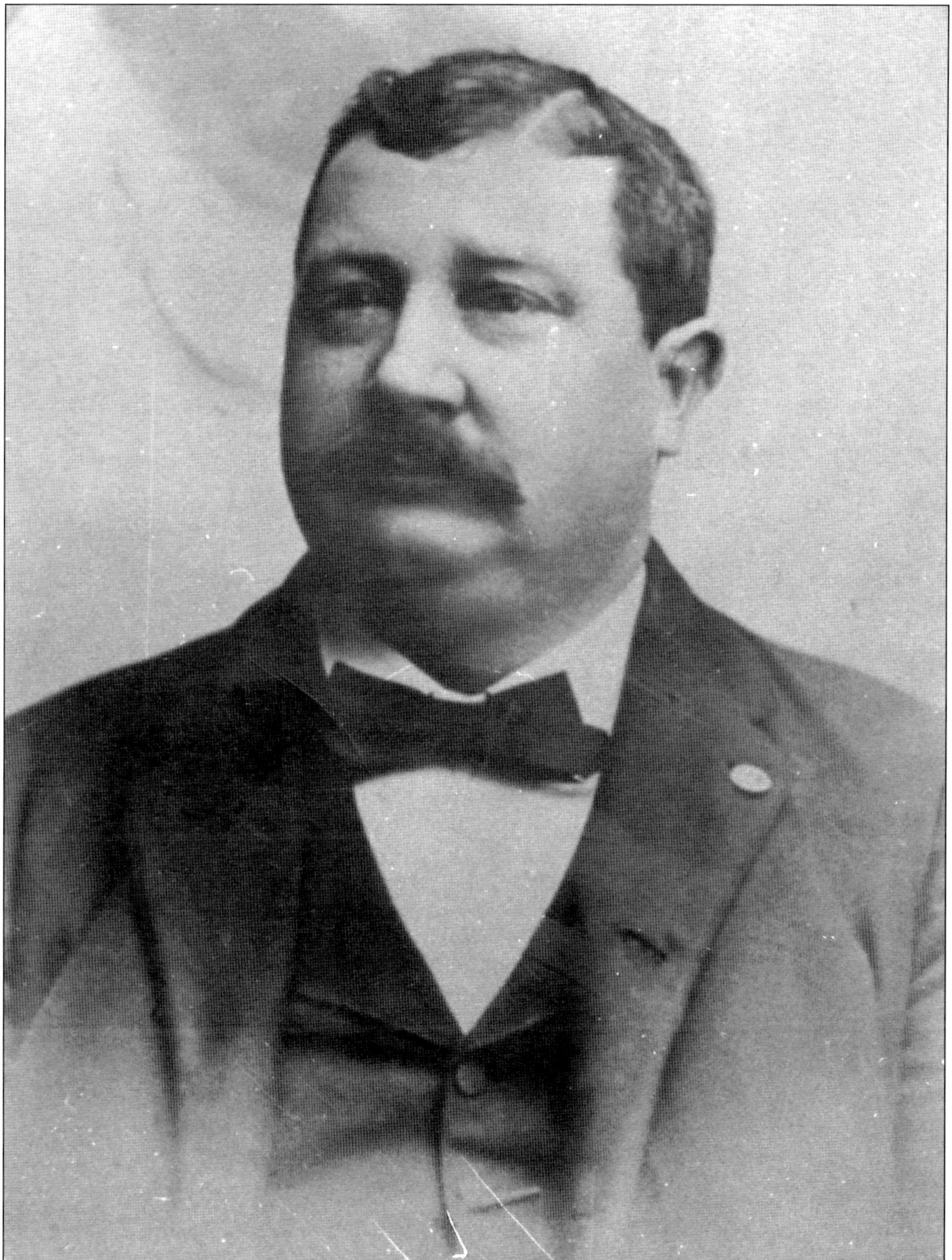

Sanders Higgins was born in July 1866, one of seven children to Gilbert and Cornelia Higgins. Sanders received his education from his mother before attending local public schools and Wheaton High School for two years. With his high school education, Sanders was made a station agent for the Winfield stop along the Chicago and North Western Railway. He married Barbara Berkes on November 30, 1889. (Courtesy of the Winfield Historical Society.)

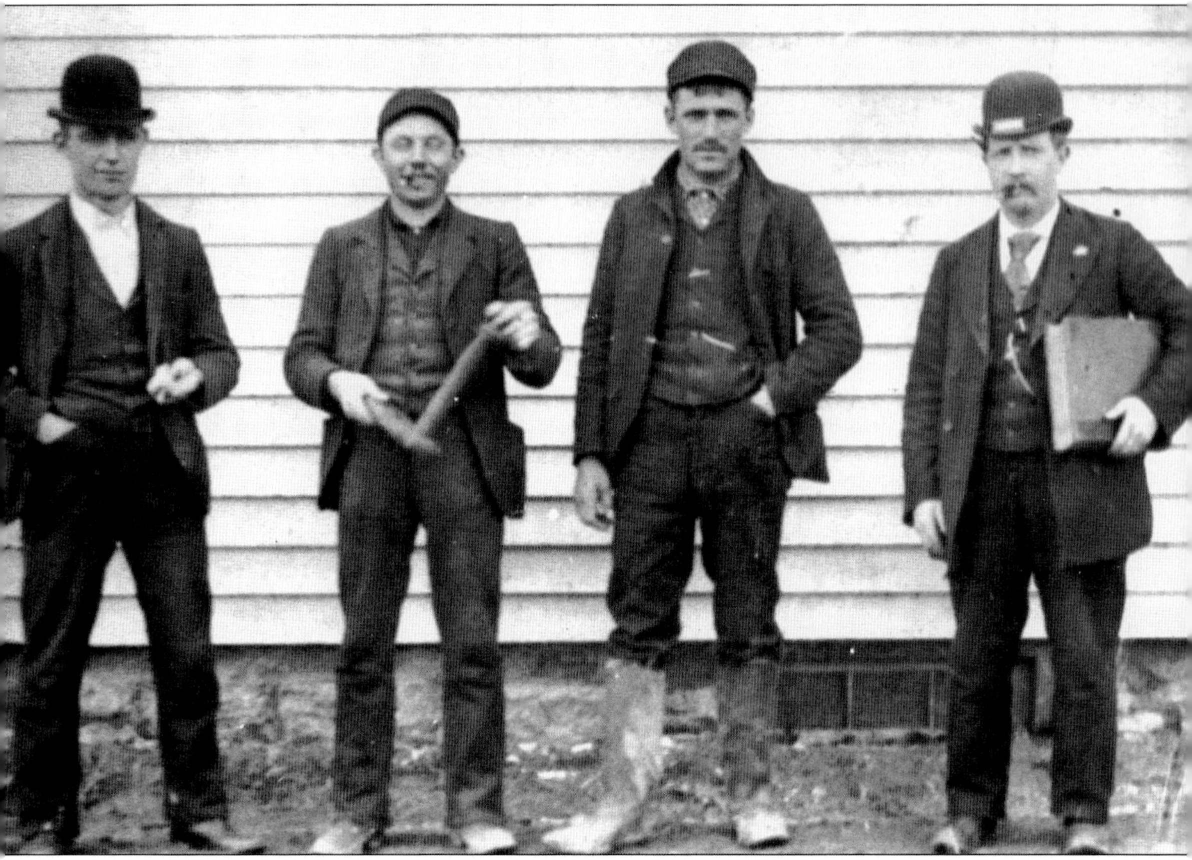

This image shows Sanders Higgins at the far right holding a ledger. From left to right, Christ Enders, Chris Miller, and J.S. Miller are standing with Sanders in this 1900 photograph. Higgins left his job as a station agent in 1894 to lease the property owned by William Fehrman on Church Street. Higgins and his wife, Barbara, ran the general store while raising their young family in the rear of the business. He died suddenly in 1908 at 42 years of age. (Courtesy of Jas. McCabe and the Winfield Historical Society.)

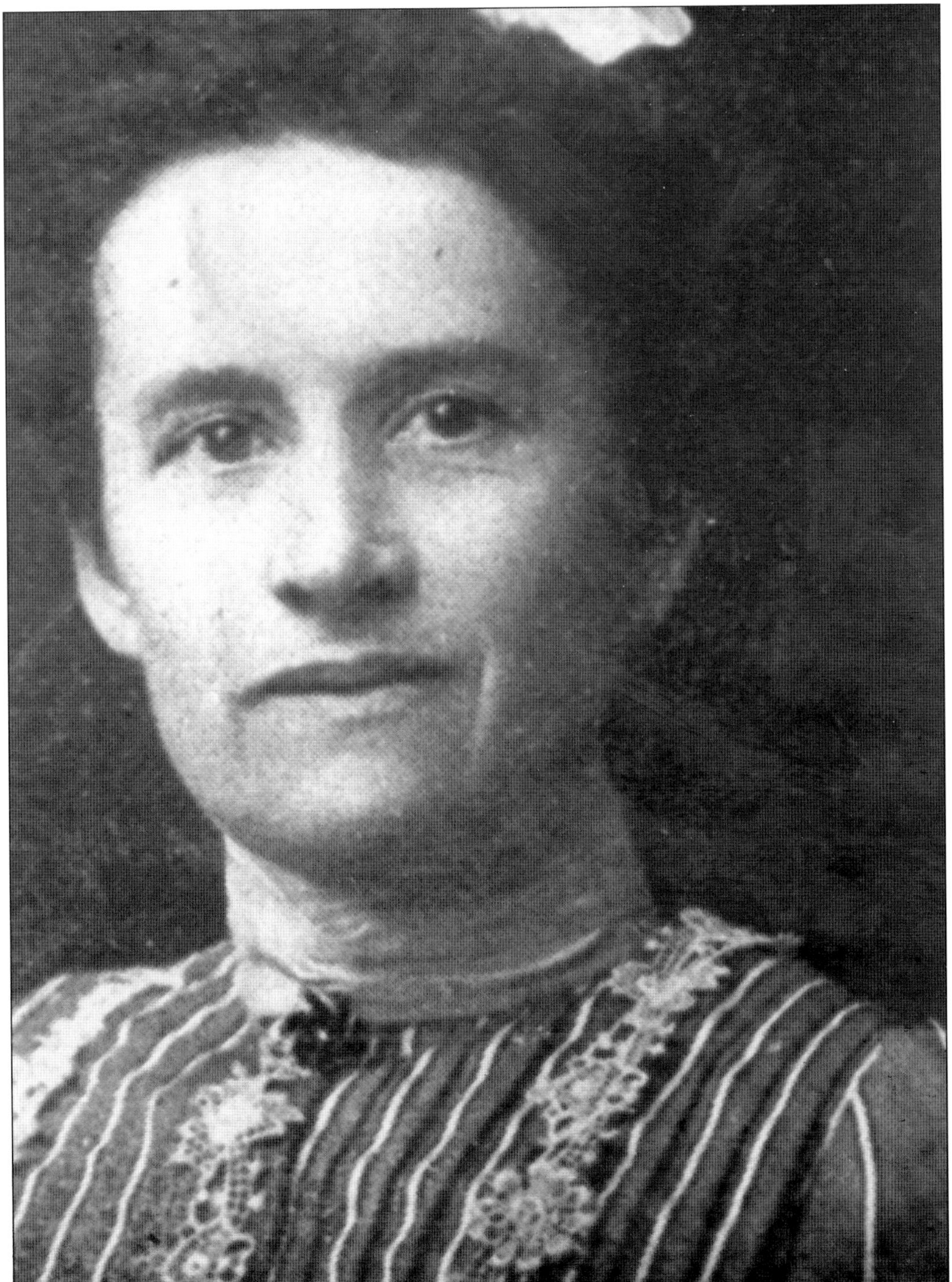

Barbara (Berkes) Higgins was born to German immigrant parents in February 1870. She was born in Winfield, lived in Winfield, married in Winfield, and died in Winfield. An active Catholic for her entire life, Barbara married Sanders Higgins on November 30, 1889, and together, the couple had nine children, though one did die in infancy. (Courtesy of the Winfield Historical Society.)

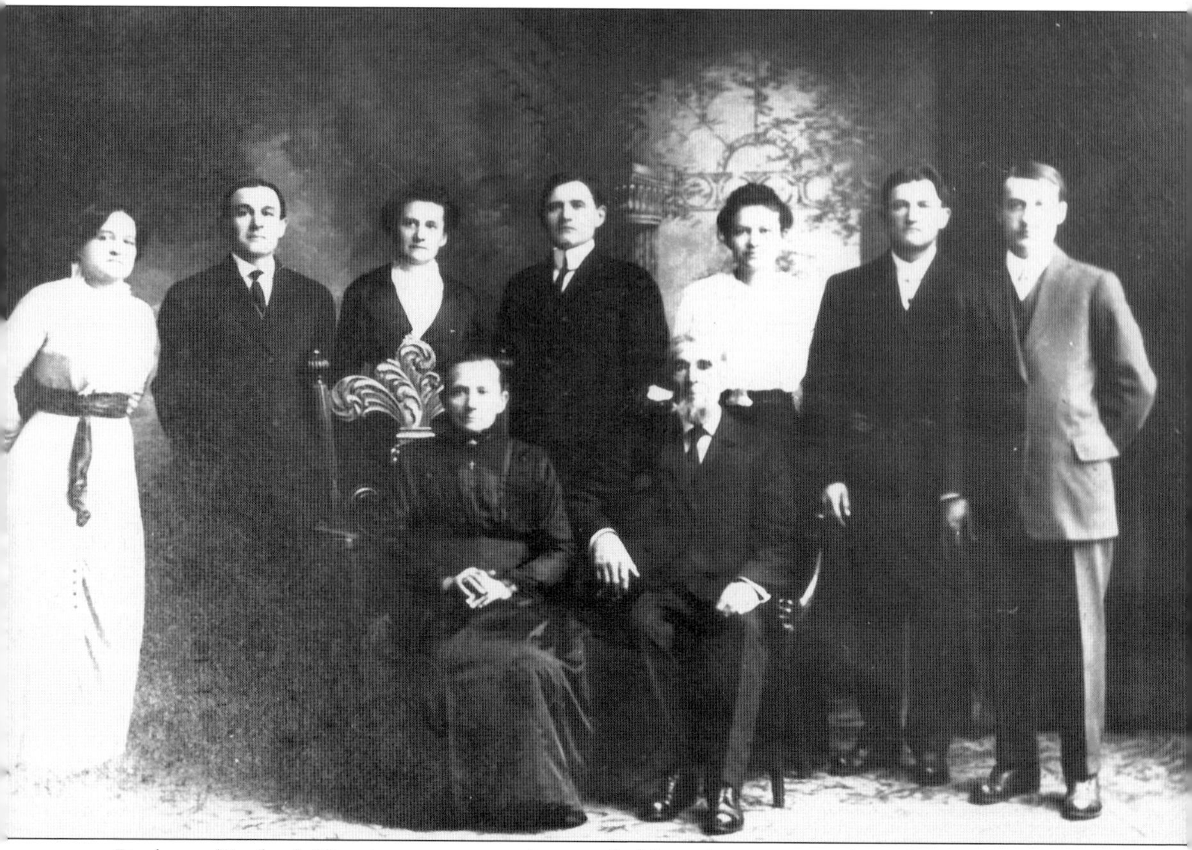

Barbara (Berkes) Higgins was one of nine children born to Jacob and Antoinette (Klein) Berkes. This photograph shows the Berkes family gathered on the 50th wedding anniversary for Jacob and Antoinette in 1914. Standing behind their seated parents are, from left to right, Katherine, Henry, Barbara, Nicholas, Mary, Leonard, and John Berkes. (Courtesy of the Winfield Historical Society.)

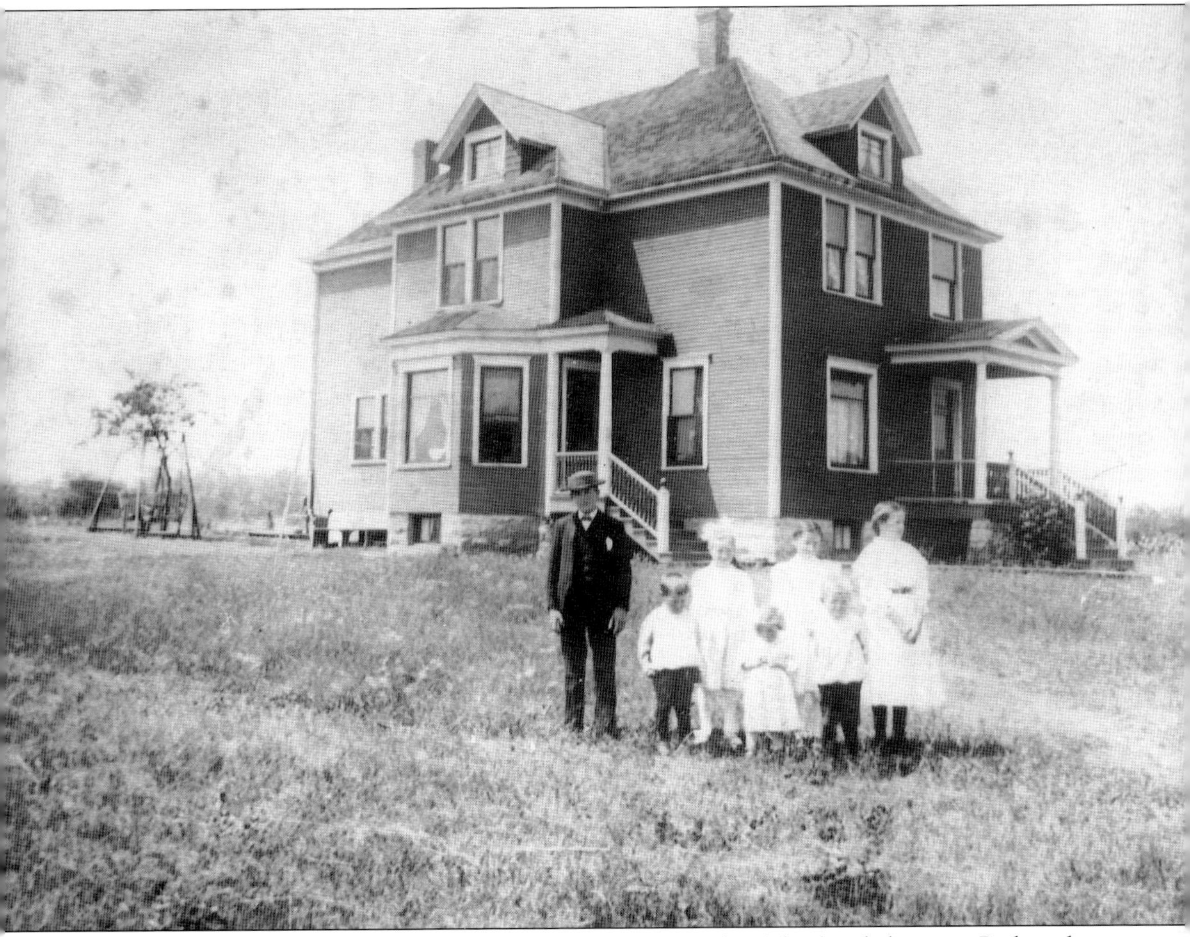

Sanders and Barbara Higgins's children are seen standing outside of the family home at Park and Beecher Streets in 1908. Sanders and Barbara were able to move into this newly constructed home following their early residence in the rear of the family store. Today, the Winfield Middle School sits on this site. The children shown here are, from left to right, George, Henry, Cornelia, Alice, Marie, Richard, and Nettie. (Courtesy of the Winfield Historical Society.)

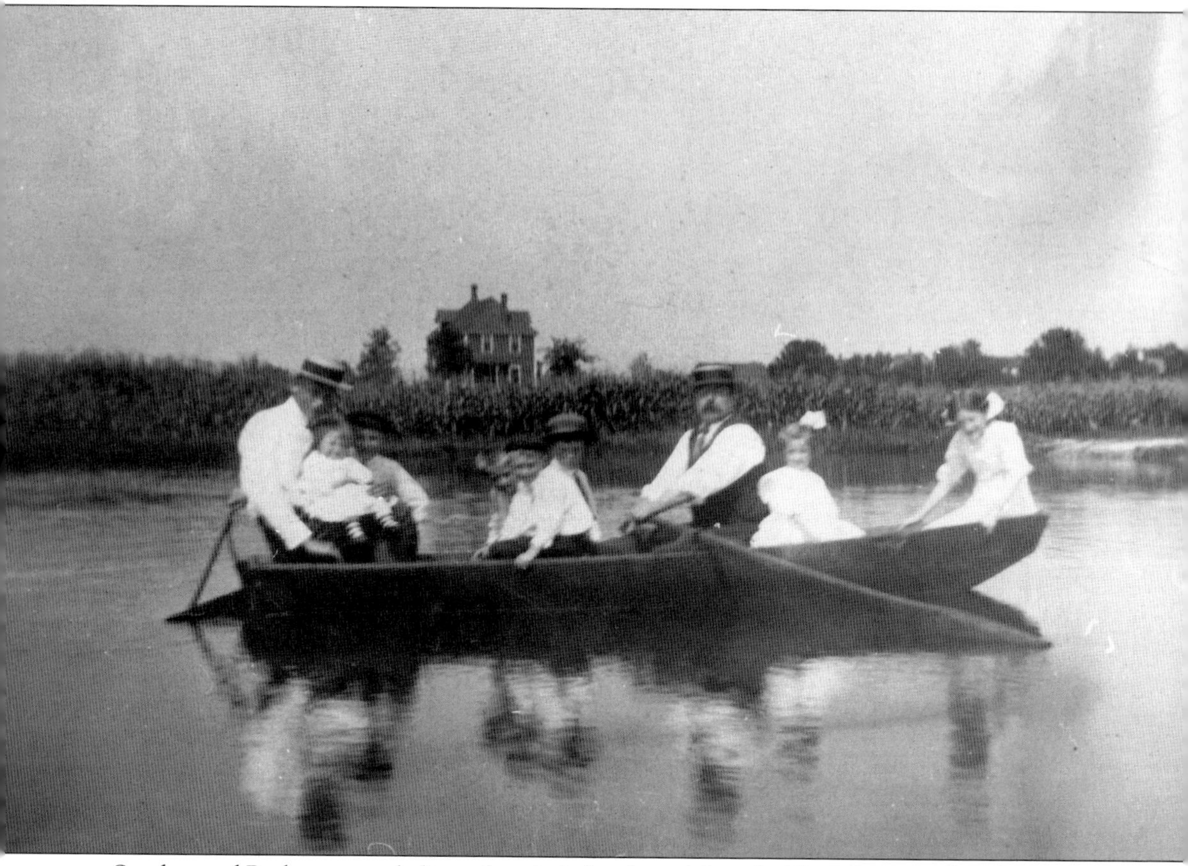

Sanders and Barbara were dedicated to their family and friends. This photograph is from the early 1900s on the Schmidt pond. Holding an unidentified baby, John Enders is at the far left in the boat. Others are, from left to right, Peter Enders, Ray Enders, George Enders, Henry Higgins, Sanders Higgins, Alice Higgins, and Cornelia Higgins. (Courtesy of the Winfield Historical Society.)

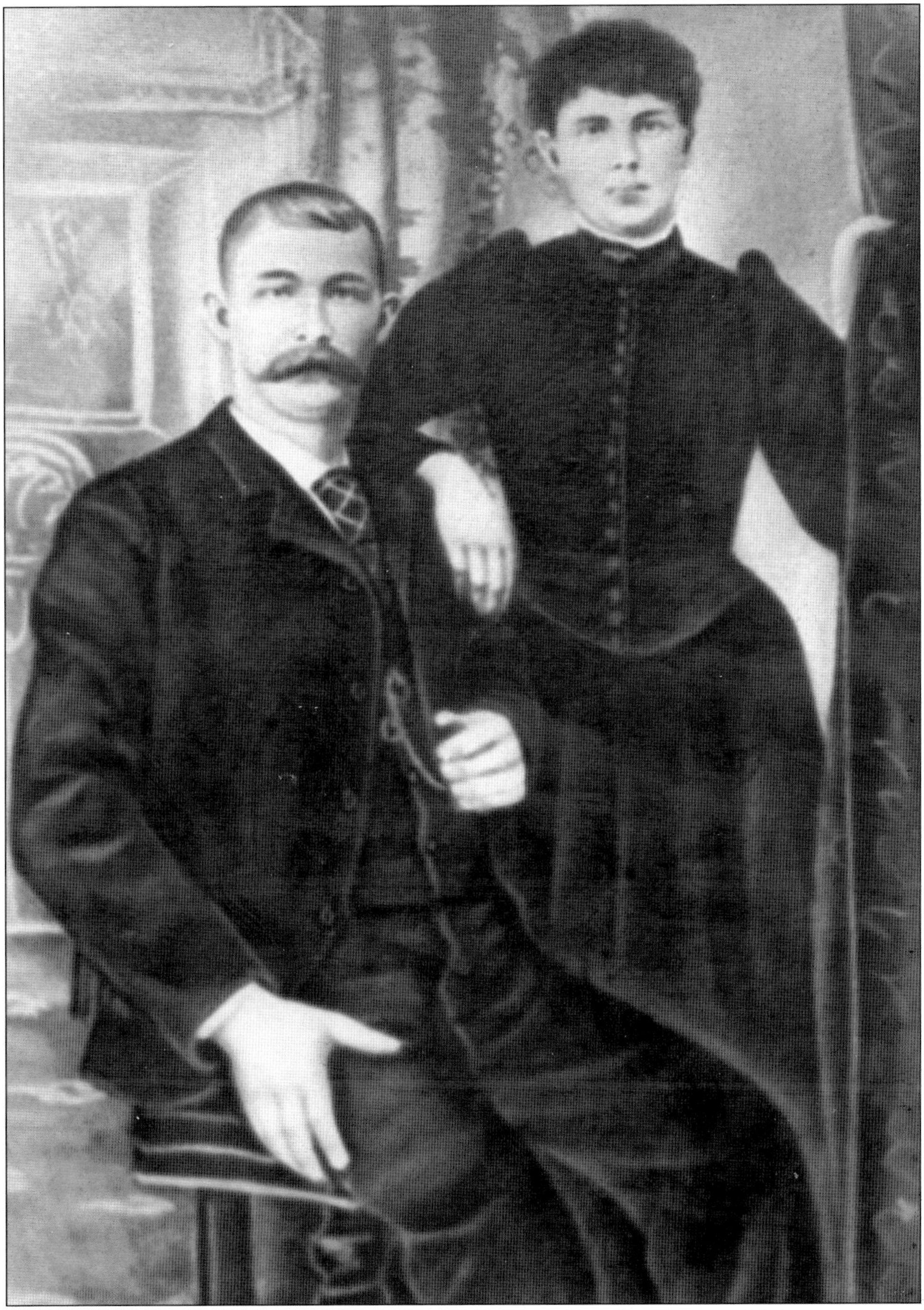

This image is a sketch portrait of John and Mary (Bollweg) Enders. John and Mary were married in February 1887. John was one of the charter members of the St. Aloysius Court No. 148 Catholic Order of Foresters. He served on the District 34 School Board for three years, from 1909 to 1912. He later served on the Winfield Board of Trustees from 1921 to 1922, and he also was appointed to the Judiciary, Police, Fire, and Health Committee when Winfield was formally incorporated in 1921. (Courtesy of the Winfield Historical Society.)

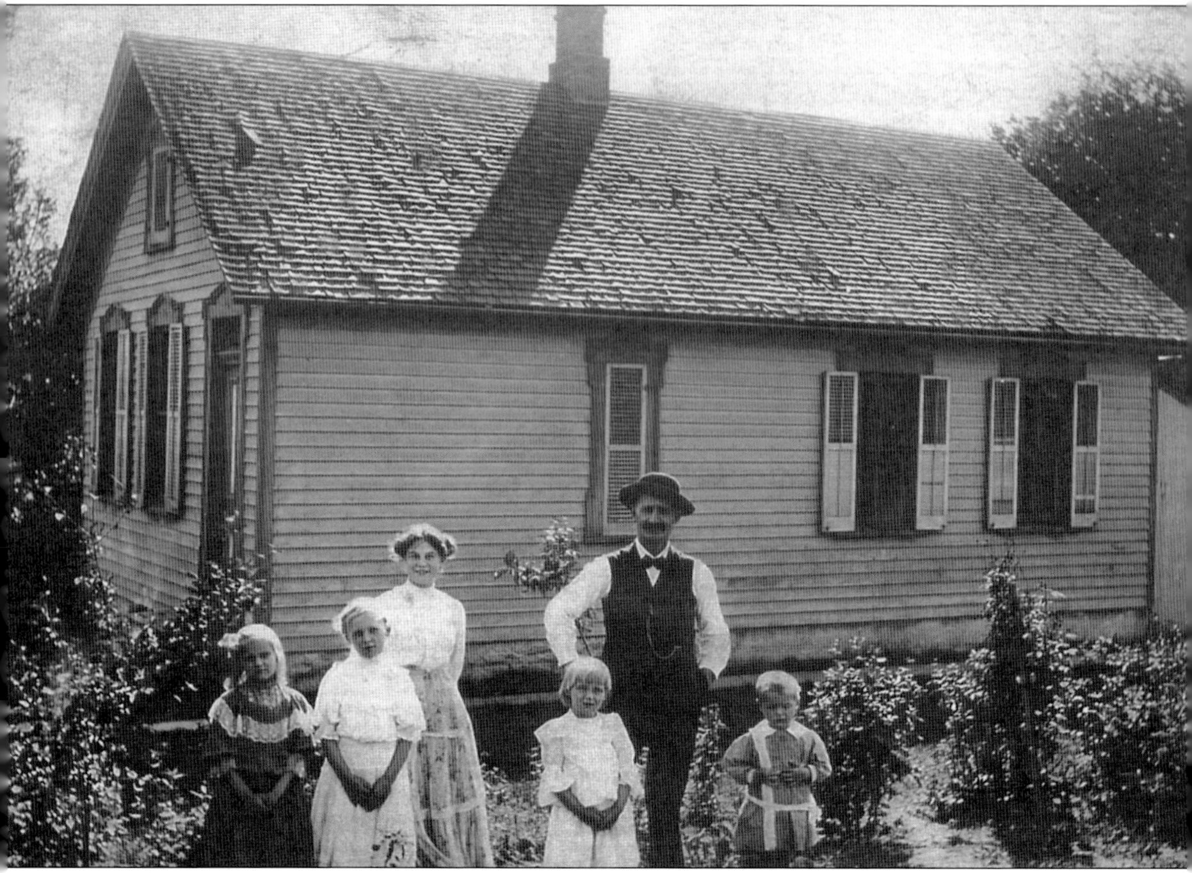

This 1905 photograph is of John Enders standing outside of his home that was located at the corner of what are now Beecher Street and Winfield Road. The gathering in the garden includes, from left to right, Emma, Therese, Mary, Alyce, John, and Peter. The home was originally built in 1891 and later remodeled by Enders. The property later became home to Stone Apple Farm Antiques and Winfield Flower Shoppe. (Courtesy of the Winfield Historical Society.)

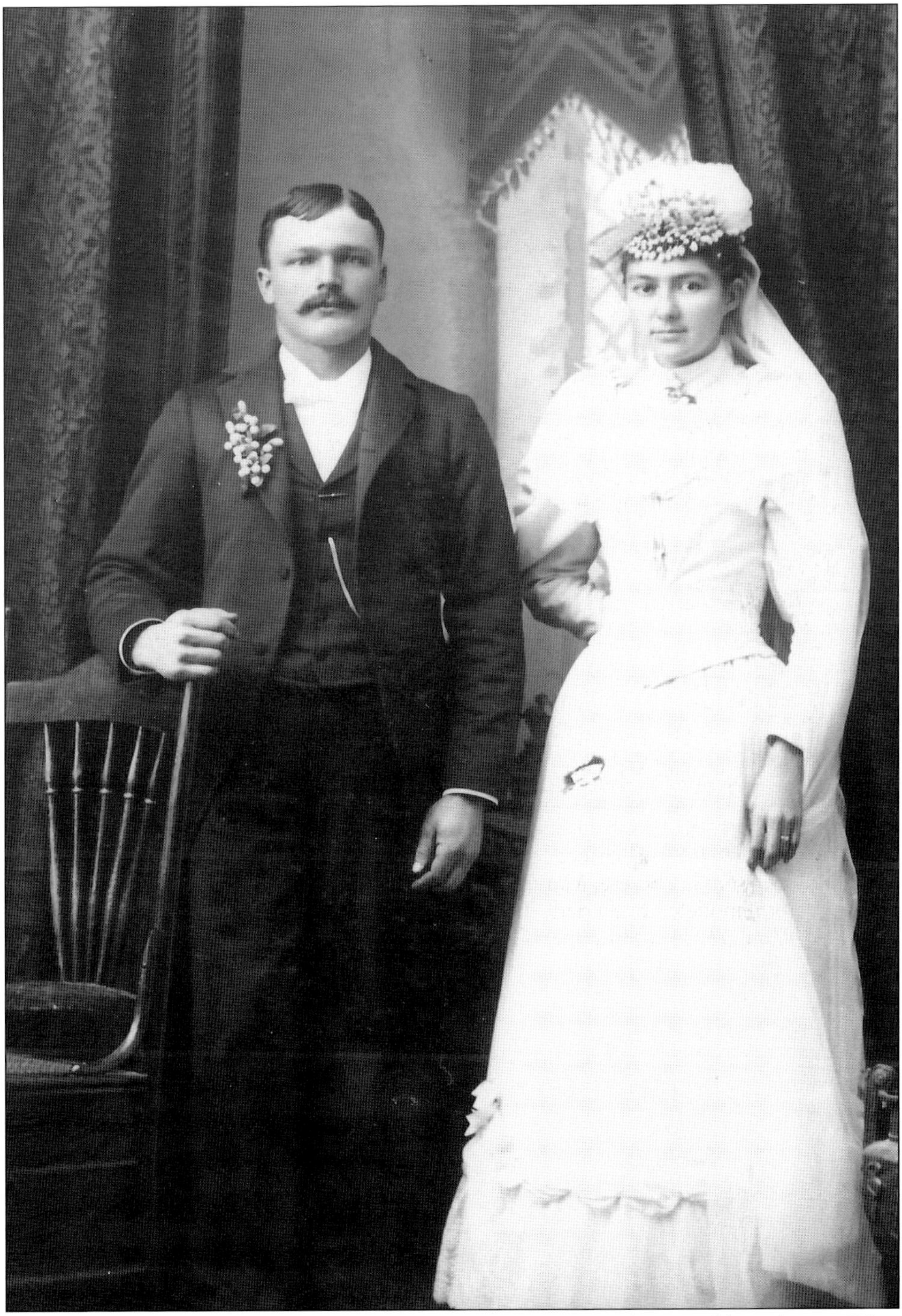

Michael Besch is standing with his new bride, Eva Huels, on their wedding day in February 1895. Michael was of six children born to Michael and Katharina Besch. The younger Michael was another charter member of the St. Aloysius Court No. 148 Catholic Order of Foresters. He worked the Chicago and North Western Railway as a member of the train crew, but he also took pride in farming. (Courtesy of the Winfield Historical Society.)

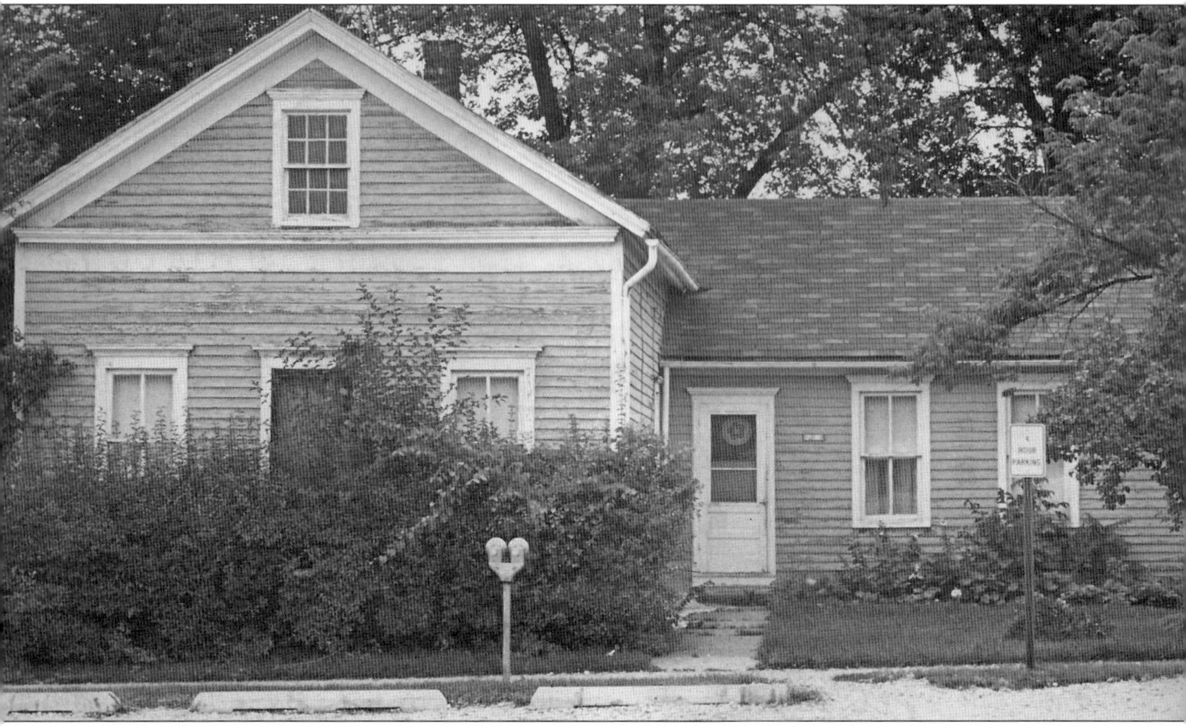

Michael and Eva raised their family at their home at 0S070 Church Street, formerly the original freight depot in Winfield that was built by John Hedges. Eva inherited the home from her sister, Mary, in 1897, and for the next 80 years, the home would be home to the Besch family. The Besch family home, also known as Hedges Station (after John Hedges), was saved by the Winfield Historical Society and moved to Oakwood Park in August 1981. It is now a local history museum for the Winfield community. (Courtesy of the Winfield Historical Society.)

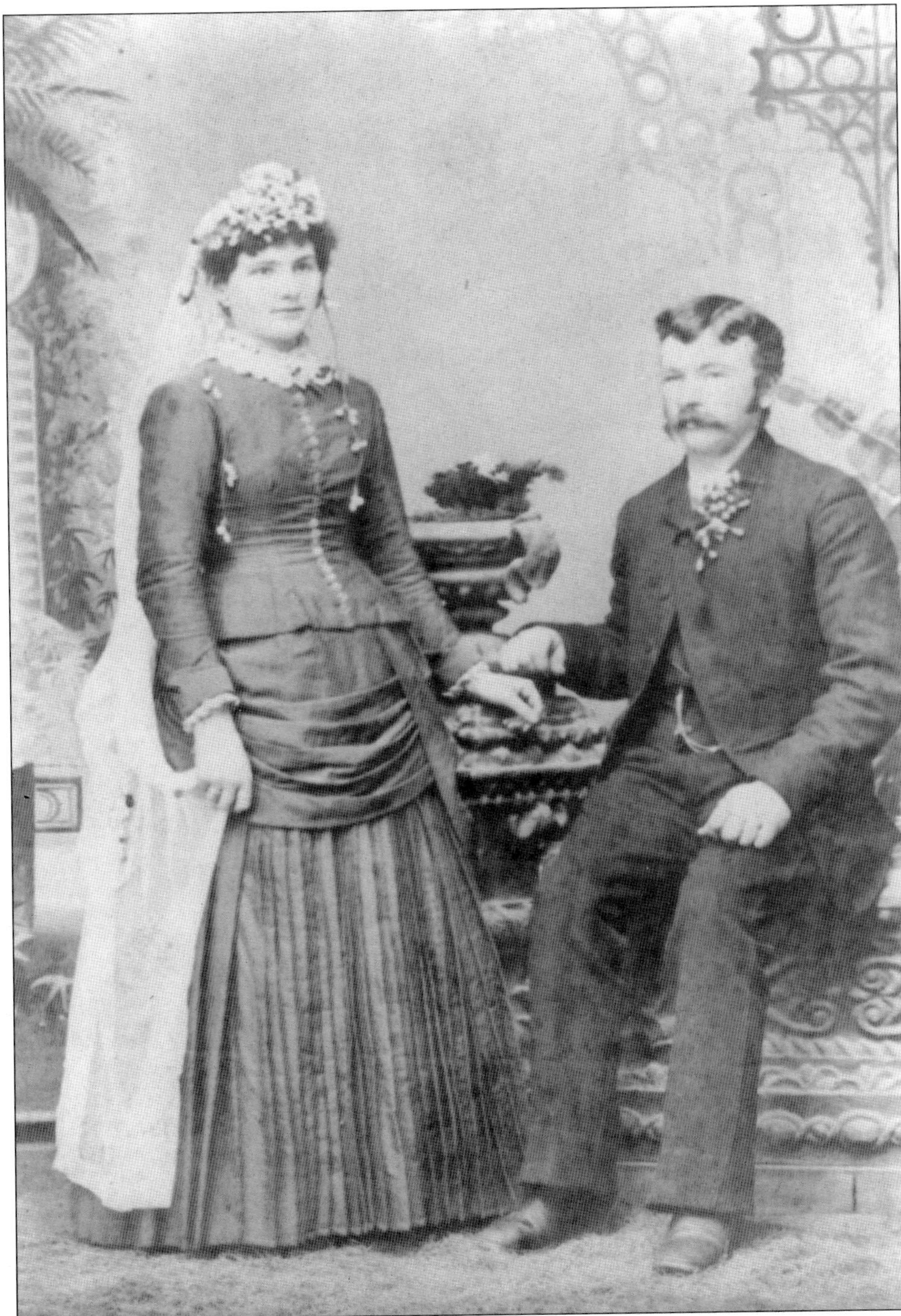

Michael Besch's brother John and Regina Besch celebrate their wedding day in 1885. John and Regina raised their 10 children on the family farm along what is now Geneva Road until 1910. They then moved to the Carson Farm on Pleasant Hill along Jewell Road until John's death in 1919. The farm was then sold, and Regina moved across the street from Michael and Eva Besch. (Courtesy of the Winfield Historical Society.)

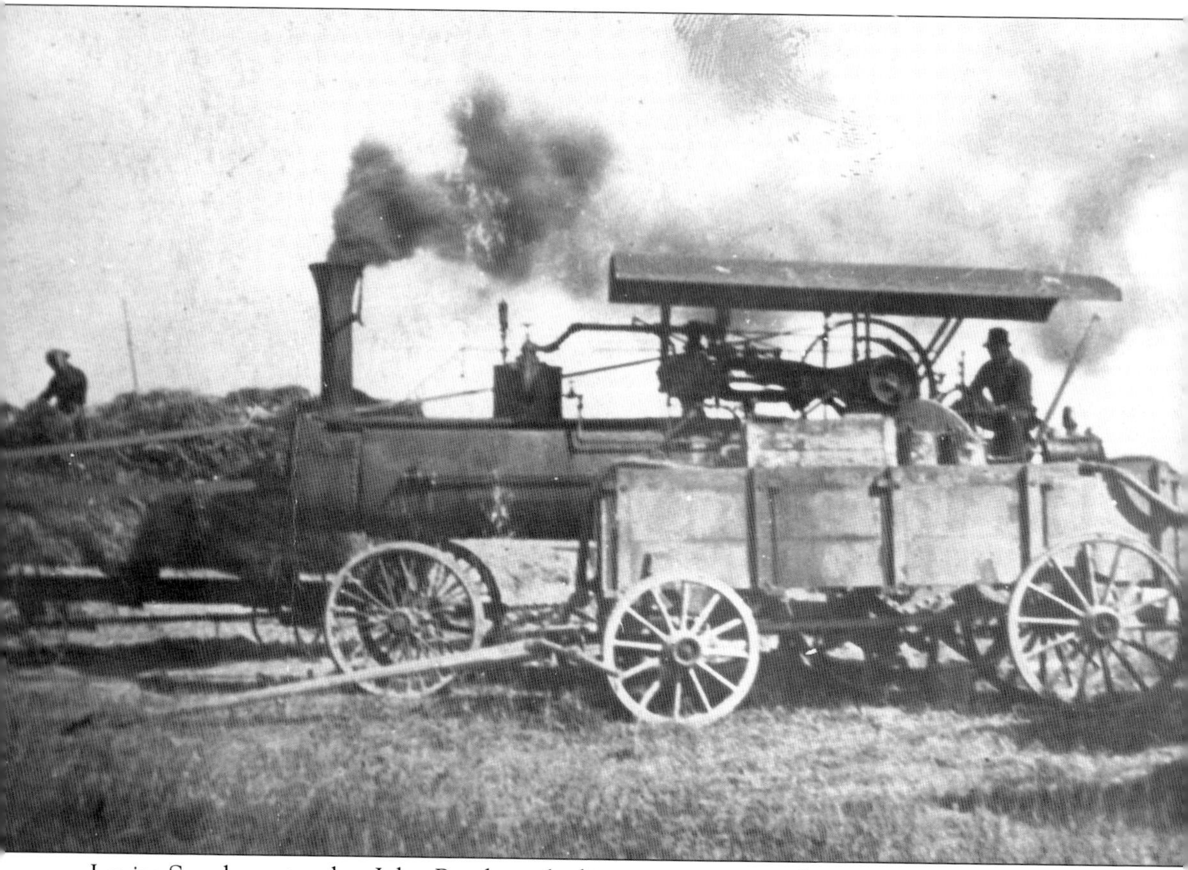

Louise Spanke notes that John Besch worked in conjunction with John Heinz, Milton Player, J.C. Schramer, and John Klein as members of a "ring" of steam thresher owners in town. Labor on the farms was shared between each farmer in the "ring." This photograph features a steam thresher at the John Besch farm. (Courtesy of the Winfield Historical Society.)

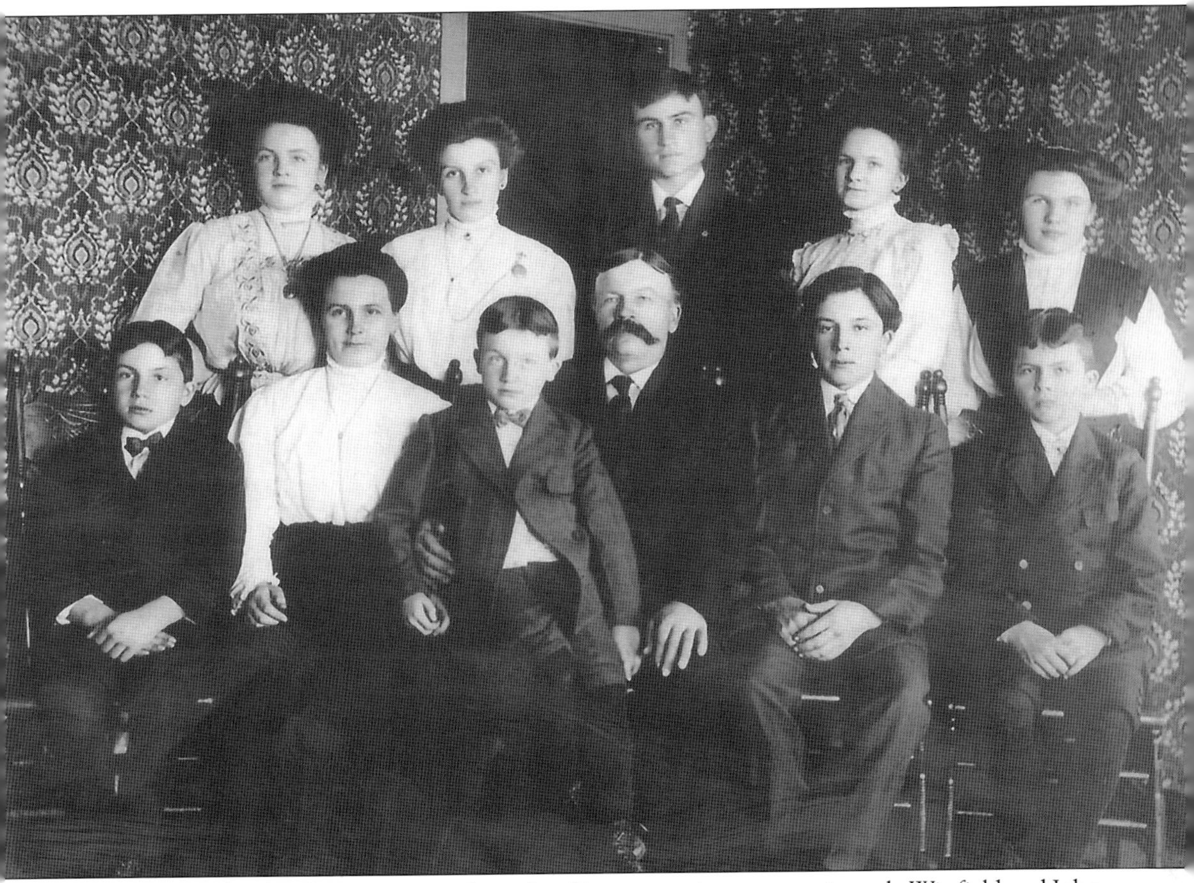

As in many other local communities, large families were quite common in early Winfield and John and Regina Besch's family was no exception. Pictured are, from left to right, (first row) Adam, Regina, Edward, John, George, and Frank; (second row) Mary Ann, Katherine, John, Helen, and Emma. (Courtesy of the Winfield Historical Society.)

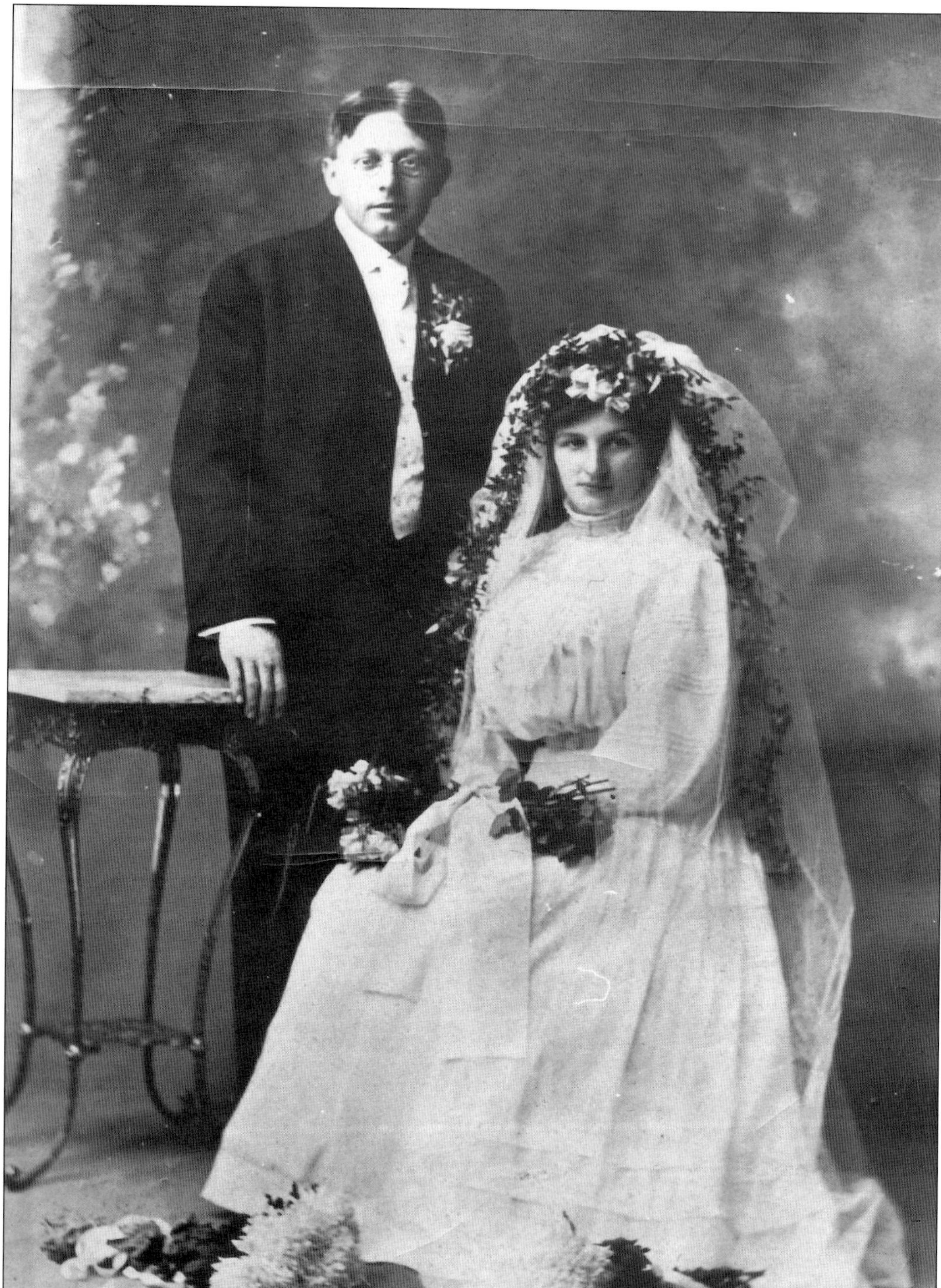

John and Regina's eldest child, Katherine, is shown here on the occasion of her wedding to Nicholas Fuchsen on October 22, 1907. Nicholas was born in November 1882 and passed at the young age of 46 on March 20, 1928. The couple had two children, a son and a daughter. Katherine was a widow for just over 35 years, with her passing coming on February 15, 1964.

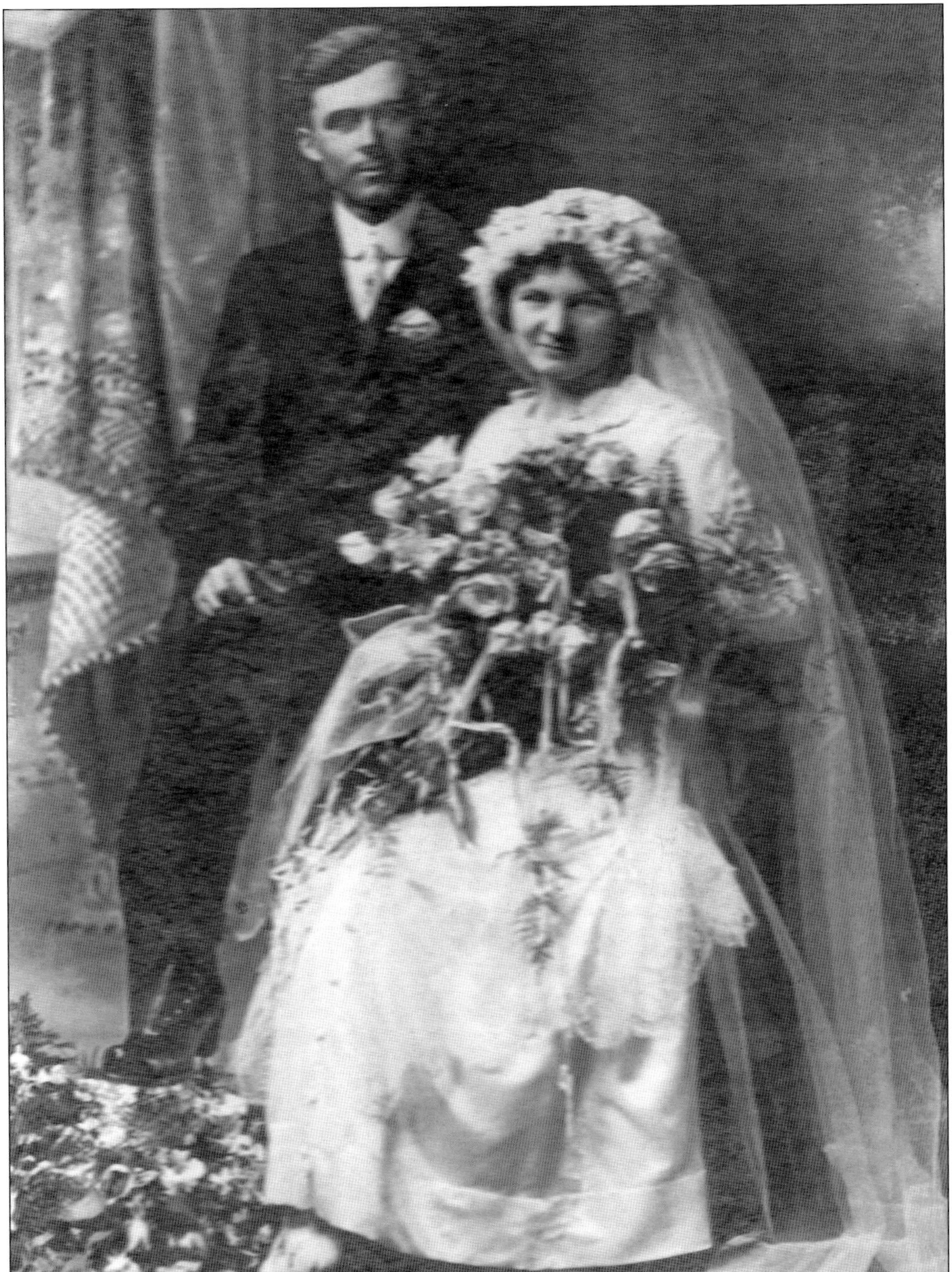

Another of John and Regina's daughters, Helen appears on her wedding day with her husband, Andrew J. Schramer, in 1919. Andrew and Helen had two daughters, Louise Regina and Audrey. Helen passed away on April 11, 1984, with Andrew following on February 5, 1985. (Courtesy of Al Besch collection and the Winfield Historical Society.)

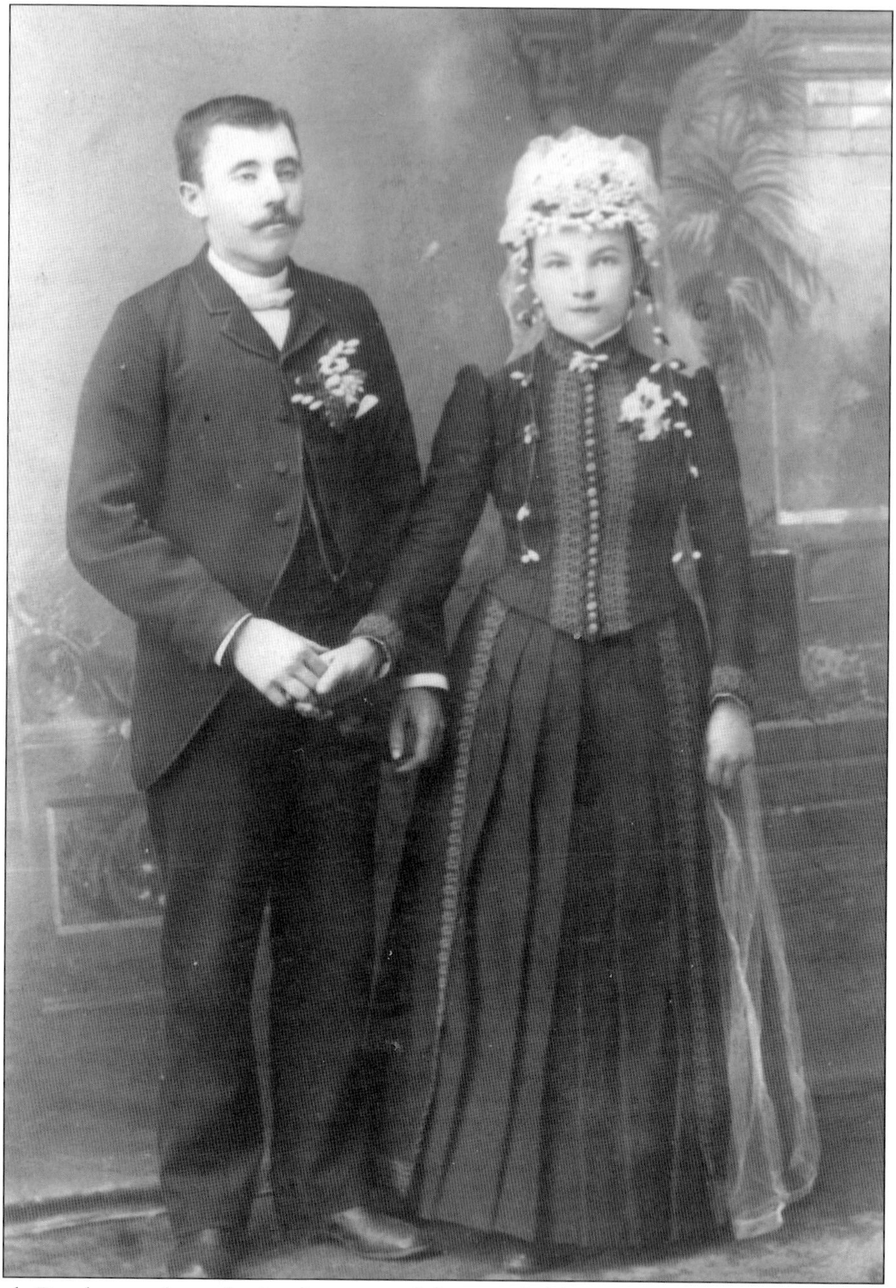

Elizabeth Besch was the only daughter out of the six children born to Michael and Katharina Besch. According to a Besch family history that was done by Otto Besch and given to the Winfield Historical Society in 1991, Elizabeth was born on November 28, 1871. She had five older brothers. Here, Elizabeth is pictured with her husband, Nicholas Bauler, on their wedding day; the exact year is not identified. Elizabeth's father passed in 1873, and for the next 17 years, Elizabeth stayed with her widowed mother. Once they were married, Elizabeth and Nicholas moved to Aurora. They had five children: one son and four daughters. They also legally adopted the two children of their daughter Margaret after she passed away suddenly in 1919. Elizabeth passed away in 1945. (Courtesy of the Winfield Historical Society.)

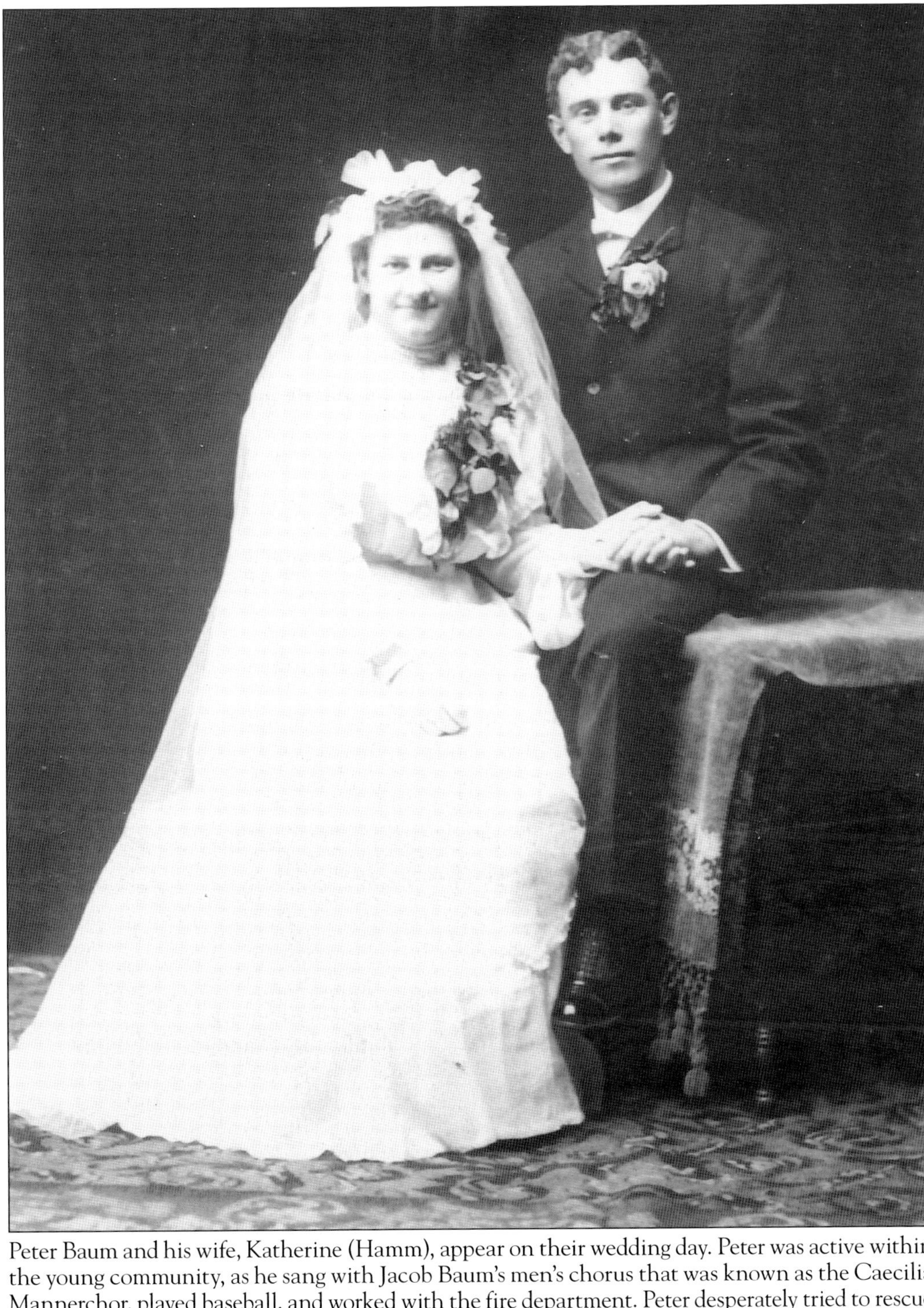

Peter Baum and his wife, Katherine (Hamm), appear on their wedding day. Peter was active within the young community, as he sang with Jacob Baum's men's chorus that was known as the Caecilia Mannerchor, played baseball, and worked with the fire department. Peter desperately tried to rescue Anthony Hamm from a disastrous fire that hit Sehnem Hall in 1931. The fire claimed Hamm's life, as it was noted by the local fire department that his body was burned beyond recognition. (Courtesy of the Winfield Historical Society.)

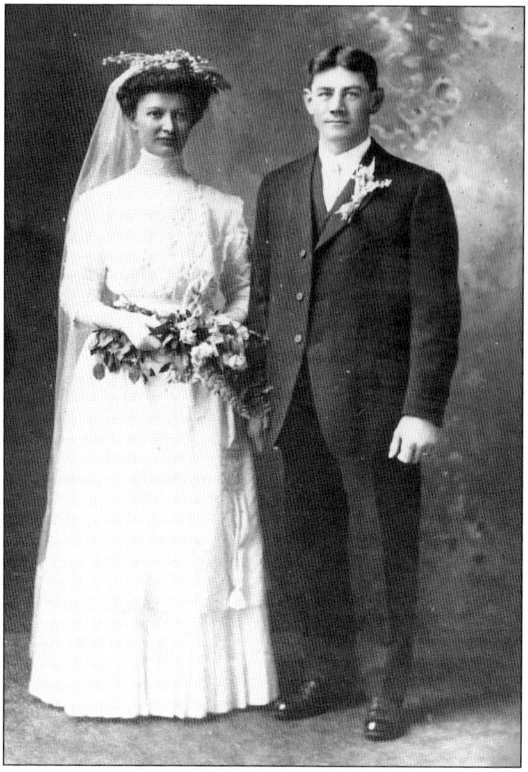

Weddings between families were quite common in the early Winfield community—as they were in other communities not just in Illinois, but across the country. The photograph at left features Matt Arends with his wife, Vernie (Lies). The image below features Peter P. Jungels with his wife, Rosa (Heinz), on their wedding day on January 27, 1914. Once again, both photographs feature beaming brides and grooms. (Both, courtesy of the Winfield Historical Society).

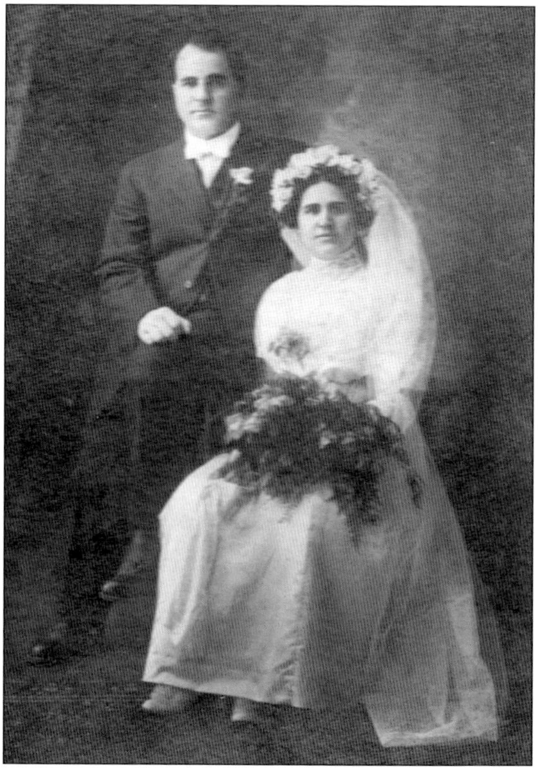

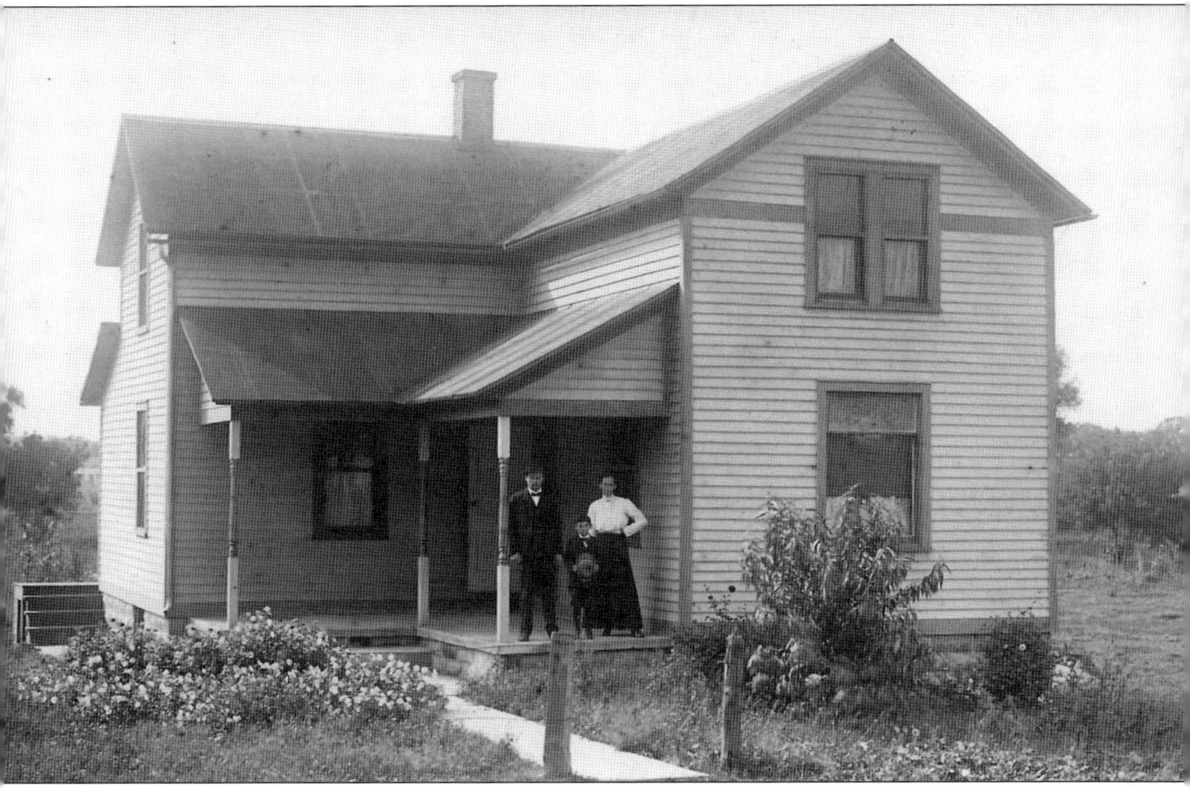

According to the identifications accompanying this image, from left to right, John, Christopher, and Kate Armbrust are standing on the front porch of this home. The year this photograph was taken is not indicated. (Courtesy of the Winfield Historical Society.)

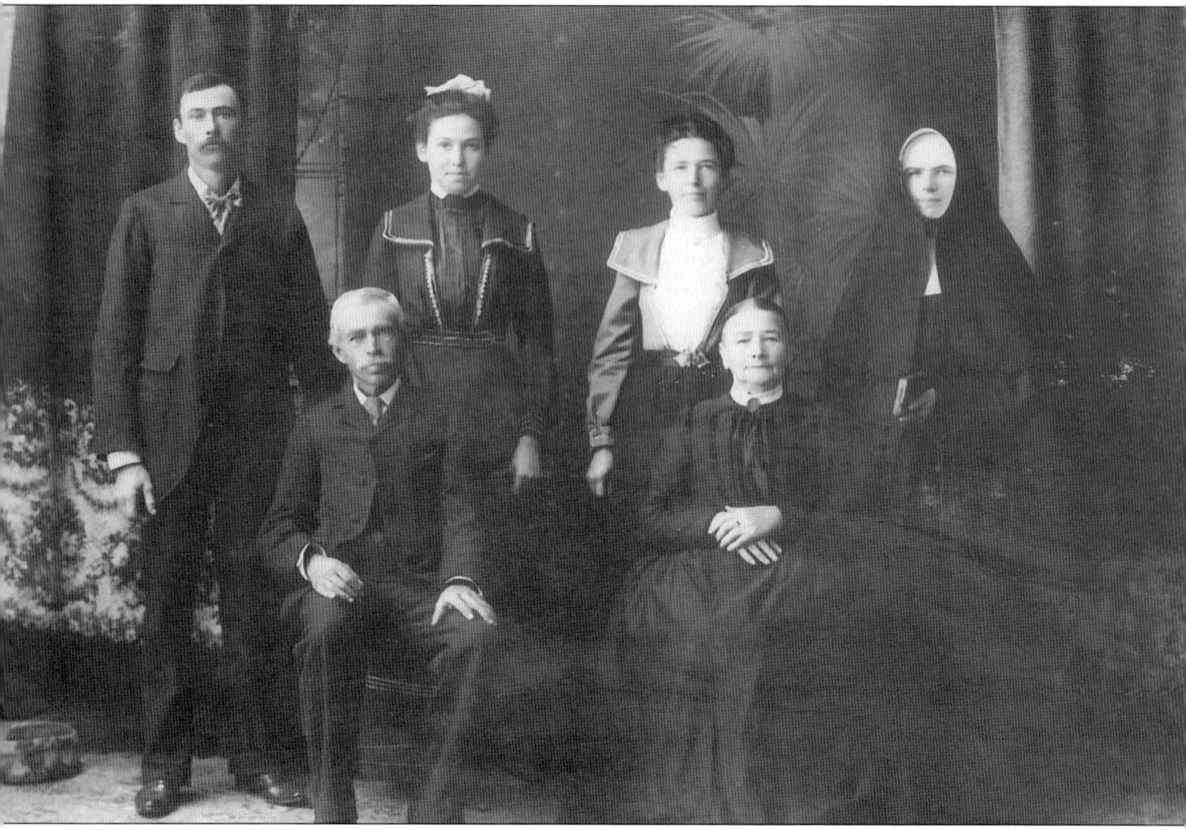

Christopher and Margaret Daleiden are shown with their family. Third from the left in back is Susan Daleiden, who would marry Caspar Schlick. Standing next to her, at far right, is Barbara Daleiden, who would become Sister Philippina. (Courtesy of Kevin Davis and the Winfield Historical Society.)

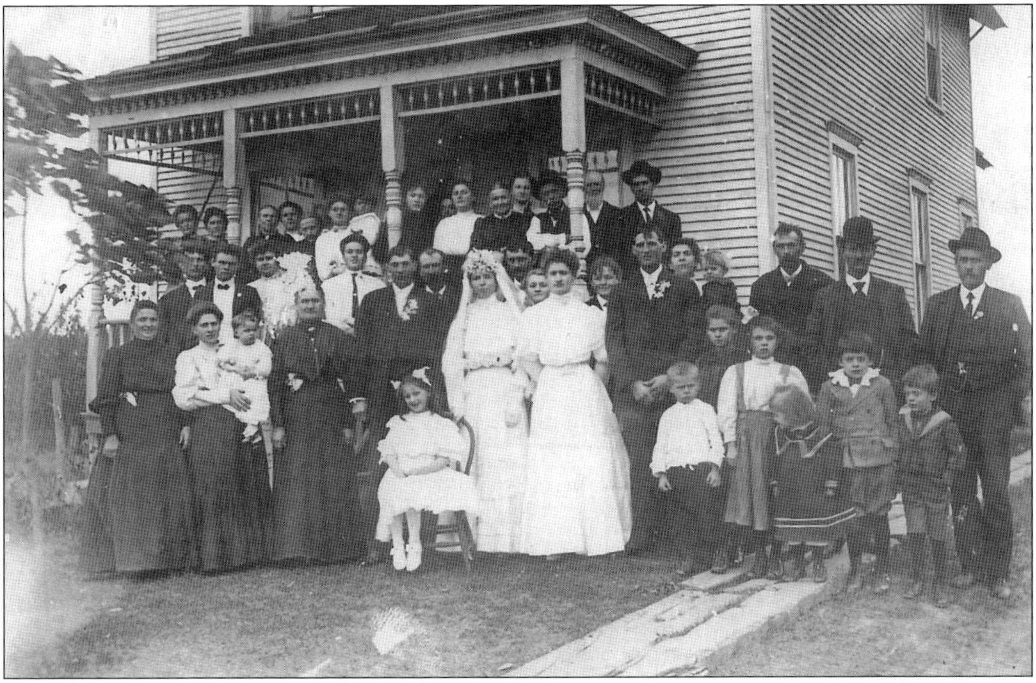

Caspar Schlick and Susan Daleiden celebrate their wedding with family and friends on October 12, 1909. This photograph was taken at the Daleiden home in Winfield near St. John the Baptist Church, where the ceremony took place. It was quite a gathering. In the image below, John Schlick (left) stands next to Susan (Daleiden) Schlick, Caspar Schlick, Katherine (Daleiden) Armbrust, and John Armbrust in front of a house on Church Street in Winfield. (Both, courtesy of Kevin Davis and the Winfield Historical Society.)

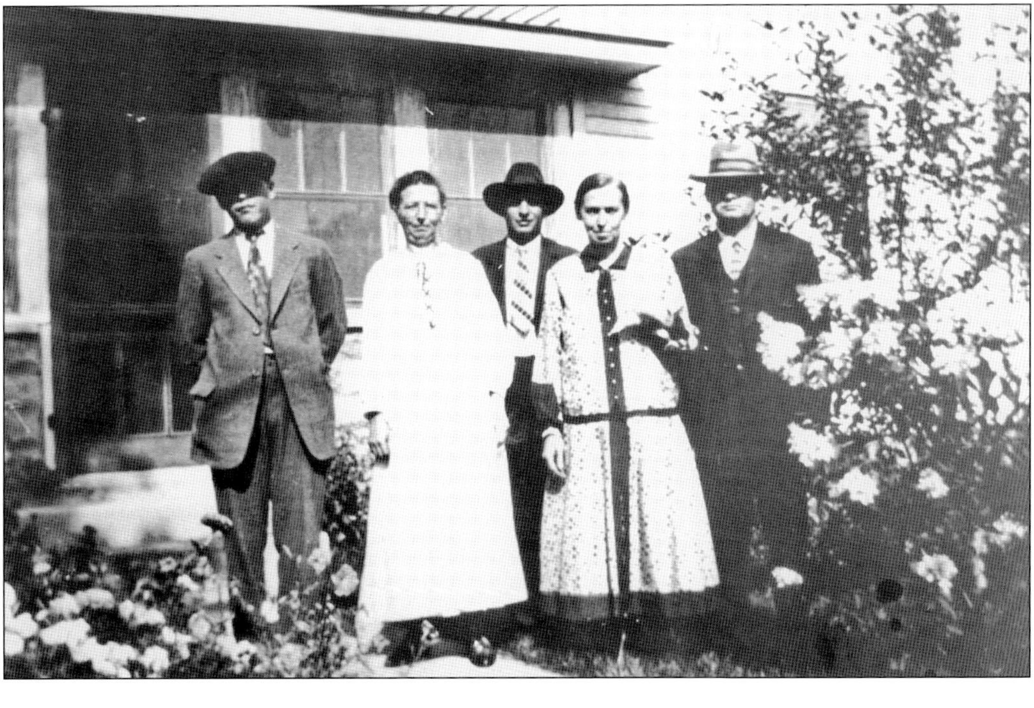

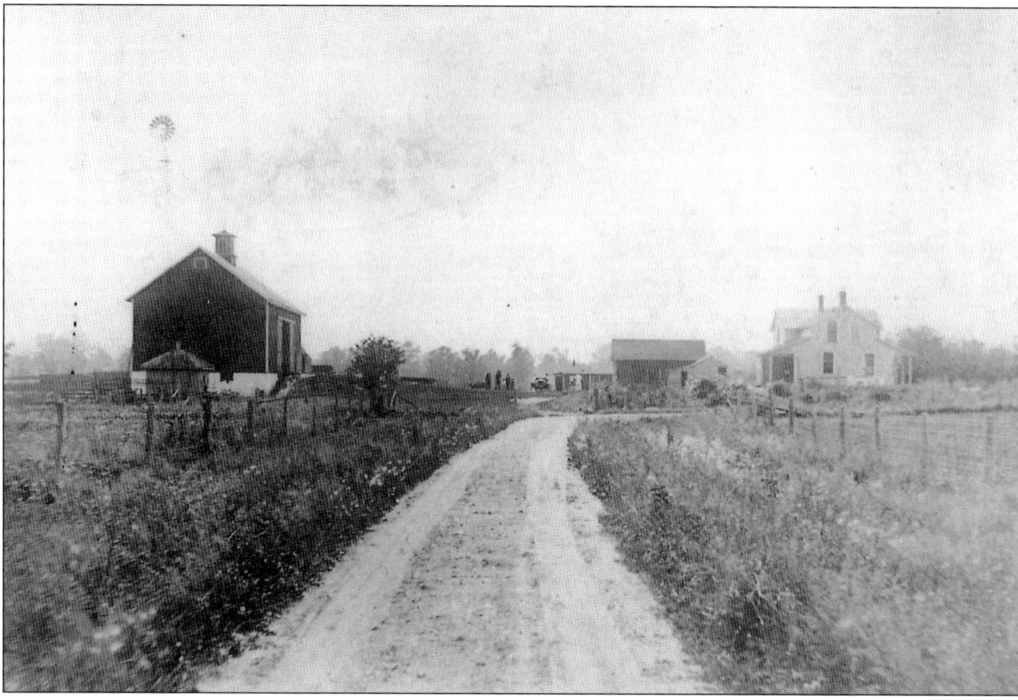

This is the farm and land that belonged to the Daleiden family before 1909. When Susan Daleiden married Caspar Schlick in 1909, the farm became their home. It was then known as the Caspar Schlick farm for the next 11 years, from 1909 to 1920. (Courtesy of Kevin Davis and the Winfield Historical Society.)

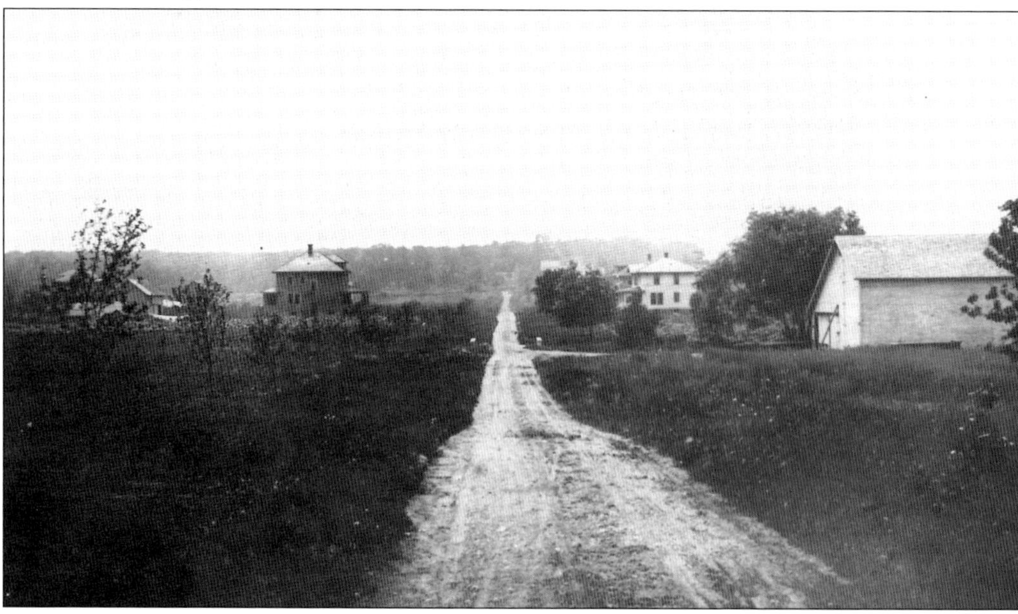

The view looks south on Park Street in Winfield. On the right are, from front to back, Peter Schmidt's icehouse, the Rutschman home, and Nicholas Schramer's home. On the left is John Kosusnik's home, with William Zeier's home being farther to the left. (Courtesy of Jas. McCabe and the Winfield Historical Society.)

Two

What Was Work in Winfield

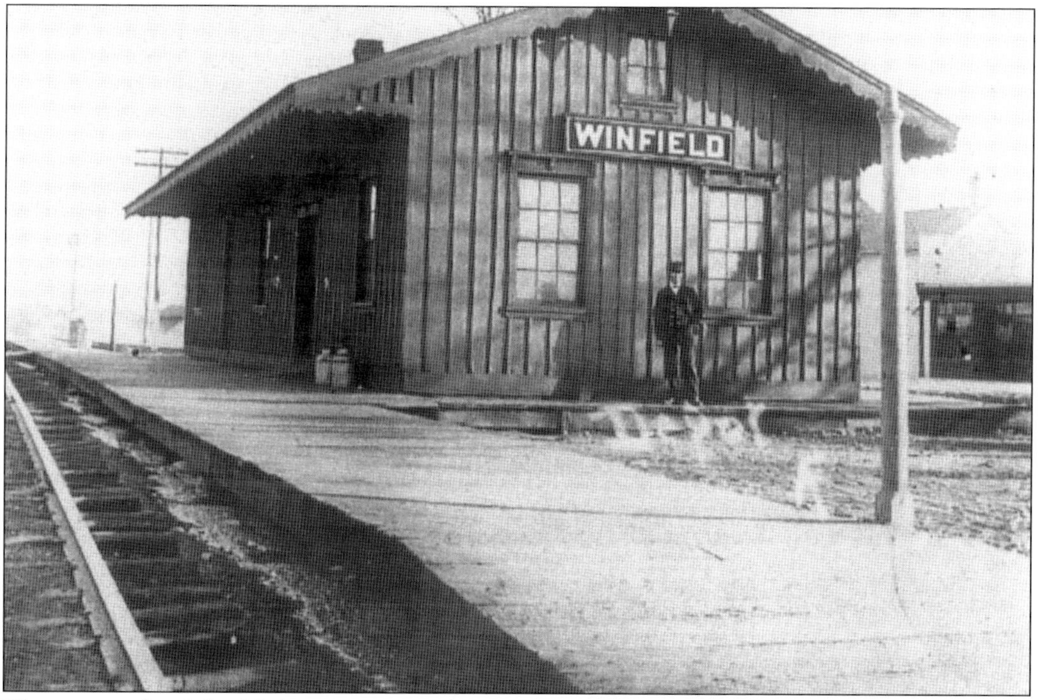

The station that John Hedges constructed in 1849 served as the local freight depot for five years. A second depot was constructed in 1854, this being on the south side of the tracks. Here, that second depot is shown, though the exact year and the station agent shown in front are unidentified. Chicago Avenue, which featured Peter Schmidt's meat market in the center of town, is seen in the background. (Courtesy of the Winfield Historical Society.)

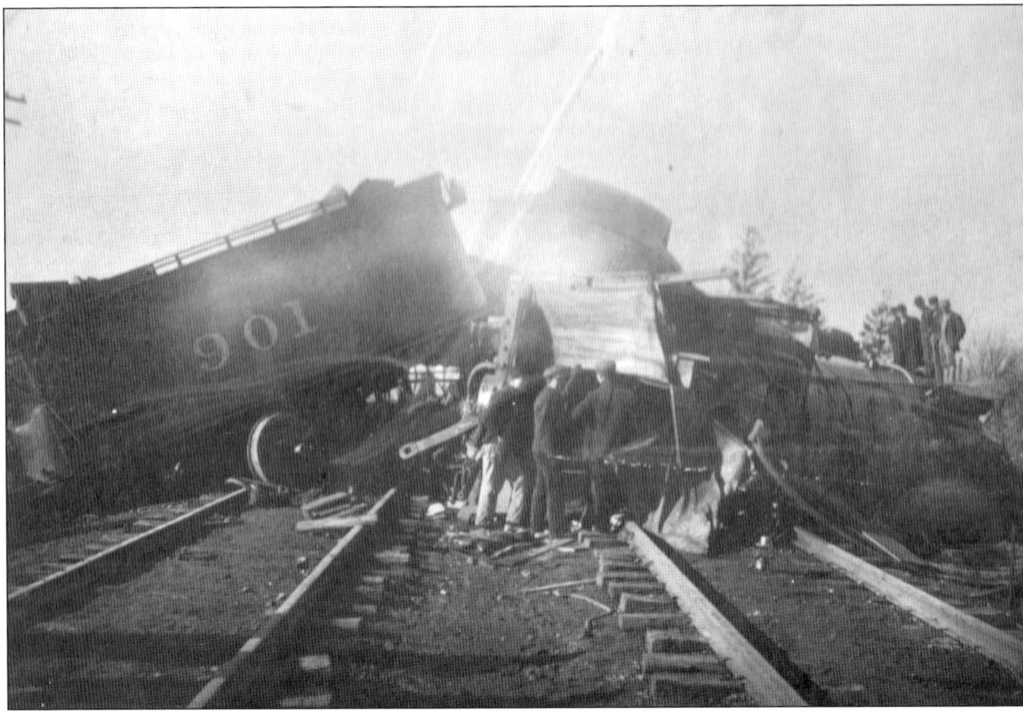

The work in the early community was not always glamorous. Accidents did happen. Here are two examples of what is described as a Sterling passenger train wreck at a Winfield rail crossing. The photograph above is listed as being taken in 1906, while the photograph below is said to have been made in 1903 and is featured in the February 23, 1975, edition of the *Sunday Journal*. According to the information specified for this photograph, the regular engineer of this train had taken the day off, but was still on board, riding coach. The substitute engineer ran the train too quickly for the turns, and the result was this wreck. A fireman and engineer (whether it is the regular or substitute is not known) perished as a result of this. Whether the actual year of the wreck was 1903 or 1906, the result was gruesome. (Both, courtesy of David and Patricia Enders and the Winfield Historical Society.)

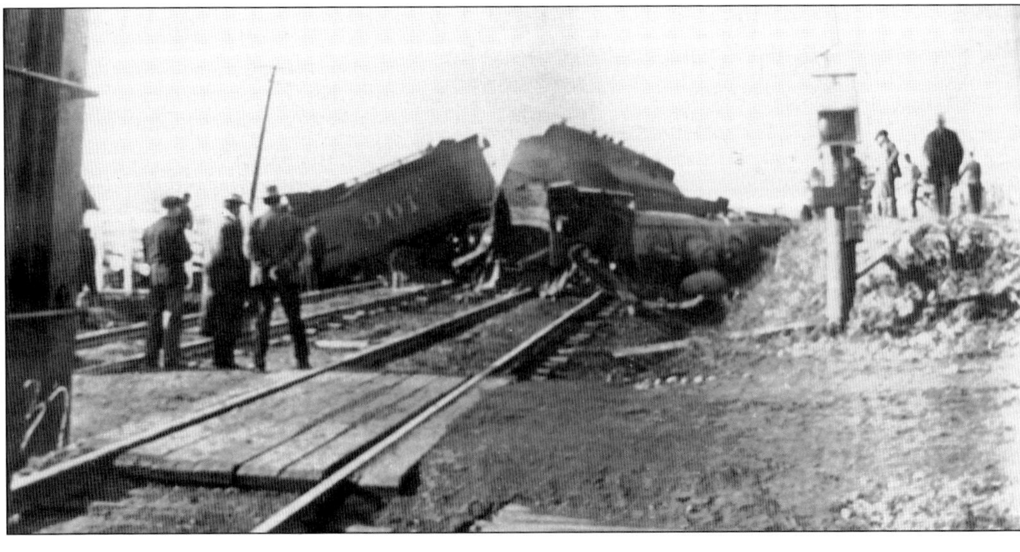

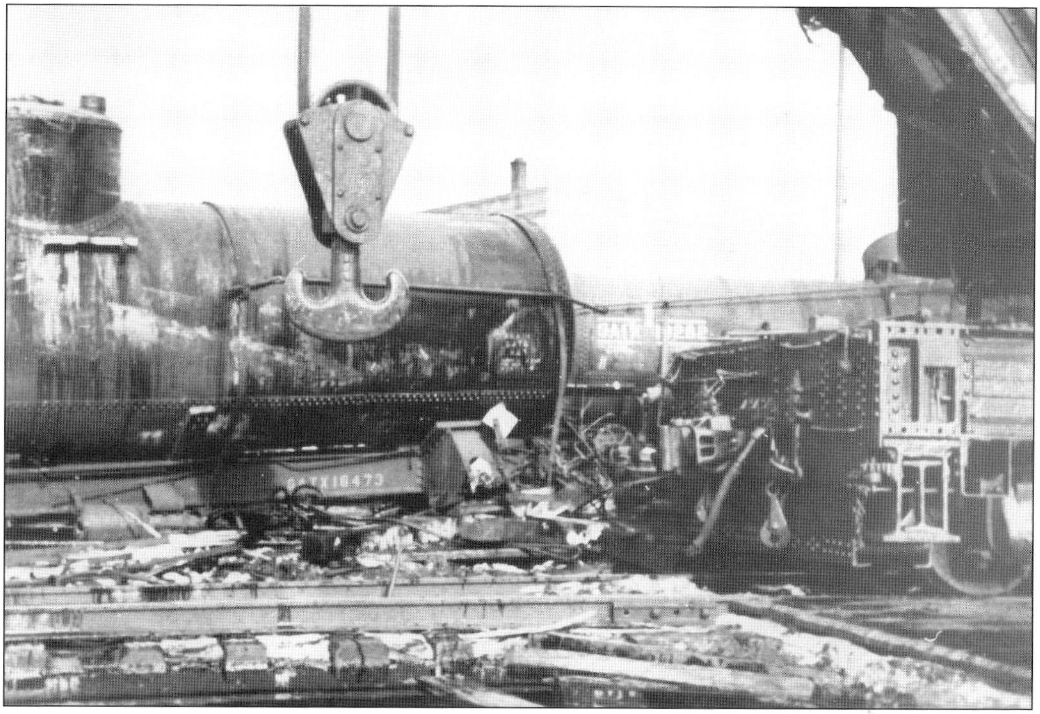

Here are two more examples of the hazards that can happen while being on the job. The image above features another train wreck in Winfield; this time, the year specified is 1943. Significant damage is evident. The photograph below features an automobile burning on a highway outside of Winfield in 1936. The said automobile collided with a cattle truck bearing a load of hogs from Iowa. The driver of the automobile was killed, while the three men manning the cattle truck suffered serious injuries. (Both, courtesy of the Winfield Historical Society.)

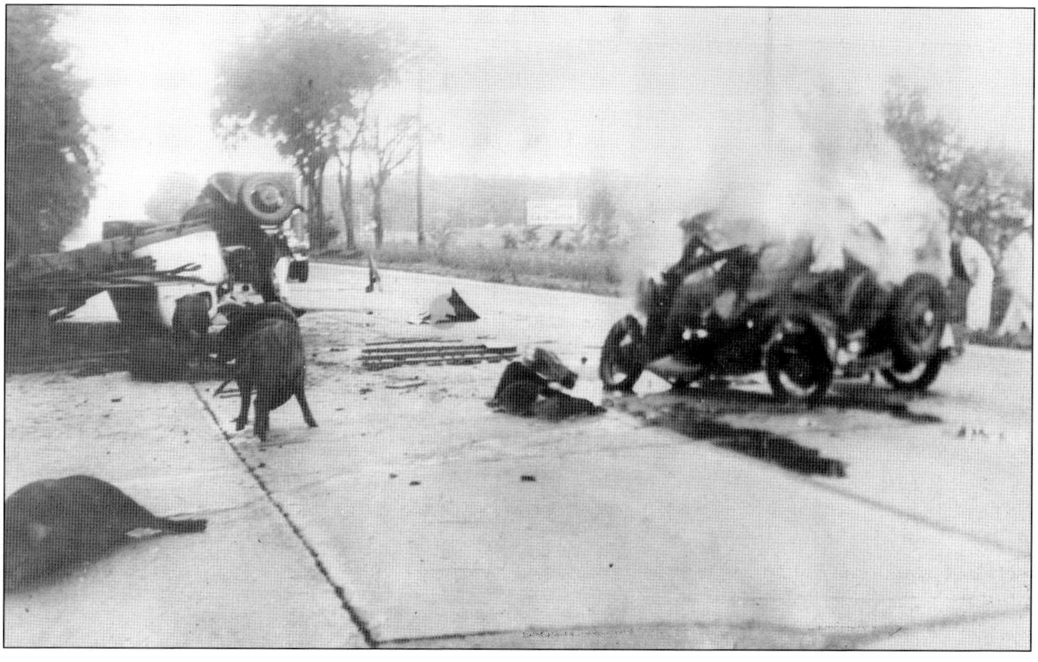

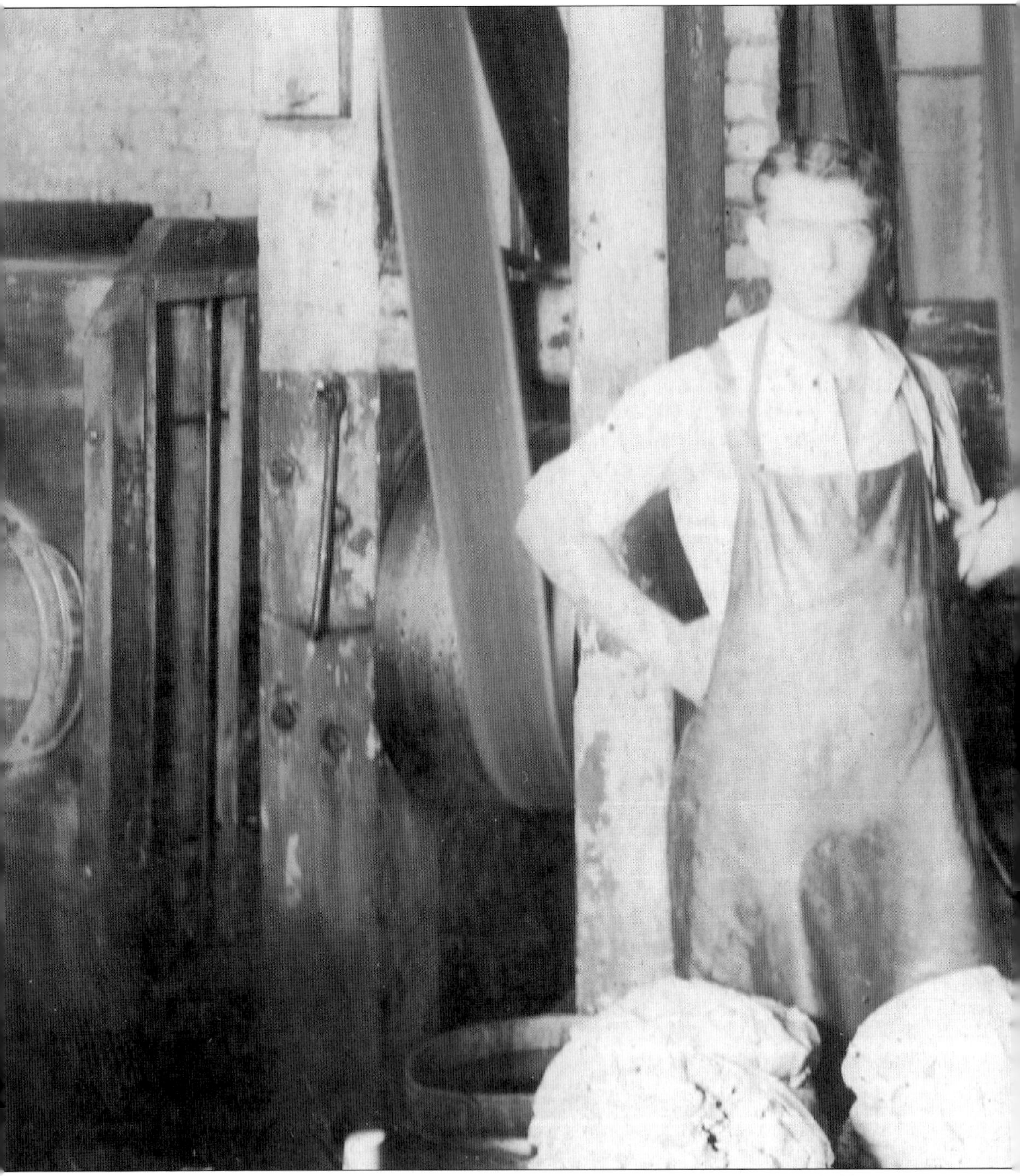

Maurice Dooley (right) and John F. Wilcox (left) were managers of the Winfield Cooperative Creamery in 1895. Located just east of town, the creamery was the preeminent local business in the early years of the village. Louise Spanke notes that, according to records done by Rufus Blanchard in 1882, the creamery's first year of operation, the creamery went through 6.000 pounds of milk on average daily in the production of 120 pounds of butter and 425 pounds of cheese on average daily. By 1884, the creamery was outbidding the Warrenville creamery by about 5¢ and

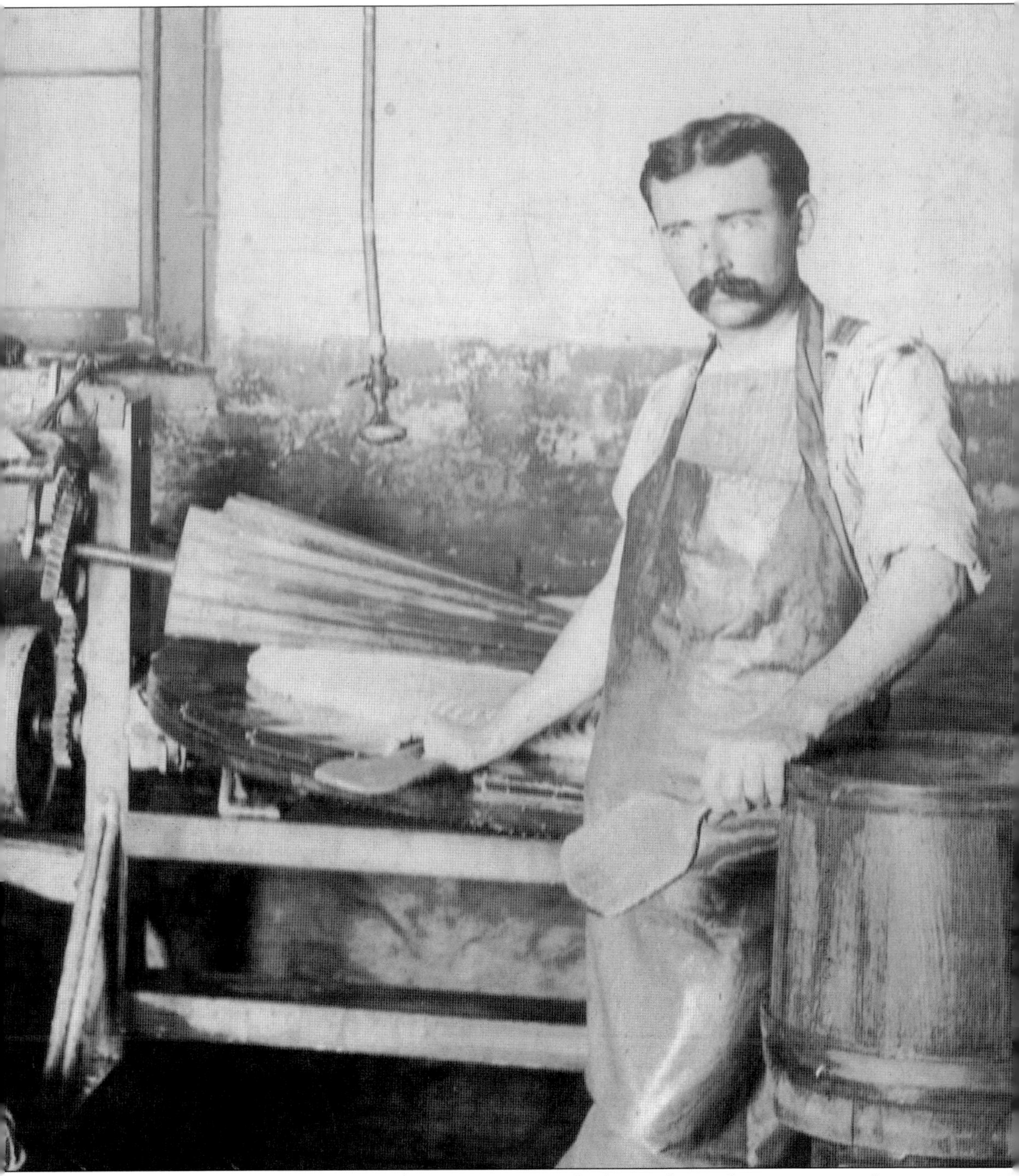

managed to pay its dairy farmers about $1.55 for every hundred pounds. Production increased even more in 1889 following the razing of the creamery in West Chicago. Winfield's creamery burned in 1895 (it is not known how long after this photograph was taken), and the living quarters of the managers pictured also burned. The creamery was rebuilt and remained in operation in the village until the early 1900s. (Courtesy of the Winfield Historical Society.)

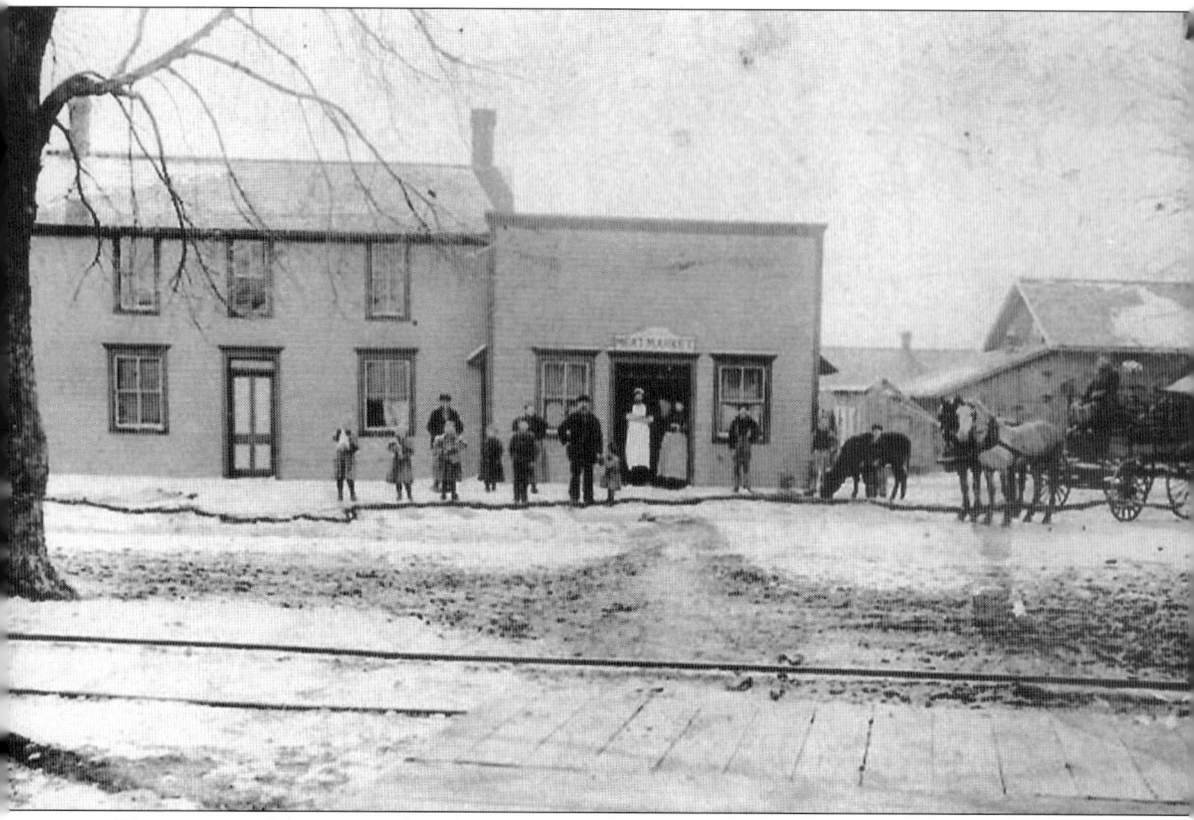

The exterior of the Peter Schmidt meat market is seen here from the platform of the second train depot that was constructed in Winfield. This photograph is from 1898. Peter would slaughter the animals that he purchased from neighboring farmers in the barn that was next door to his market. His family would assist in the butchering, curing, and marketing of the final product to the community. The meat market was at the corner of Chicago Avenue and what is now Winfield Road, part of the commercial hub of this young community. (Courtesy of the Winfield Historical Society.)

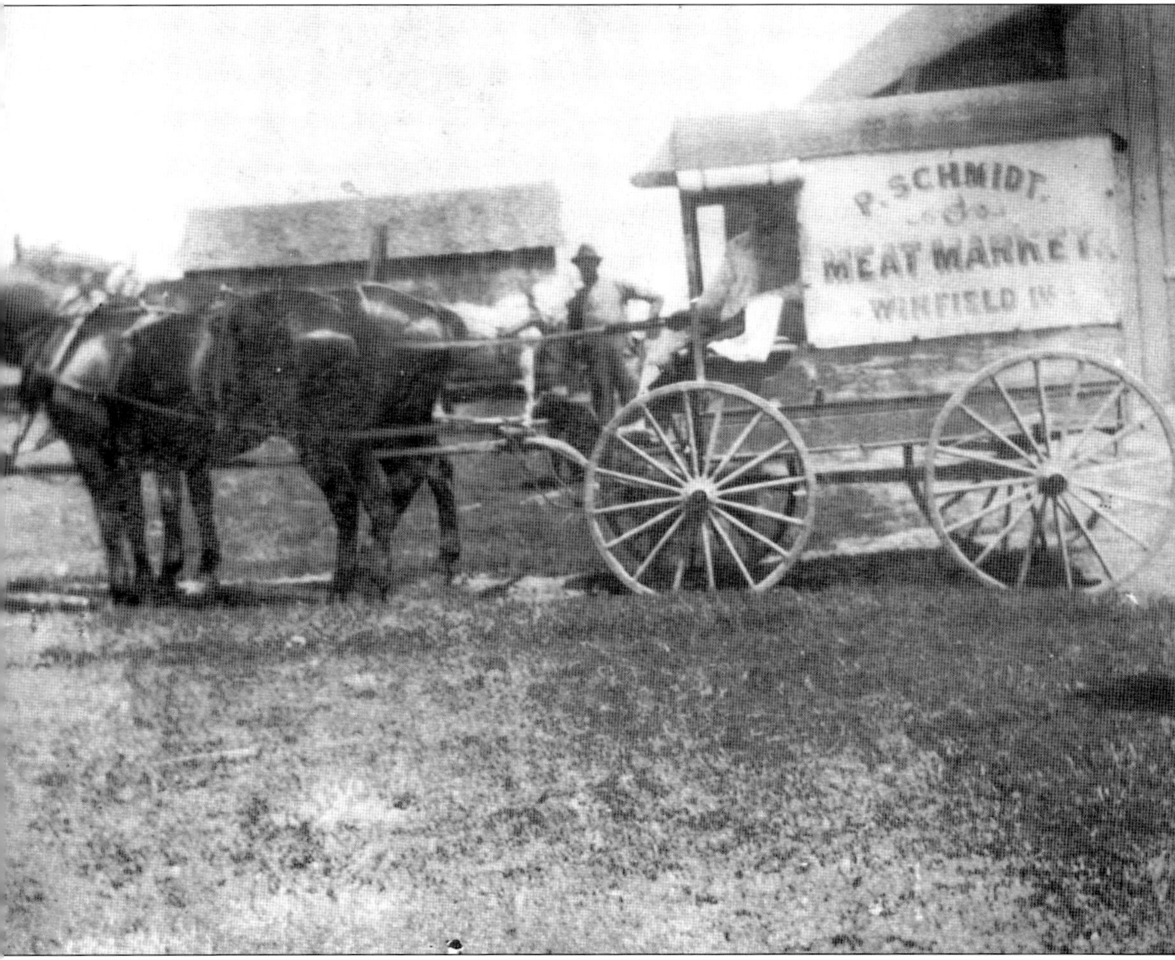

This is one of the meat market wagons that belonged to Peter Schmidt's business. These modes of transportation would often carry the ice that was cut from nearby Schmidt's pond over to the butcher shop for use, as well as to the community for use. The Schmidt family worked hard not only in their business but also in caring for their home, where the family would often take in boarders to assist with their income. (Courtesy of the Winfield Historical Society.)

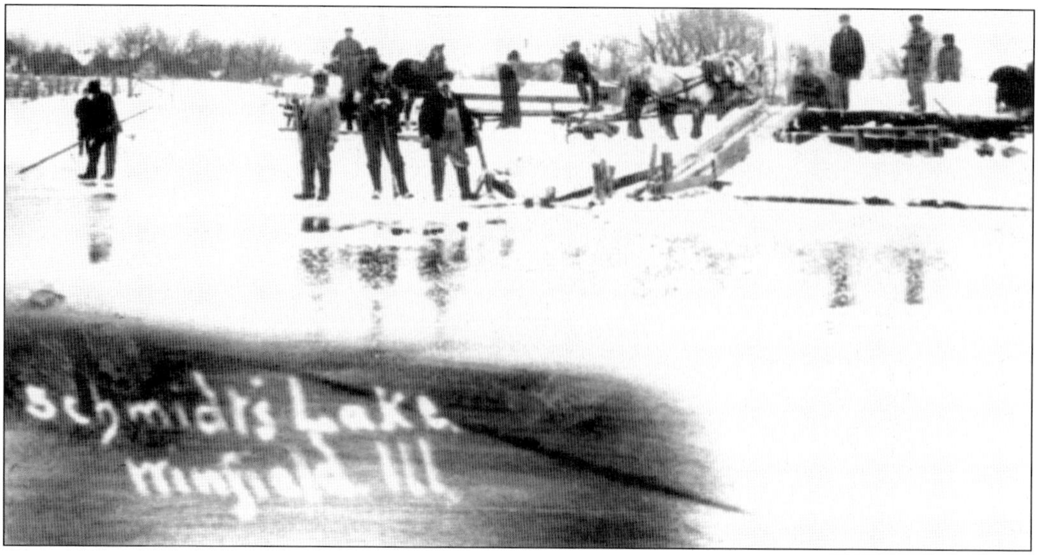

These photographs show the Schmidt pond and ice-cutting crew. Schmidt's pond was located along Park Street. This was a man-made pond created by Peter Schmidt himself. Each winter, his crew would work to cut blocks of ice to supply not only his market in the summer months but also the village. These blocks of ice were kept in an icehouse and buried in sawdust. The icehouse later became the residence of Robert Enders. One story that made the rounds regarding the icehouse was that more than ice was stored there. It was speculated that, during Prohibition, Peter may have helped his brother hide some alcohol from a federal raid in Elmhurst, where his brother had a tavern. Whether this is a true story or not is open to debate. (Both, courtesy of the Winfield Historical Society.)

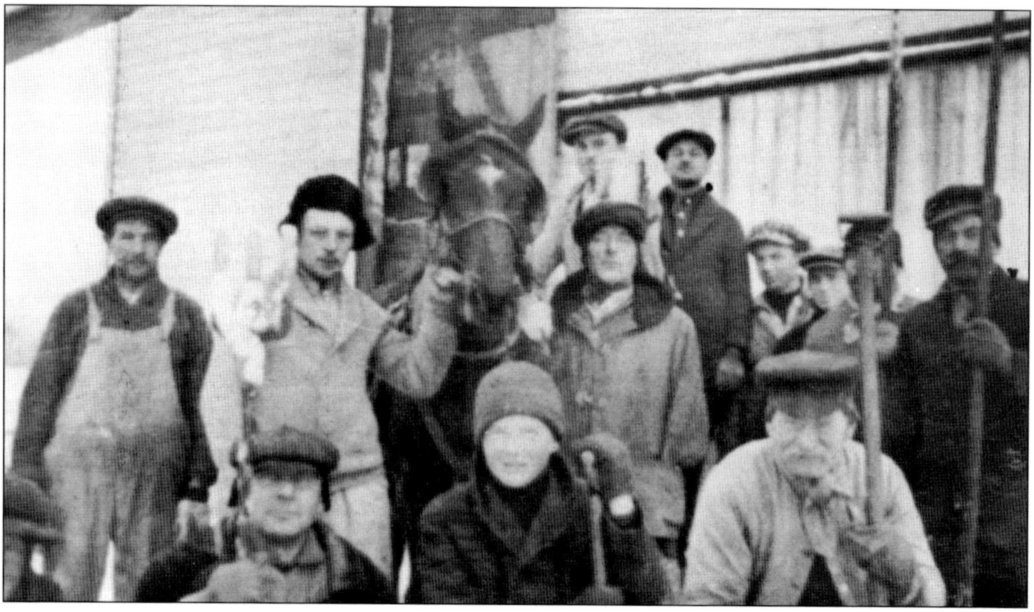

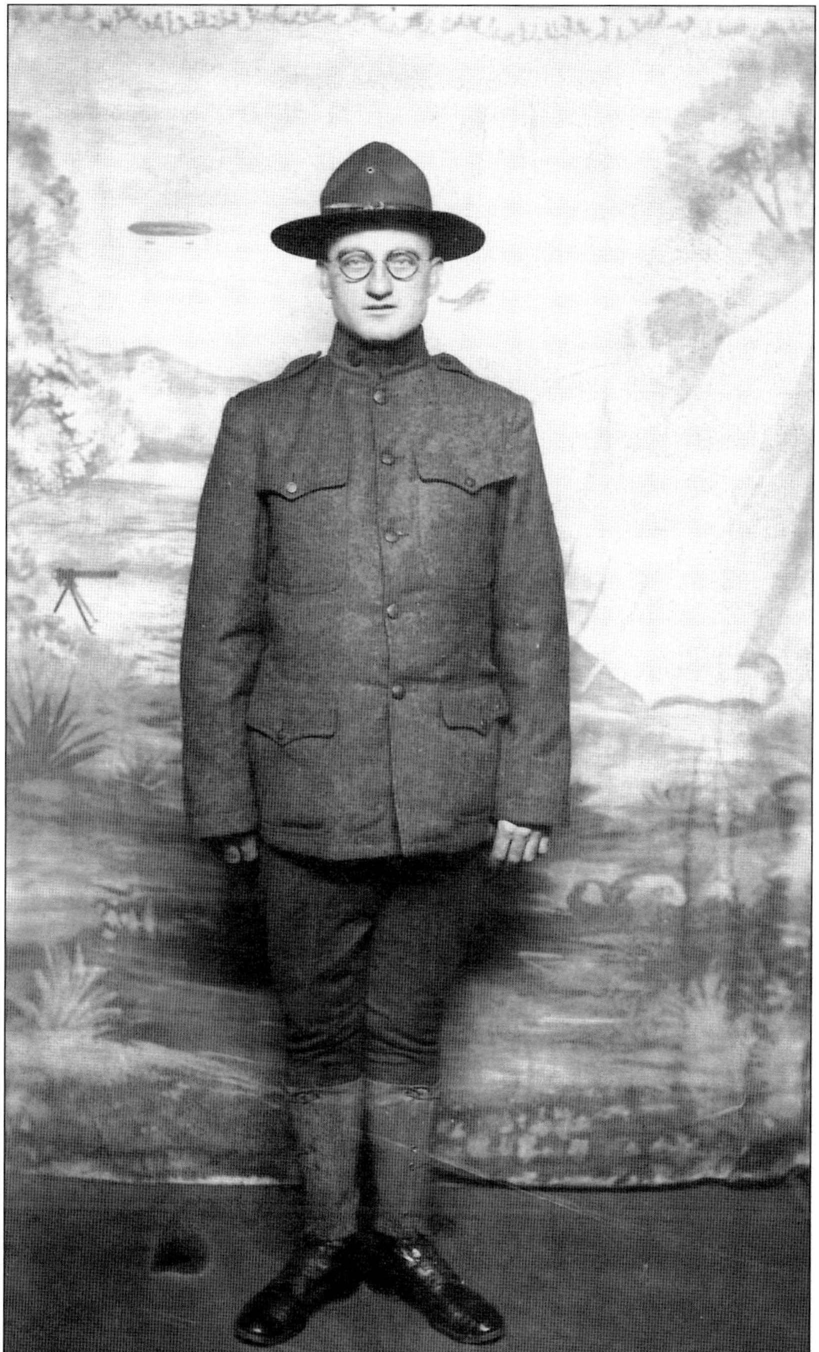

Al Schmidt was born in 1888. For many years, he assisted his father in the operations of the family meat market. He also served our country as a private in the army for a year and a half, being stationed at Camp Grant, Illinois, during World War I. This photograph features Al in his uniform while he was in military service. While stationed there, Al was the butcher on the base, no doubt drawing on his experience helping his father at their shop in Winfield. (Courtesy of the Winfield Historical Society.)

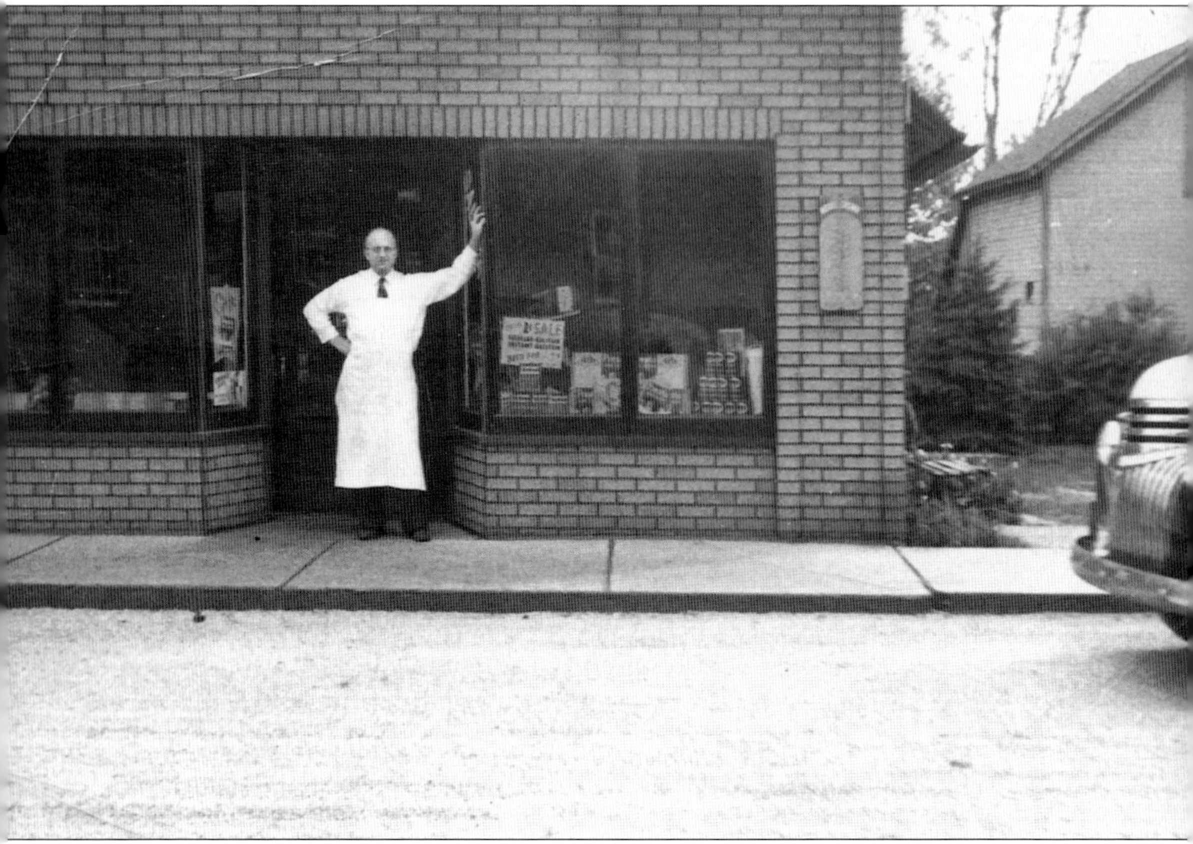

Peter Schmidt turned the ownership of his market to his son, Al Schmidt, following a stroke that Peter suffered in 1937. Along with his wife, Martha, Al expanded the business to carry more groceries and sundries over the course of the next 10 years before retiring in 1949. The photograph here shows Al standing outside the family market in 1943. Years before, Al was one of the key figures in helping to organize the Winfield Volunteer Fire Department in the early 1920s after the Bluebird Confectionery, a store just across Winfield Road not far from the meat market, burned in a blaze. The Wheaton Fire Department, the closest organized fire department to Winfield in the early 1920s, was late in responding. (Courtesy of the Winfield Historical Society.)

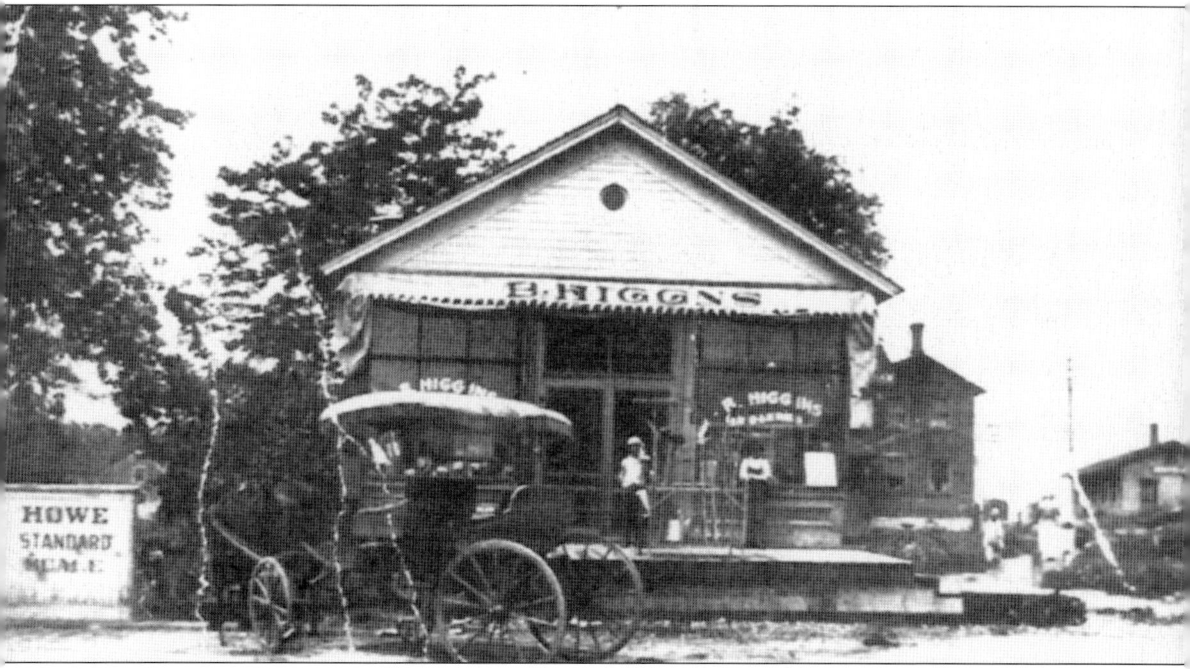

The Higgins Store became the complete general store in early Winfield. The photograph here shows the exterior of the business in 1914. Note the misspelling of the Higgins name on the store front, as the second *i* is missing. Shoppers coming to Higgins Store would find a variety of products for sale. Clothing and candy, hardware and feed, dress goods and stationery, medicine, kerosene, flour, yeast cakes, and groceries could all be found within the store. Coal was marketed in boxcars on the siding across the street. A drive-in scale was also here, and it can be seen to the left of the store in this photograph. Farmers paid 10¢ a load to weigh the grain that they were going to ship. Higgins Store was an integral part of the community until its sale and closing on August 15, 1956. (Courtesy of the Winfield Historical Society.)

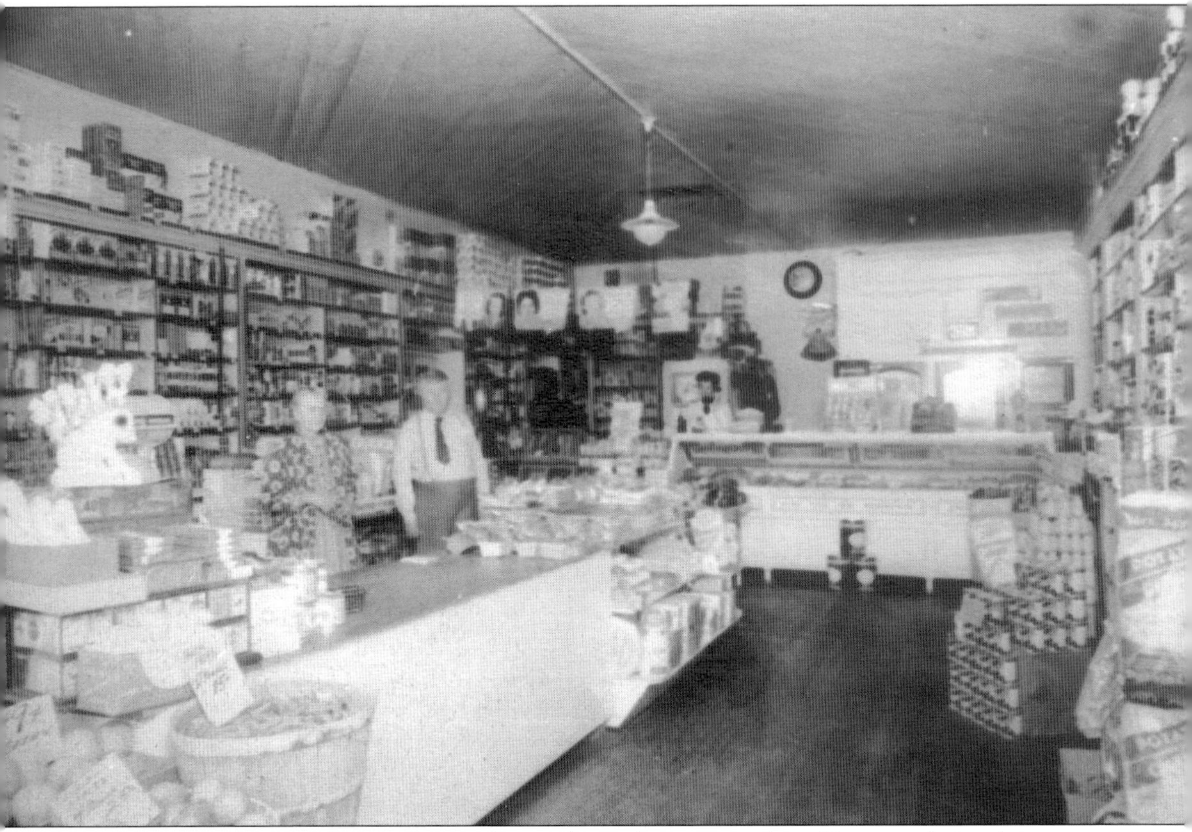

This is the interior of Higgins Store during the early 1940s. Barbara Higgins is behind the counter on the left, along with two of her children. She ran the store operations and raised her family following the sudden passing of her husband, Sanders, in 1908. Her children, in turn, helped in the housekeeping as well as in the store. Barbara made sure that all her children received their education and attended Catholic school. She continued to lease the store from the Fehrman family for the next 11 years following Sanders's death. Barbara was able to purchase ownership of the store outright in August 1919, and she was a staple there until retiring in 1956. Barbara had an affable reputation throughout the community, and residents would affectionately refer to her as "Grandma" in her later years because of her sincere generosity to all. (Courtesy of the Winfield Historical Society.)

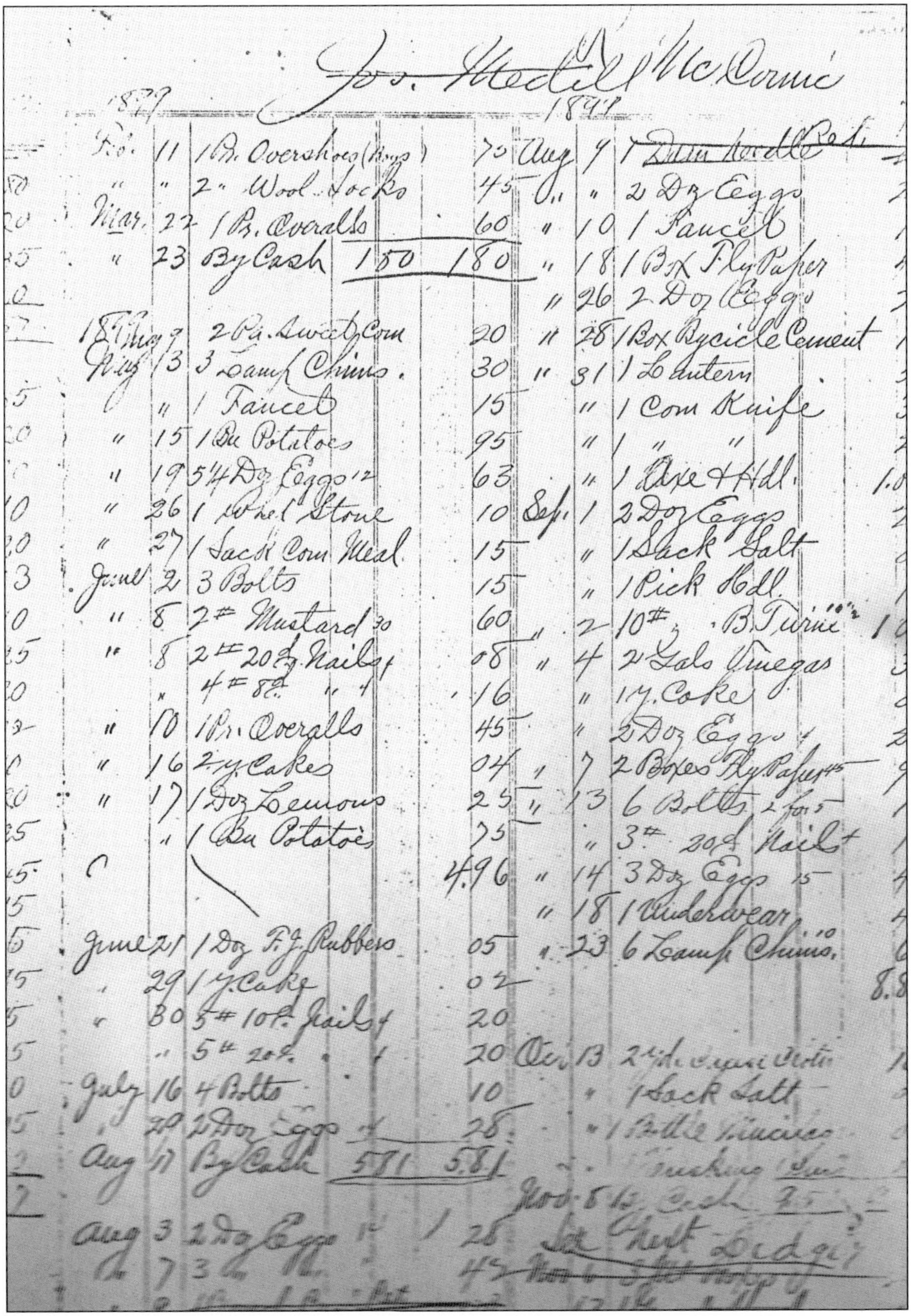

Jos. Medill McCormic

1879 — 1897

Feb. 11 1 Pr. Overshoes (Boys) 70
" " 2 " Wool Socks 45
Mar. 22 1 Pr. Overalls 60
" 23 By Cash 1 80 1 80
May 7 2 Pk. Sweet Corn 20
May 13 3 Lamp Chims. 30
" 1 Faucet 15
" 15 1 Bu Potatoes 95
" 19 5 1/4 Doz Eggs 12 63
" 26 1 Whet Stone 10
" 27 1 Sack Corn Meal 15
June 2 3 Bolts 15
" 8 2# Mustard 30 60
" 8 2# 20d Nails 4 08
4# 8d " 4 16
" 10 1 Pr. Overalls 45
" 16 2 Y. Cakes 04
" 17 1 Doz Lemons 25
" 1 Bu Potatoes 75
4.96
June 21 1 Doz F.J. Rubbers 05
" 29 1 Y. Cake 02
" 30 5# 10d Nails 4 20
" 5# 20d " 4 20
July 16 4 Bolts 10
" 20 2 Doz Eggs 14 28
Aug 11 By Cash 5 81 5.81
Aug 3 2 Doz Eggs 14 28
" 7 3 [illegible] 45

Aug 9 1 [illegible]
" " 2 Doz Eggs
" 10 1 Faucet
" 18 1 Box Fly Paper
" 26 2 Doz Eggs
" 28 1 Box Bycicle Cement
" 31 1 Lantern
" 1 Corn Knife
" 1 " "
" 1 Axe & Hdl.
Sep. 1 2 Doz Eggs
" 1 Sack Salt
" 1 Pick Hdl.
" 2 10#, B. Twine 10 1/2
" 4 2 Gals Vinegar
" 1 Y. Cake
" 2 Doz Eggs
" 7 2 Boxes Fly Paper 15
" 13 6 Bolts 2 for 5
" 3# 20d Nails
" 14 3 Doz Eggs 15
" 18 1 Underwear
" 23 6 Lamp Chims.
Oct 13 [illegible]
1 Sack Salt
Nov 8 By Cash
See Next Ledger

This is an example of one of the pages in the Higgins Store ledges that kept track of purchase per customer account. This particular page features account belonging to Col. Robert McCormick's farm. Among purchases listed are potatoes, eggs, cornmeal, and salt. Even when payments were made, this was noted, as well, such as the line featuring the date March 23. The specification "by cash" has been made. Colonel McCormick's farm took the account over from McCormick's grandfather Joseph Medill. All visitors to Higgins Store who made purchases had a page like this one created for them. (Courtesy of the Winfield Historical Society.)

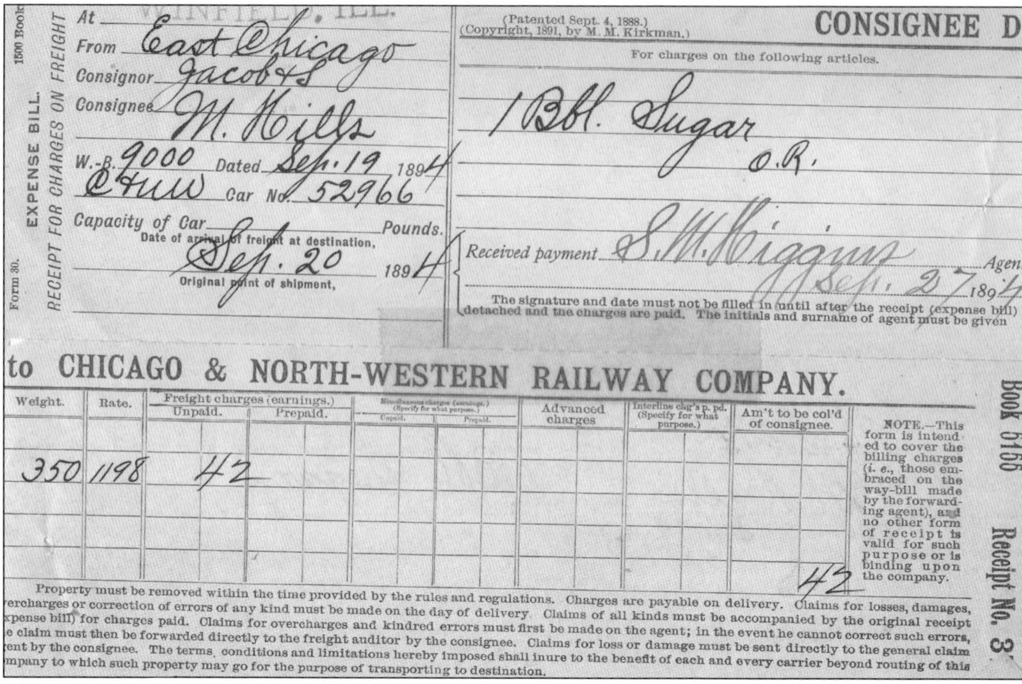

1500 Book

Form 30. EXPENSE BILL. RECEIPT FOR CHARGES ON FREIGHT

At WINFIELD, ILL.
From East Chicago
Consignor Jacob & S
Consignee M. Hills
W.-B. 9000 Dated Sep. 19 1894
C&NW Car No. 52966
Capacity of Car Pounds.
Date of arrival of freight at destination, Sep. 20 1894
Original point of shipment,

(Patented Sept. 4, 1888.)
(Copyright, 1891, by M. M. Kirkman.)

CONSIGNEE D

For charges on the following articles.

1 Bbl. Sugar
O.R.

Received payment S. M. Higgins Agent
Sep. 27 1894

The signature and date must not be filled in until after the receipt (expense bill) is detached and the charges are paid. The initials and surname of agent must be given

to CHICAGO & NORTH-WESTERN RAILWAY COMPANY.

Weight.	Rate.	Freight charges (earnings.) Unpaid.	Prepaid.	Miscellaneous charges (earnings.) (Specify for what purpose.) Unpaid.	Prepaid.	Advanced charges	Interline chg's p. pd. (Specify for what purpose.)	Am't to be col'd of consignee.
350	1198	42						
								42

NOTE.—This form is intended to cover the billing charges (i. e., those embraced on the way-bill made by the forwarding agent), and no other form of receipt is valid for such purpose or is binding upon the company.

Book 6155 Receipt No. 3

Property must be removed within the time provided by the rules and regulations. Charges are payable on delivery. Claims for losses, damages, overcharges or correction of errors of any kind must be made on the day of delivery. Claims of all kinds must be accompanied by the original receipt (expense bill) for charges paid. Claims for overcharges and kindred errors must first be made on the agent; in the event he cannot correct such errors, the claim must then be forwarded directly to the freight auditor by the consignee. Claims for loss or damage must be sent directly to the general claim agent by the consignee. The terms, conditions and limitations hereby imposed shall inure to the benefit of each and every carrier beyond routing of this company to which such property may go for the purpose of transporting to destination.

This is an example of a receipt of purchase that was made by Sanders Higgins on September 27, 1894. This receipt is for the purchase of sugar. The seller of the sugar is noted, as are the location, weight, railroad, and railroad car number. Sanders's signature appears in the box on the right. (Courtesy of the Winfield Historical Society.)

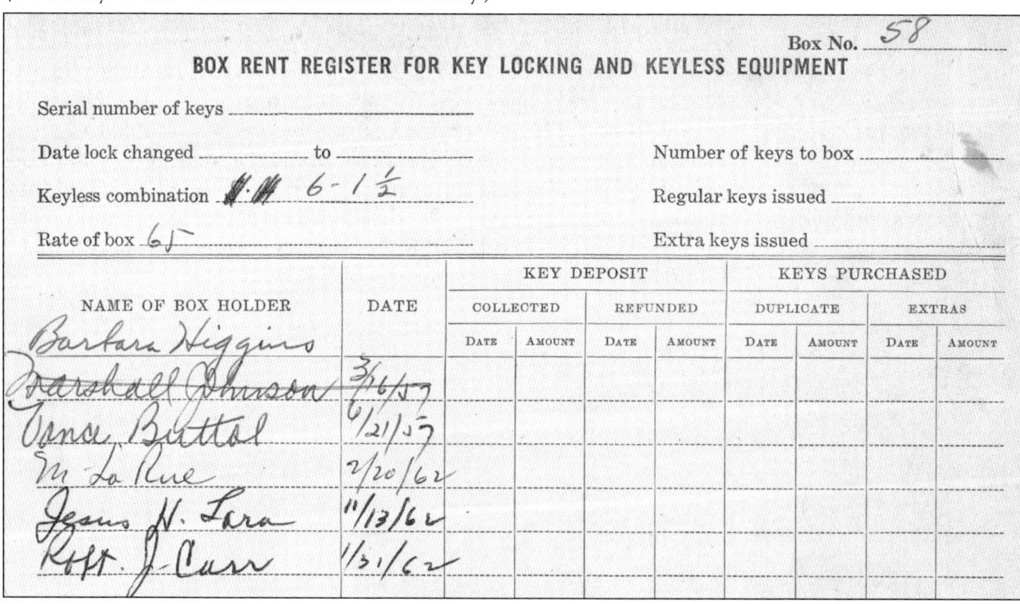

Box No. 58

BOX RENT REGISTER FOR KEY LOCKING AND KEYLESS EQUIPMENT

Serial number of keys
Date lock changed to
Number of keys to box
Keyless combination H-M 6-1½
Regular keys issued
Rate of box 65
Extra keys issued

NAME OF BOX HOLDER	DATE	KEY DEPOSIT Collected Date	Collected Amount	Refunded Date	Refunded Amount	KEYS PURCHASED Duplicate Date	Duplicate Amount	Extras Date	Extras Amount
Barbara Higgins									
~~Marshall Johnson~~	3/16/57								
Vance Buttol	6/21/57								
M. LaRue	2/20/62								
Jesus N. Lara	11/13/62								
Robt. J. Carr	1/31/62								

This is an example of a post office box rent register card that many residents of early Winfield had. Prior to 1966, the post office was a revolving institution, moving to different locales around the village. Residents would stop in to pick up their mail from their respective boxes or give mail to send out to the postmaster on duty behind the stand. This card shown here belonged originally to Barbara Higgins. (Courtesy of the Winfield Historical Society.)

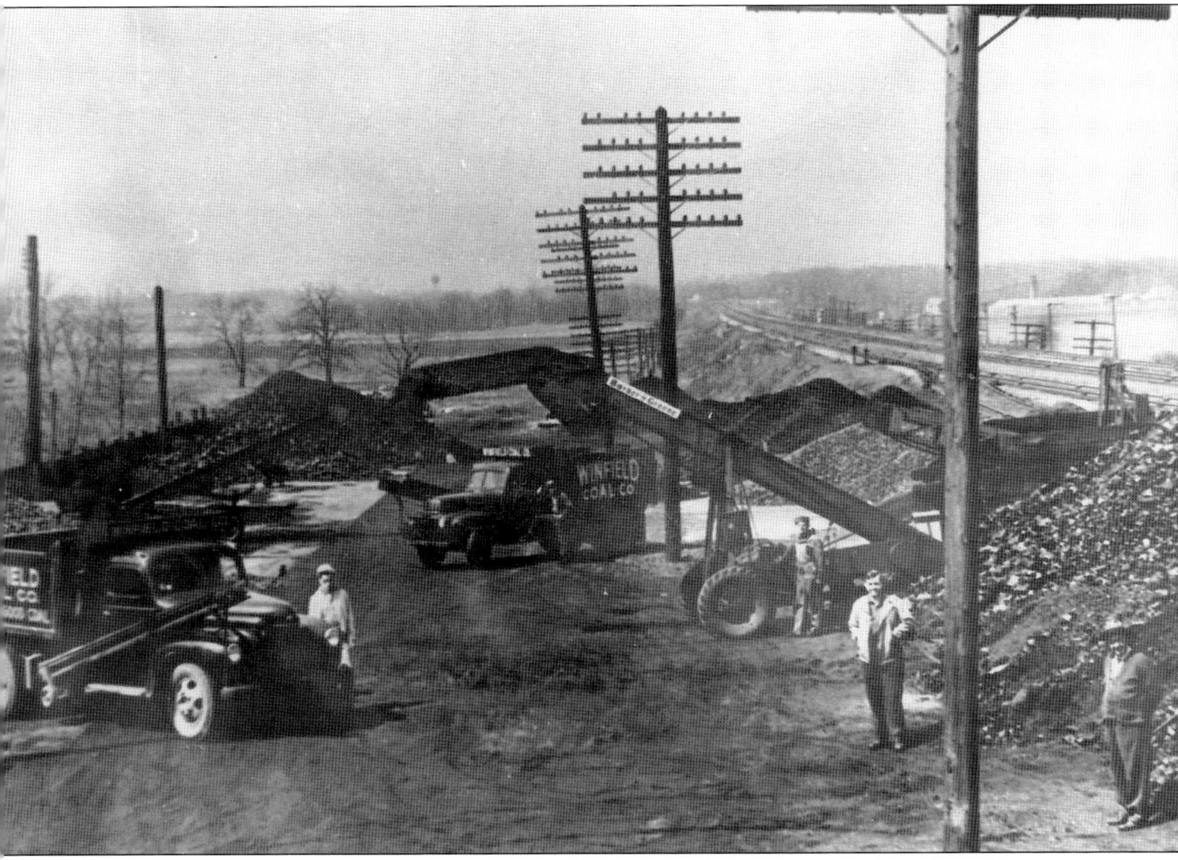

This is a view looking west at the Winfield Fuel & Material Company yard. Barbara Higgins turned over control of the coal operations at Higgins Store to her eldest son, George Higgins, in 1912. George ran the coal business from the Higgins Store counter before he was able to get his own place of operation. In 1938, George moved out of the store and into a small office that had been built at the new coal yard. In 1947, a warehouse for sand, gravel, heating oil, and building materials was built along the railroad tracks. The exact year this photograph was taken is unknown. The coal yard sat along what is now Winfield Road, and the business evolved into the Winfield Fuel & Material Company. (Courtesy of the Winfield Historical Society.)

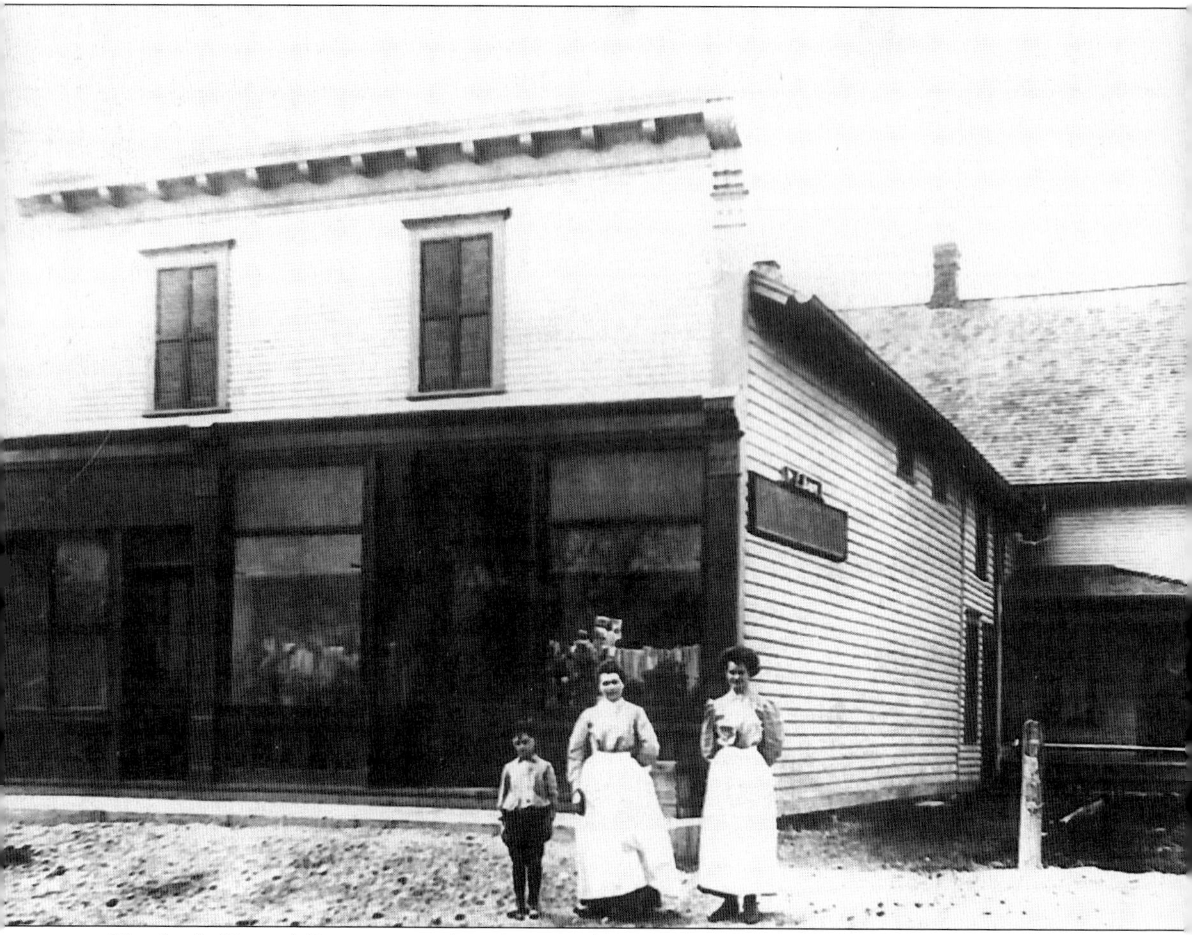

Elizabeth (Foxen) Baum is standing front and center with her son John and sister-in-law Angela (Baum) Wicke in front of the Baum store, which was located along Main Street (now Winfield Road) in 1909. Elizabeth was married to Jacob Baum, who was Winfield postmaster in 1898. After Jacob's sudden death, Elizabeth became the first woman postmaster in Winfield in 1905. She later married Christopher Enders. According to information provided in Louise Spanke's Winfield history book, the front section of the Baum store was moved across the railroad tracks to become the Bluebird Confectionery. The other portion of this building, which was residential, continued as the home to the Christopher Enders family into the 1960s. It was later used as an office for the Winfield Fuel and Material Company. (Courtesy of the Winfield Historical Society.)

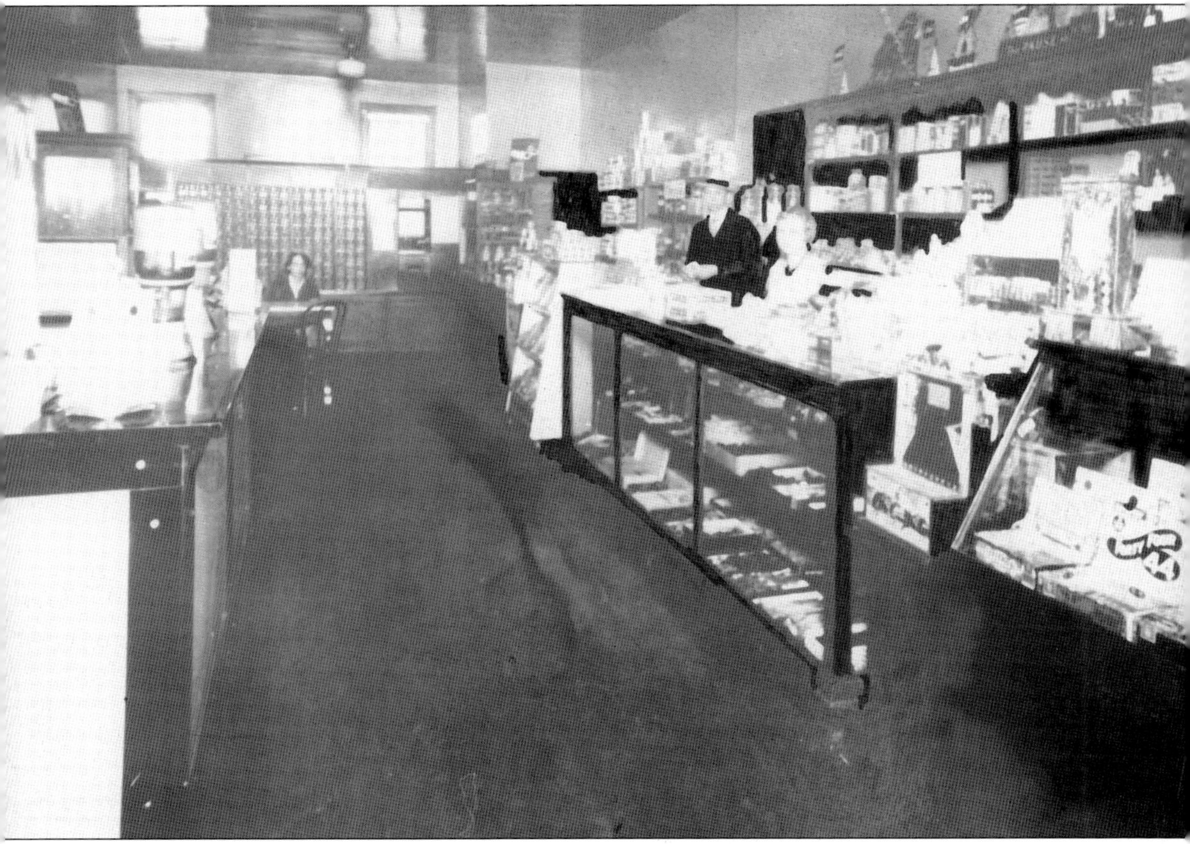

Oftentimes, an owner of a particular business in early Winfield would serve dual roles. For example, prior to 1966, the post office in Winfield revolved to different locales throughout the community. If the post office was in a general store, the owner of that particular store would often serve as the postmaster. In this particular photograph of William Daleiden's store in 1931, Daleiden, who was proprietor of the store, also served as the postmaster in the community. The post office is shown at the rear of the store. Daleiden stands behind the counter with Marguerite Roth. (Courtesy of the Winfield Historical Society.)

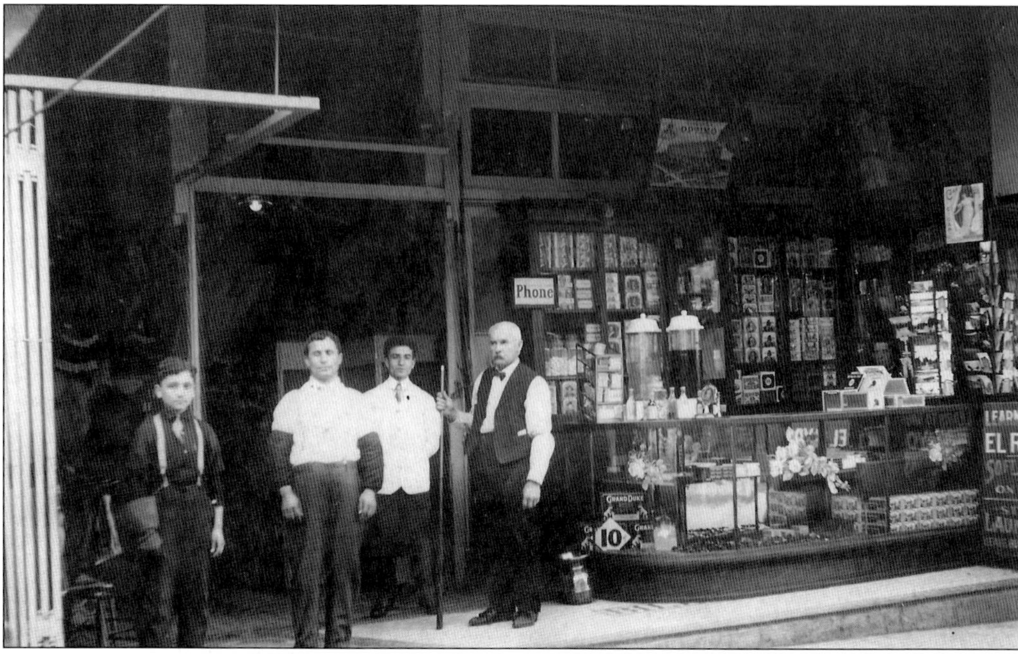

Two examples of additional stores that existed in the community are pictured. The year and those pictured are not identified, but the images highlight the different products that were available for residents to purchase. One could say that they served as general stores in the community—maybe not on the level of Higgins Store, but they still attracted customers nonetheless. (Both, courtesy of the Winfield Historical Society.)

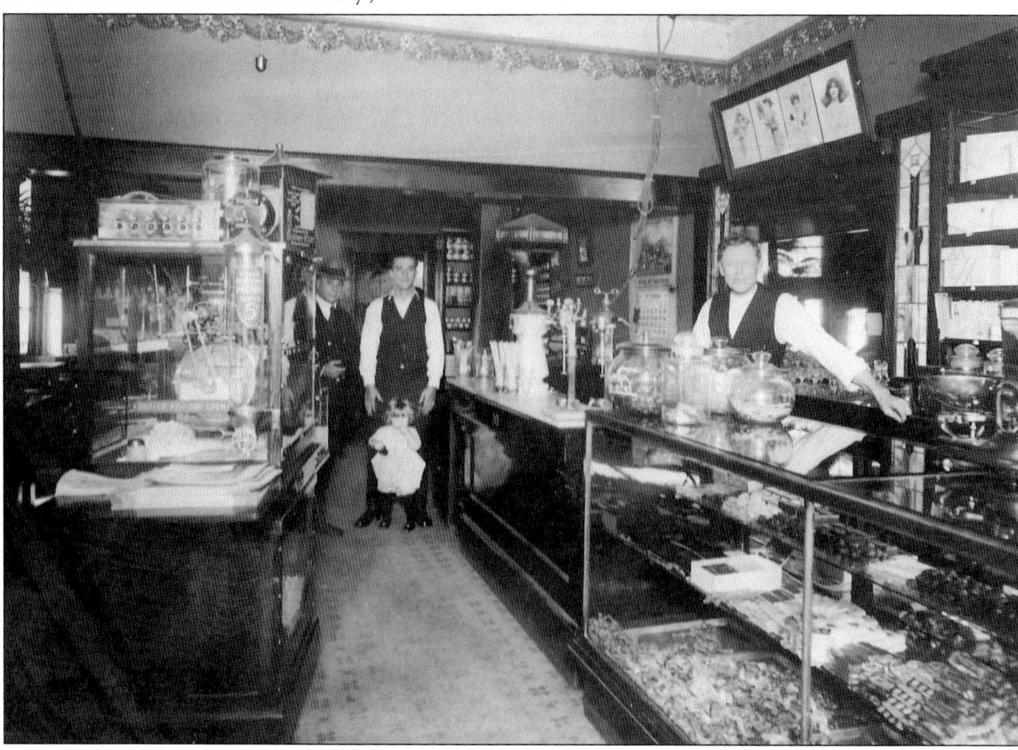

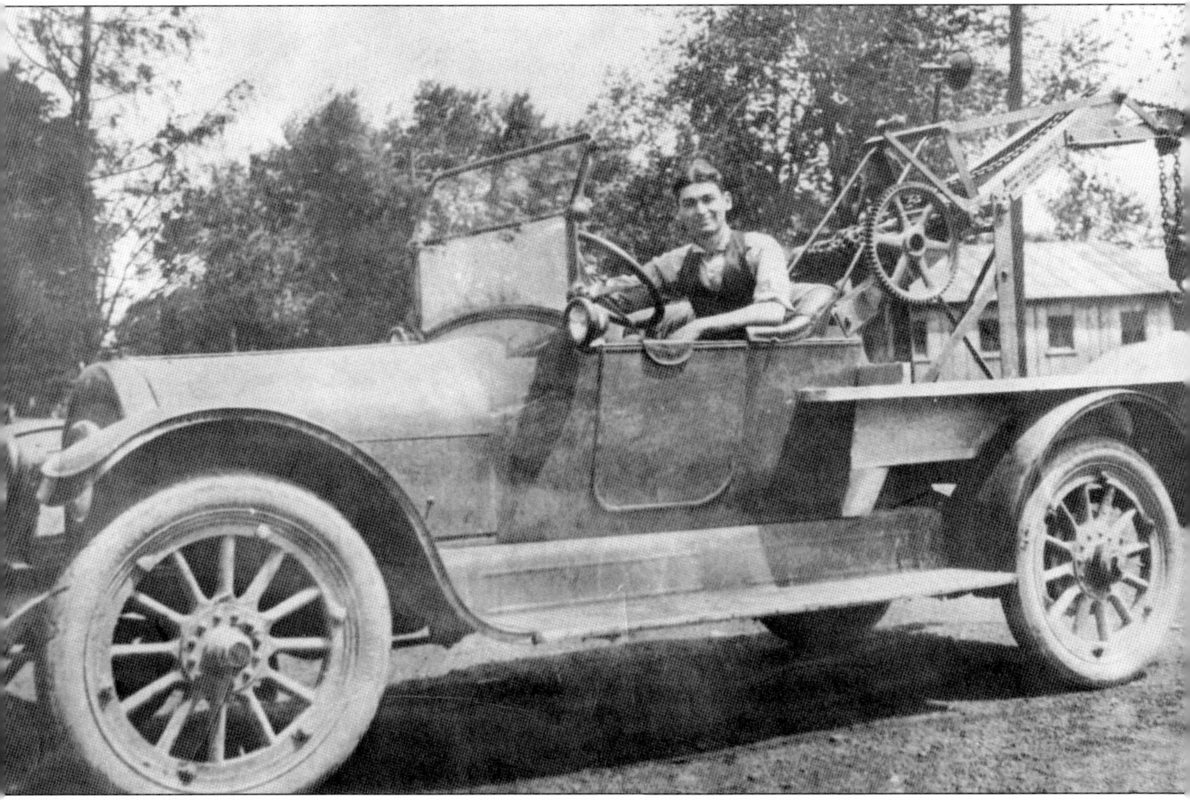

This is a photograph of the first tow truck in Winfield. It was owned and operated by Chris Armbrust, with the exact year of this photograph not indicated. The location of where this image was captured is not identified, but the subject serves as an example of the progress the young village was making. Armbrust additionally served in the village government. (Courtesy of the Winfield Historical Society.)

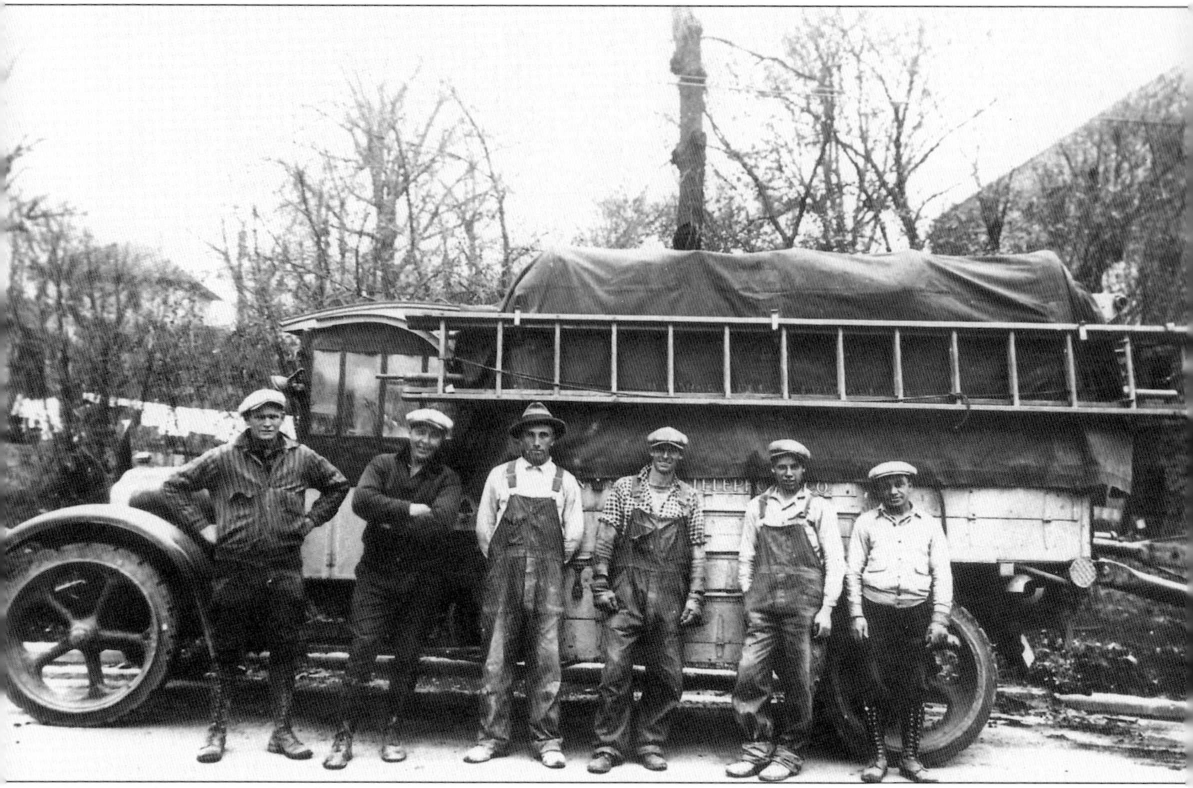

Members of the local telephone service in Winfield pose for this 1928 photograph. According to the February 23, 1975, edition of the *Sunday Journal*, in which a copy of this photograph appears, the men shown here work for the Illinois Bell Telephone Company. Carl Jerdee is pictured on the far left, next to Jacob J. Zeier. The other crew members are unidentified. (Courtesy of the Winfield Historical Society.)

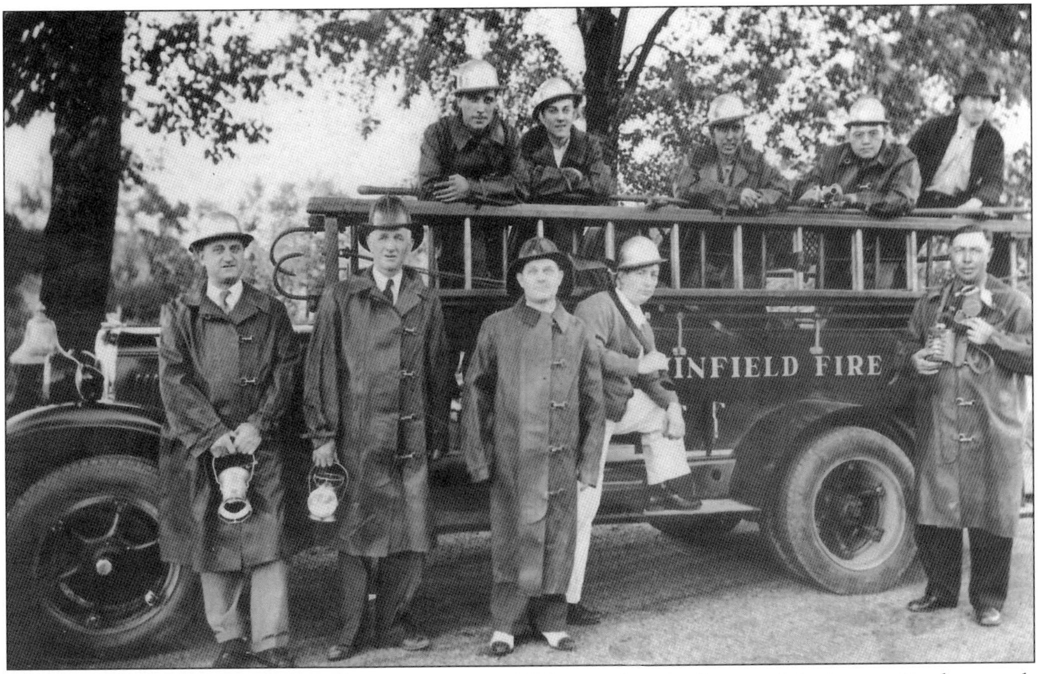

Members of the Winfield Fire Department in 1931 standing in front of their new Dodge truck are, from left to right, Al Schmidt, George Brehm, Chief John Karwoski, Herbert Zeier, and Jacob Zeier. Pictured in the truck from left to right are Charles Abbott, Chester Karwoski, L.C. Abbott, Clarence Beggs, and Joseph Zeier. The image below features the Winfield Fire Department's Engine No. 4, similar to the truck in the photograph with the crew, as evidenced by the ladder placements on the sides and bell placement up front. This image is believed to be from the 1930s. Information specified with this photograph states that this truck was later moved to Clearwater, Florida. (Both, courtesy of the Winfield Historical Society.)

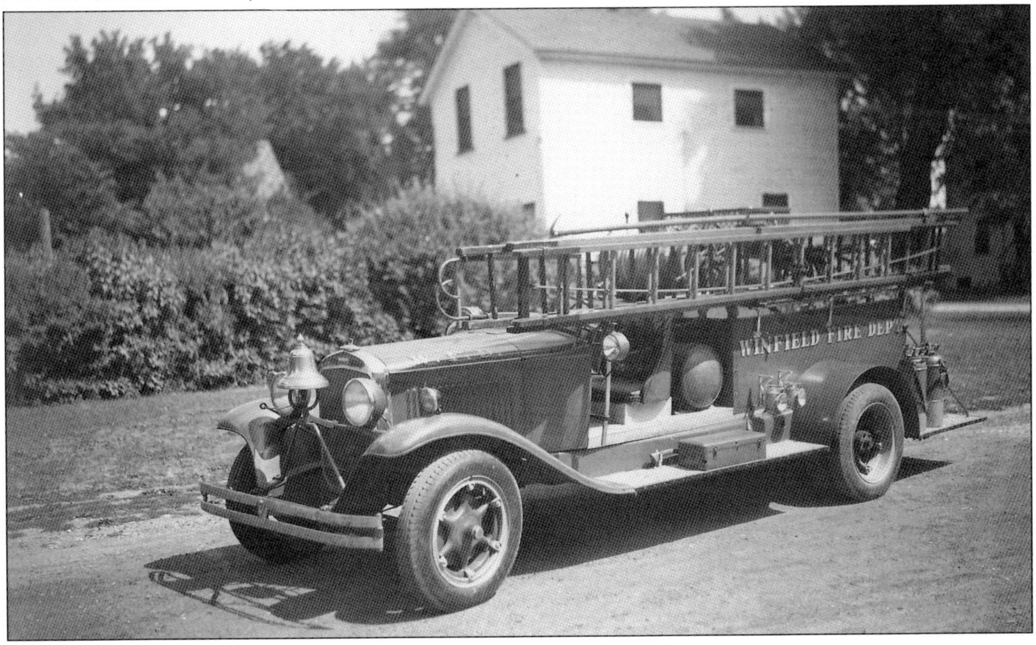

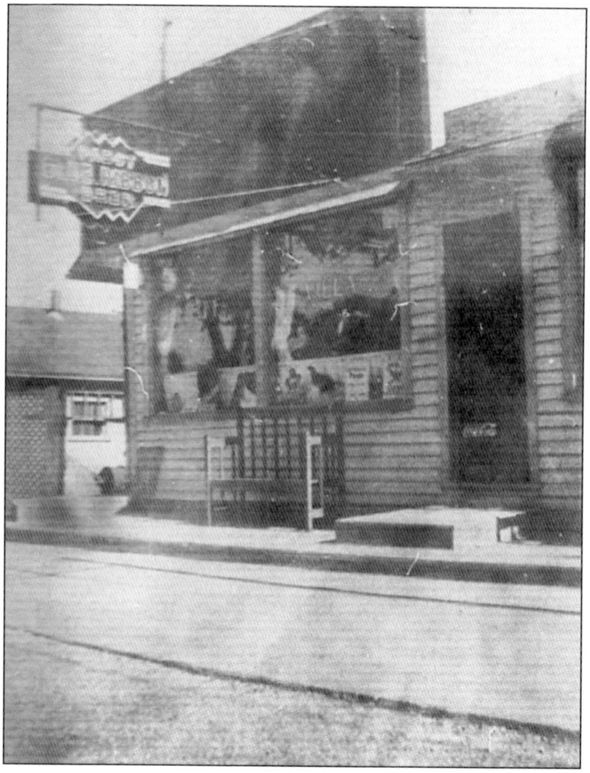

John T. Karwoski and his wife, Cecilia, operated a multifaceted barbershop and refreshment establishment that is pictured at left. According to Louise Spanke, John purchased this building, which had formerly been the John Besch store. This establishment stood on what is now the site of the Winfield Village Hall. Below, Cecilia is shown standing outside, with the Hedges Station/ Besch home in the background. This photograph was taken in 1947, the same year that John opened his new location. (Left, courtesy of the Winfield Historical Society; below, courtesy of the Winfield Historical Society and Fritz Karwoski.)

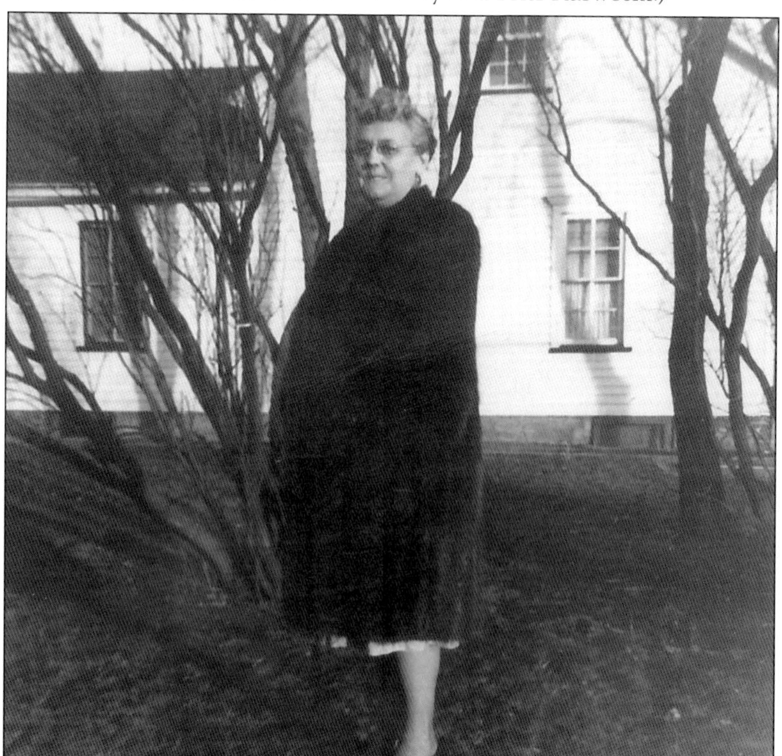

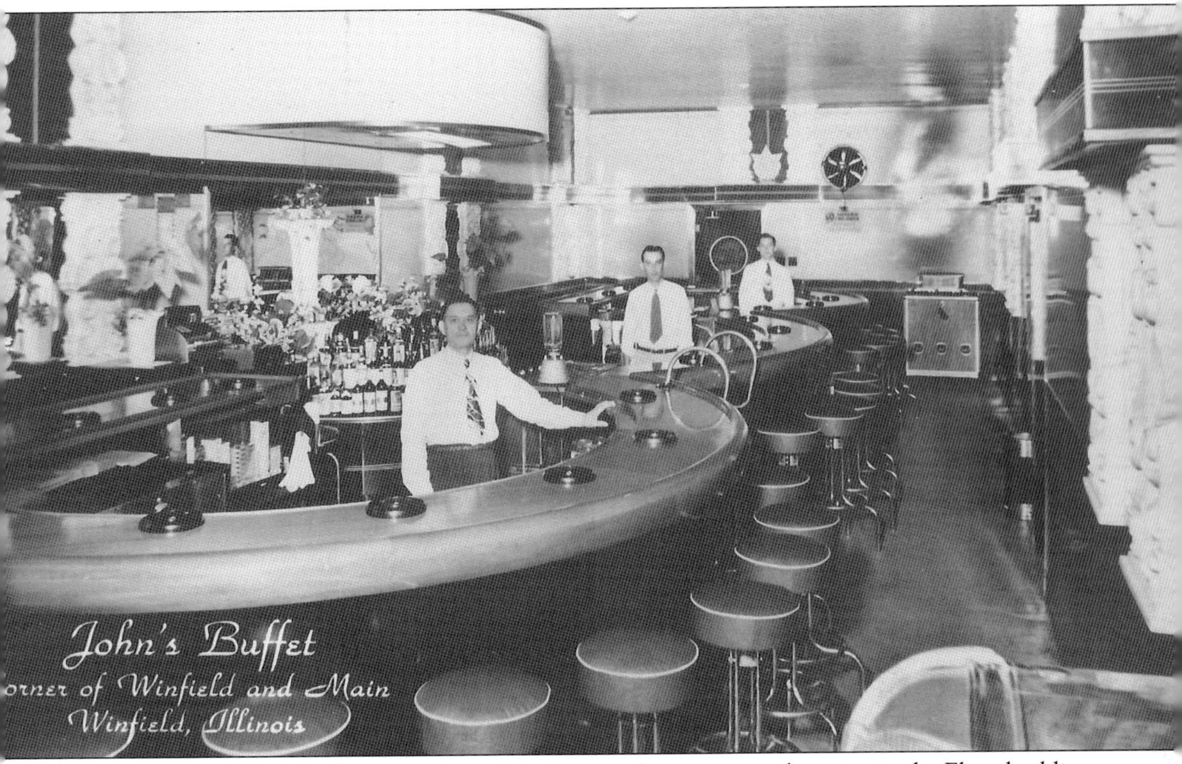

The interior of John's Buffet is seen here. John's opened at its current location in the Elsen building on Easter Sunday in 1947. William Daleiden formerly operated his store out of this location. John T. Karwoski owned and operated this business (later transferring ownership to his son, John N. Karwoski). There was no newspaper in the community in 1947, as the *Winfield Glimpses* would not start publication until July 1, 1947. Despite this, reports did circulate that there was toasts with free champagne to commemorate the grand opening in the new locale. This establishment is still in business in Winfield in 2017. (Courtesy of the Winfield Historical Society.)

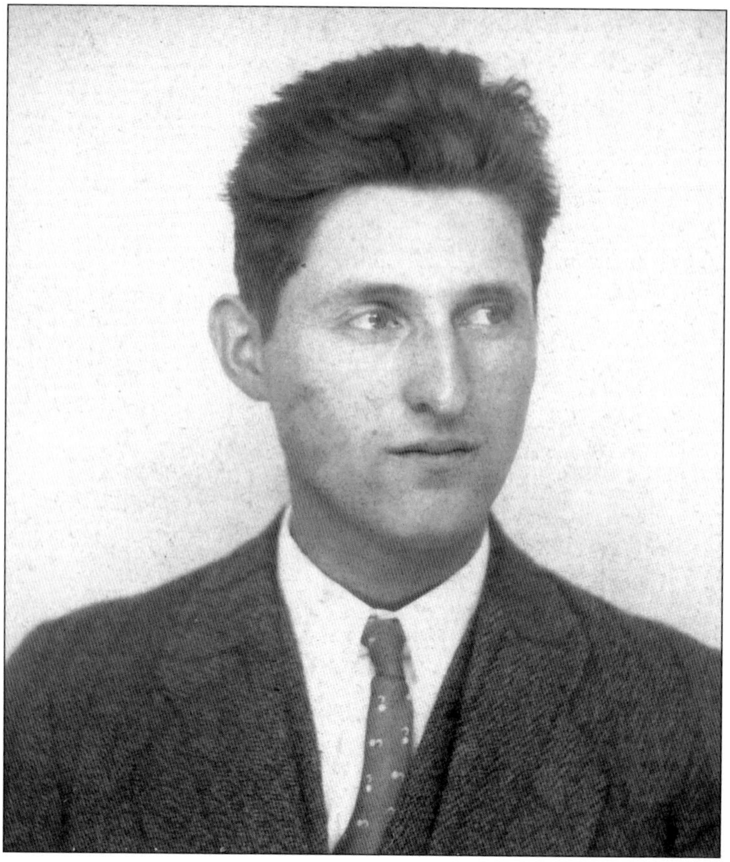

During the spring and summer of 1932, William Biel (at left) established a one-page newspaper that was complete with advertisements for community businesses. Originally titled the *Bulletin*, the paper was renamed the *Reporter*. Biel lived at this home (below) in Winfield. Despite the *Reporter* carrying a news story amongst its advertisements, it was not considered Winfield's newspaper. That distinction, as Louise Spanke notes, went to the *Winfield Glimpses* in July 1947. (Both, courtesy of Helen Biel and Winfield Historical Society.)

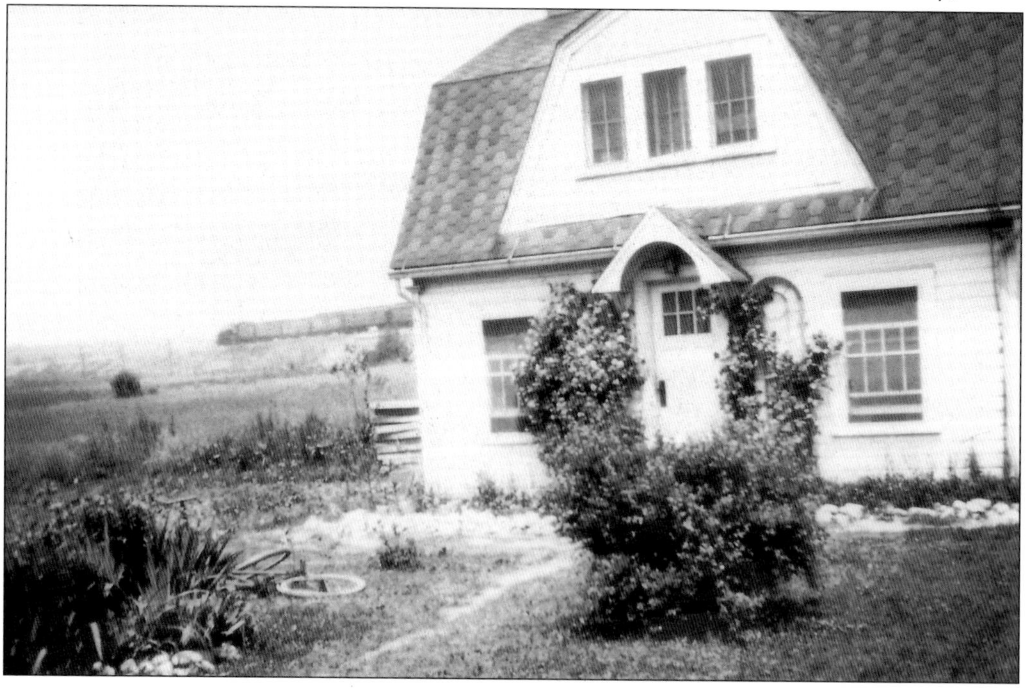

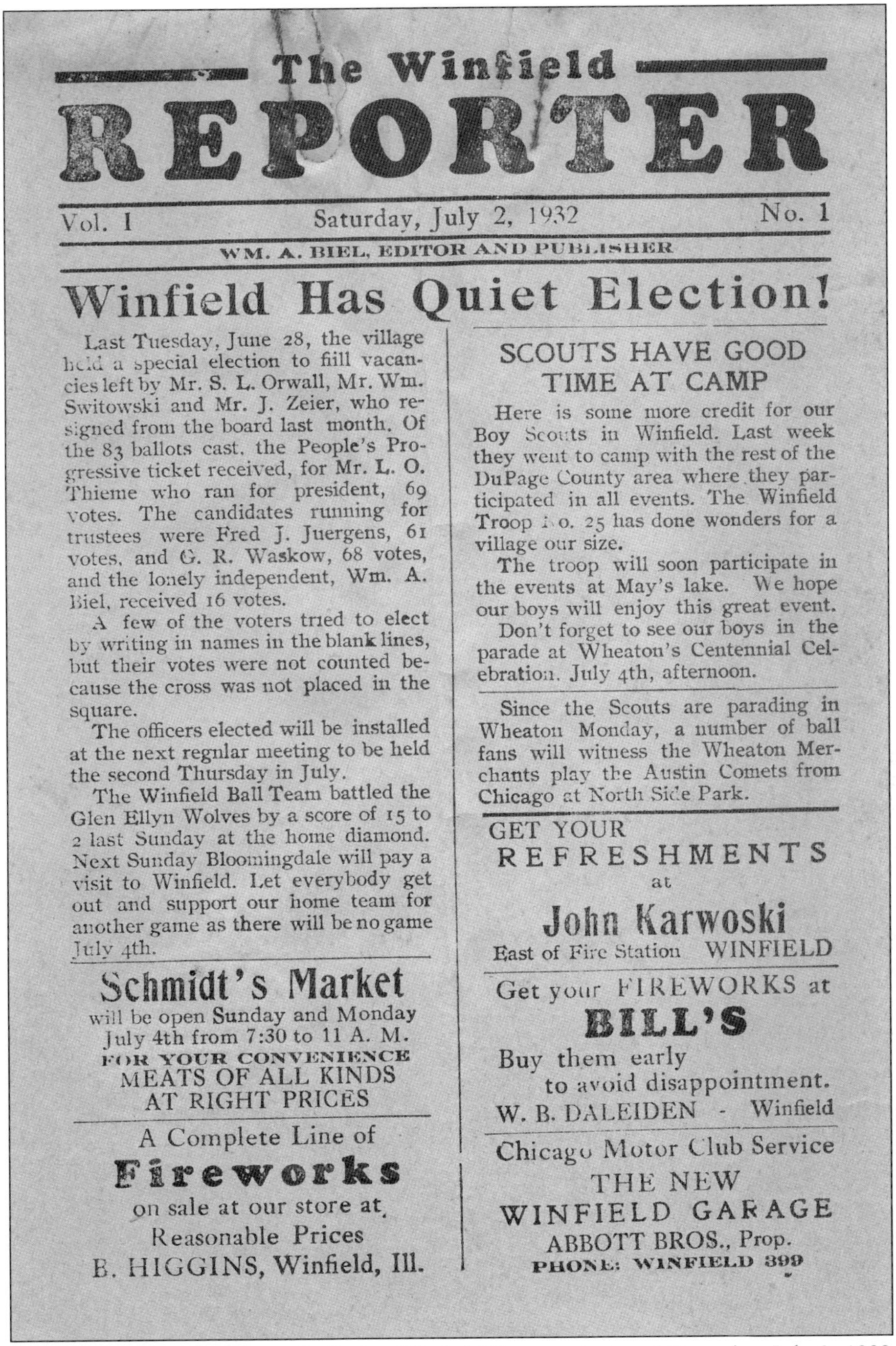

The Winfield

REPORTER

Vol. I — Saturday, July 2, 1932 — No. 1

WM. A. BIEL, EDITOR AND PUBLISHER

Winfield Has Quiet Election!

Last Tuesday, June 28, the village held a special election to fill vacancies left by Mr. S. L. Orwall, Mr. Wm. Switowski and Mr. J. Zeier, who resigned from the board last month. Of the 83 ballots cast, the People's Progressive ticket received, for Mr. L. O. Thieme who ran for president, 69 votes. The candidates running for trustees were Fred J. Juergens, 61 votes, and G. R. Waskow, 68 votes, and the lonely independent, Wm. A. Biel, received 16 votes.

A few of the voters tried to elect by writing in names in the blank lines, but their votes were not counted because the cross was not placed in the square.

The officers elected will be installed at the next regular meeting to be held the second Thursday in July.

The Winfield Ball Team battled the Glen Ellyn Wolves by a score of 15 to 2 last Sunday at the home diamond. Next Sunday Bloomingdale will pay a visit to Winfield. Let everybody get out and support our home team for another game as there will be no game July 4th.

SCOUTS HAVE GOOD TIME AT CAMP

Here is some more credit for our Boy Scouts in Winfield. Last week they went to camp with the rest of the DuPage County area where they participated in all events. The Winfield Troop No. 25 has done wonders for a village our size.

The troop will soon participate in the events at May's lake. We hope our boys will enjoy this great event.

Don't forget to see our boys in the parade at Wheaton's Centennial Celebration, July 4th, afternoon.

Since the Scouts are parading in Wheaton Monday, a number of ball fans will witness the Wheaton Merchants play the Austin Comets from Chicago at North Side Park.

This particular issue of William Biel's the *Winfield Reporter* is dated Saturday, July 2, 1932. The news story covered is the special election that was held to fill the vacant board seat that was the result of S.L. Orwall's resignation as Winfield's board of trustees president. This issue also carries advertisements for Peter Schmidt's Meat Market on Chicago Avenue, as well as for John T. Karwoski's pre–John's Buffet establishment in the center of town where the village hall now stands. (Courtesy of Helen Biel and Winfield Historical Society.)

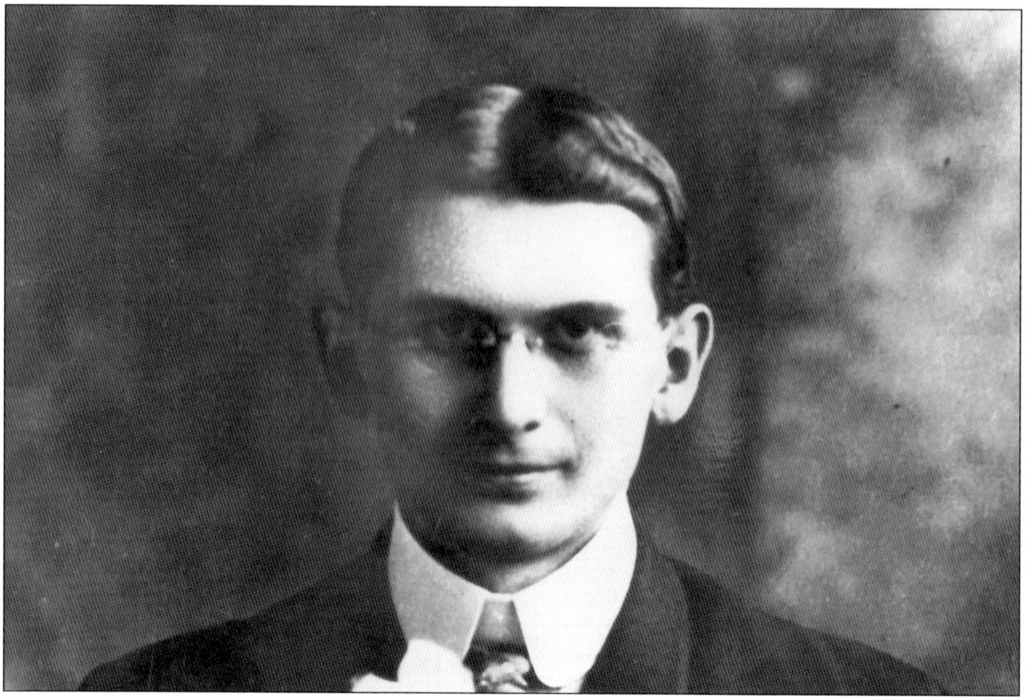

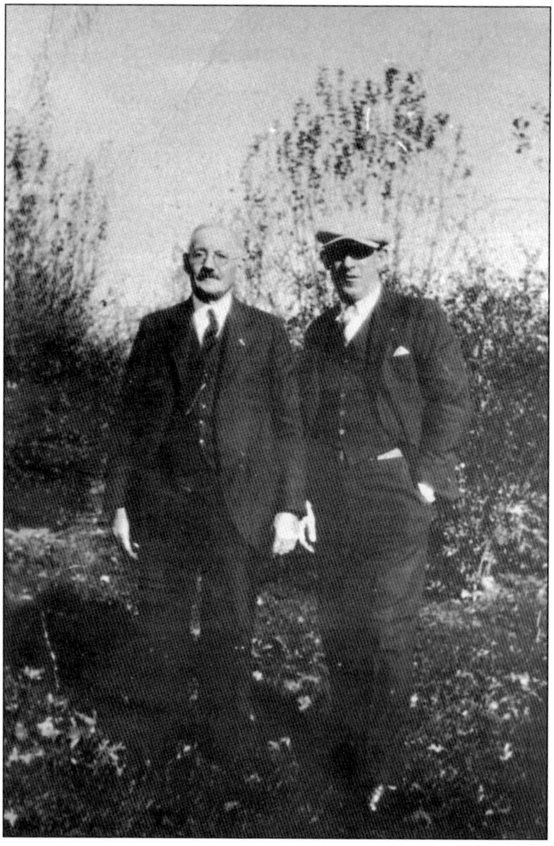

Oliver Atkinson (above) and Albert Hopkins (on the left, at left) were two of Winfield's early village presidents. Atkinson served two separate four-year terms, both times succeeding L. Oscar Thieme. Atkinson served from 1923 to 1927 and from 1933 to 1937. Prior to his tenure as village president, Atkinson served on the board of trustees from 1921 to 1923. Albert Hopkins served as village president from 1927 to 1929, succeeding Atkinson's first term. (Both, courtesy of the Winfield Historical Society.)

Three

Recreation and Play in Winfield

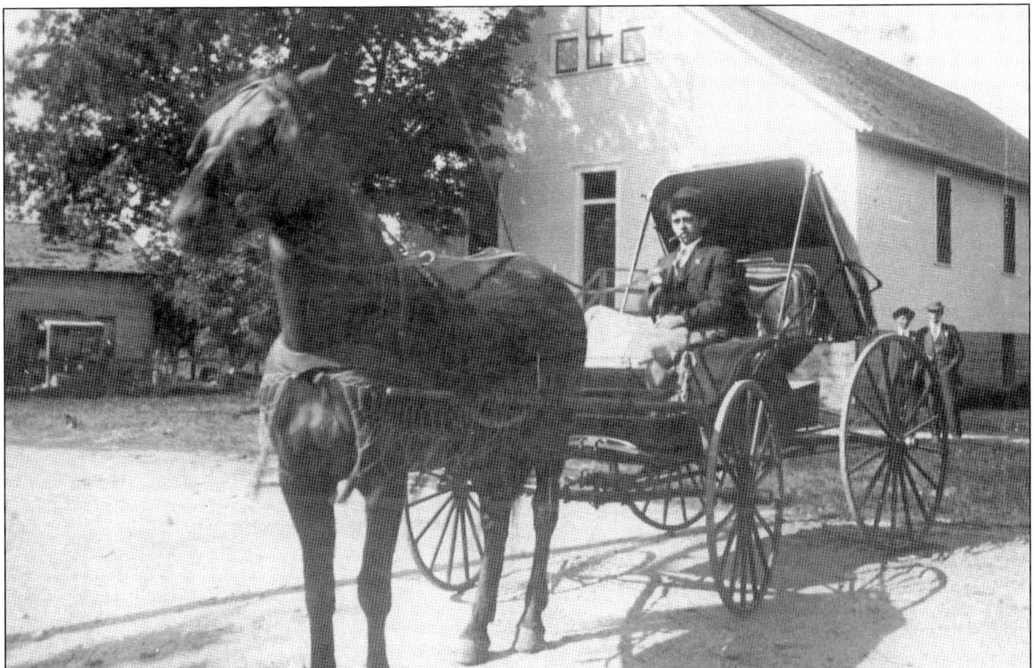

John Schramer operates a horse-drawn buggy in front of Forester Hall in Winfield. This particular photograph has on its reverse the inscription of "John [V.?] Schramer," though it is not definitive. Should this be John V. Schramer, he served on the Winfield Board of Trustees in 1925–1927. (Courtesy of the Winfield Historical Society.)

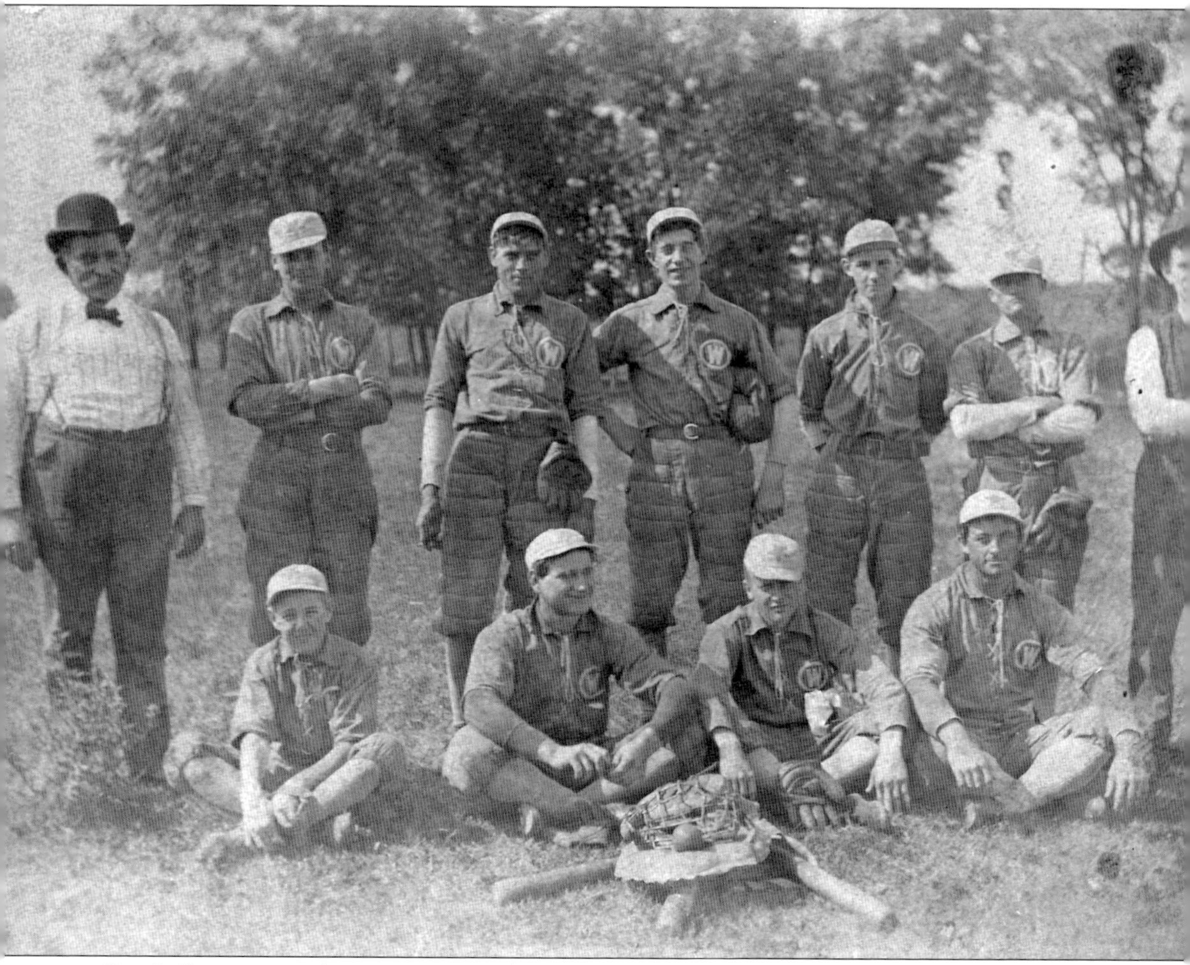

Baseball was a popular pastime in early Winfield. Louise Spanke notes in her book that games were often found on vacant lots, with Sunday afternoon games being a popular draw at the field on Matt Schramer's farm. Roger Higgins shared with Louise that Tinnes corner was also popular for games. Finding a spot to play baseball was seemingly quick and easy. Younger players, according to Roger Higgins, were often stuck in right field, but everybody got to play. This image features a local team from 1894, with no identifications listed for the players. (Courtesy of the Winfield Historical Society.)

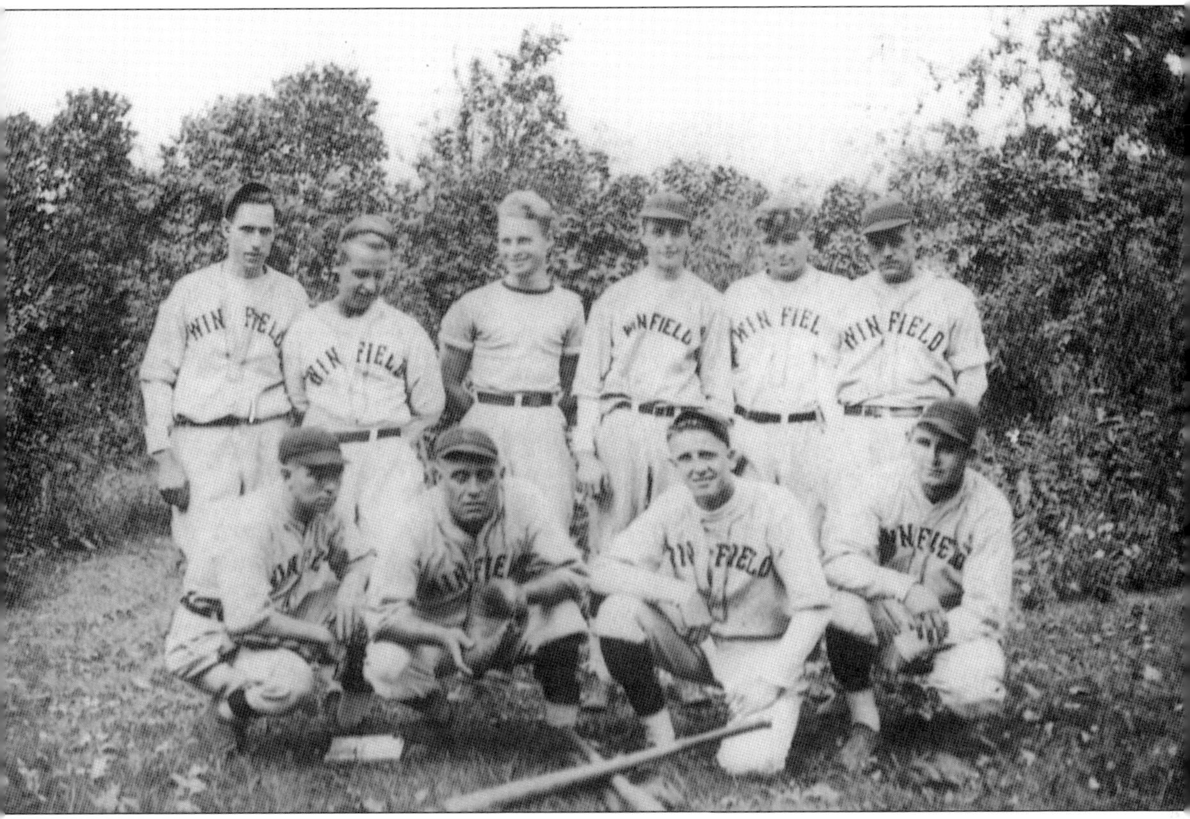

This photograph features a local 1933 team that participated in the Third Rail baseball league (Chicago Aurora & Elgin Railroad). From left to right are (first row, kneeling) Herbert Zeier, Peter Baum, Ray Werdell, and William Enders; (second row, standing) Edward Roth, Joseph Enders, Ray Klein, Ed Burton, Ernest Besch, and Robert Stuart. Lawrence Enders was the manager of this team, but he is not pictured. (Courtesy of the Winfield Historical Society.)

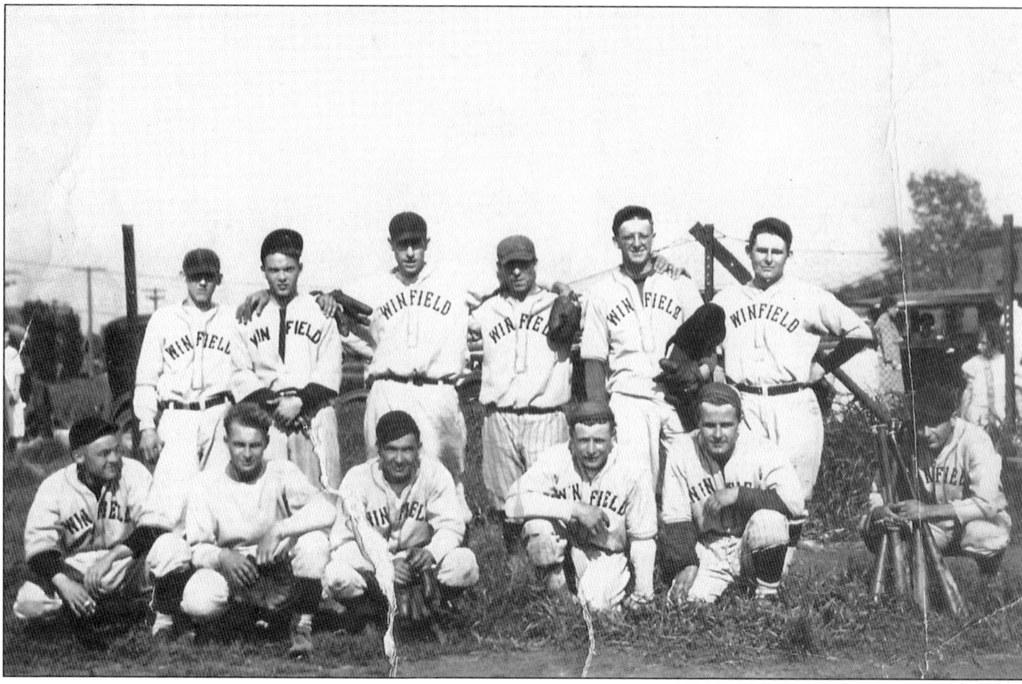

These are two more photographs that highlight the popularity of baseball in the young community. This image above features a Winfield baseball team in 1934. From left to right are (first row) Bob Stuart, Ray Klein, Eddie Burton, Vernon Arends, Joe Enders, and Ernest Besch; (second row) Chet Karwoski, Joe Burton, Ed Roth, Al McAleese, Ray Werdell, and Bill Enders. The photograph below features the Winfield Merchants baseball team from 1936. Many of the players from the 1934 team played on this team. (Above, courtesy of Peg Hernandy; below, courtesy of David "Skip" Higgins.)

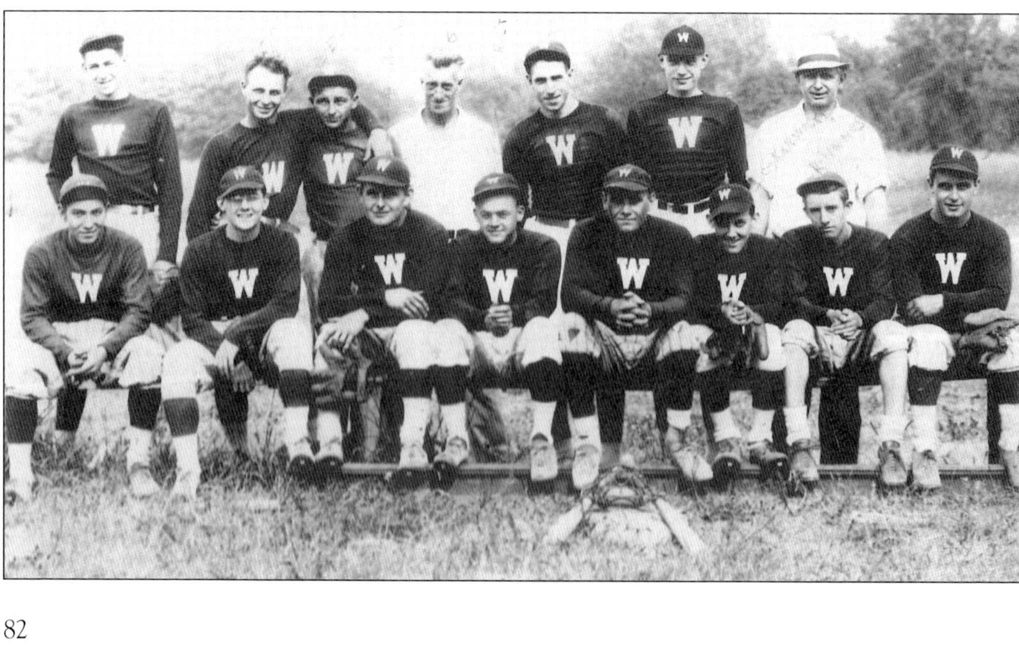

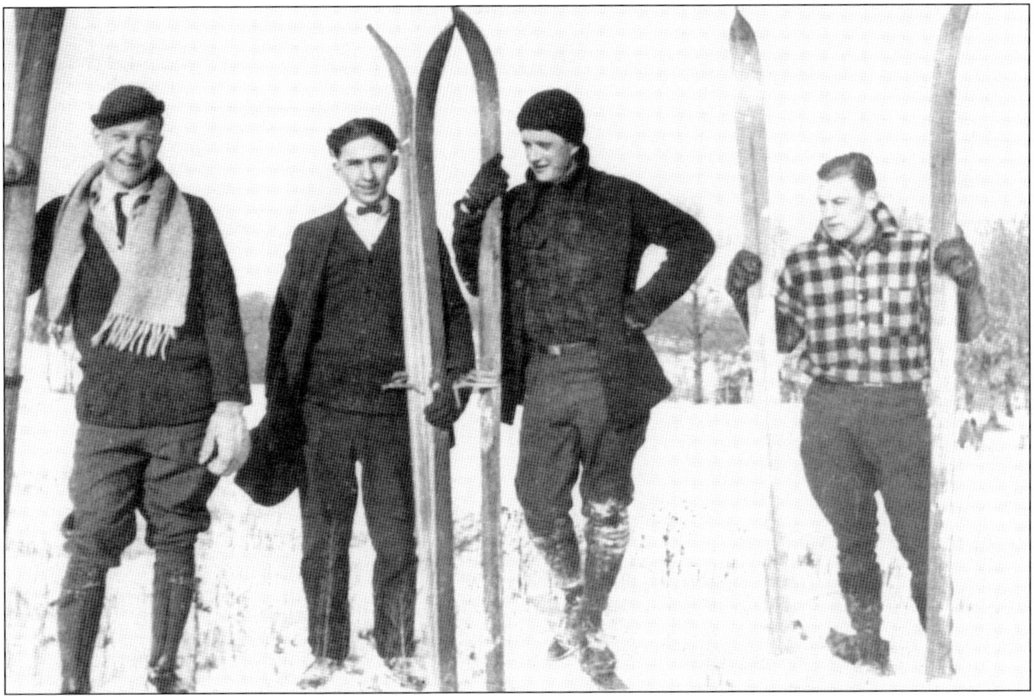

Skiing was quite popular, also. The image above features, from left to right, Clemen Mueller, Al Besch, Henry Higgins, and Robert Stuart taking a break from skiing on Boie's Hill in Winfield. Boie's Hill was also popular in the winter for sledding. This locale was near a popular spot for picnics that was just north of Gary's Mill Road. In photograph below, Edward Enders and Henry Higgins seem to be having a good time sitting atop of what looks to be a pile of wood in the back of a truck. The Higginses and Enderses were two of the families having the longest ties to Winfield, along with the Besches. (Above, courtesy of the Winfield Historical Society; below, courtesy of Mrs. Al Sennett and the Winfield Historical Society.)

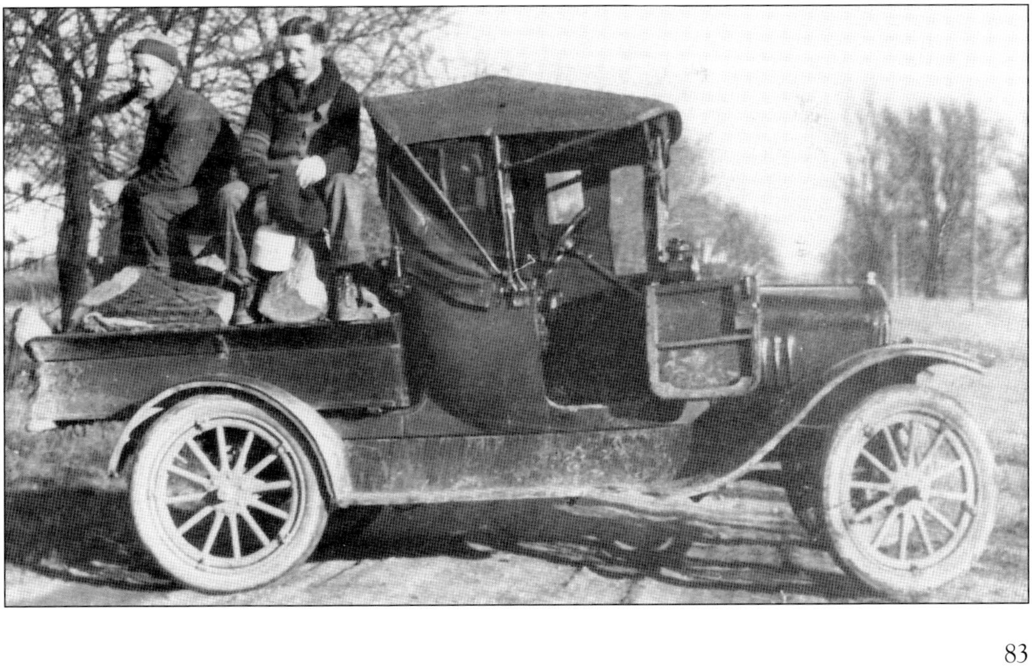

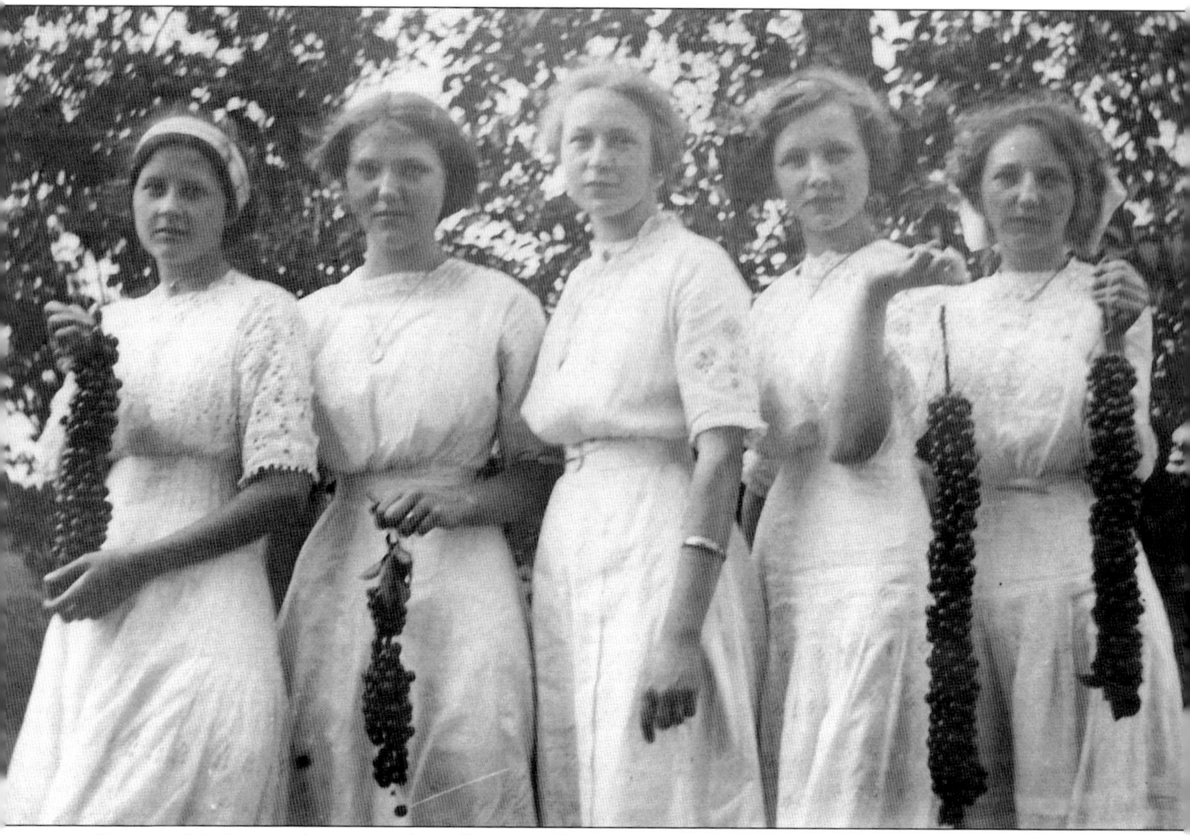

It is a girls' day out featuring, from left to right, Marie (Higgins) McCabe, Jennie Fortman, Alma Wakeman, Therese (Enders) Kruger, and Lillian Heinz. This was taken on the farm that was owned by George Fortman, though the exact year is unknown. The girls appear to have been picking some berries. (Courtesy of the Winfield Historical Society.)

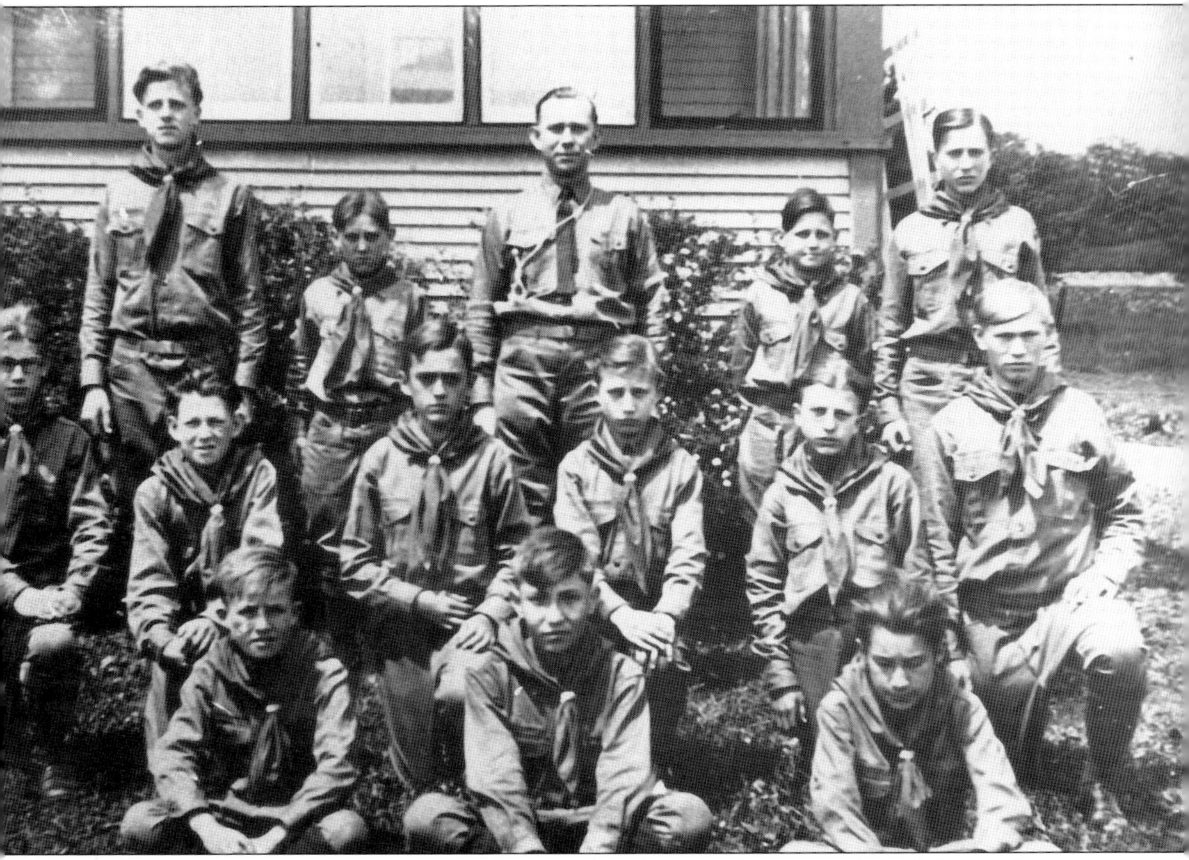

The first Boy Scout troop in Winfield gathers for this photograph in 1931. From left to right are (front row) Richard Tinnes, Waldemar Hirt, and James Berkes; (middle row) Richard Kosusnick, Donald Zeier, Raymond Schramer, Joseph Meyers, Otto Meyers, and Edward Kosusnik; (back row) Ray Werdell, Chester Karwoski, William Swiatowski (troop leader), Marion Karwoski, and Francis Werdell. (Courtesy of the Winfield Historical Society.)

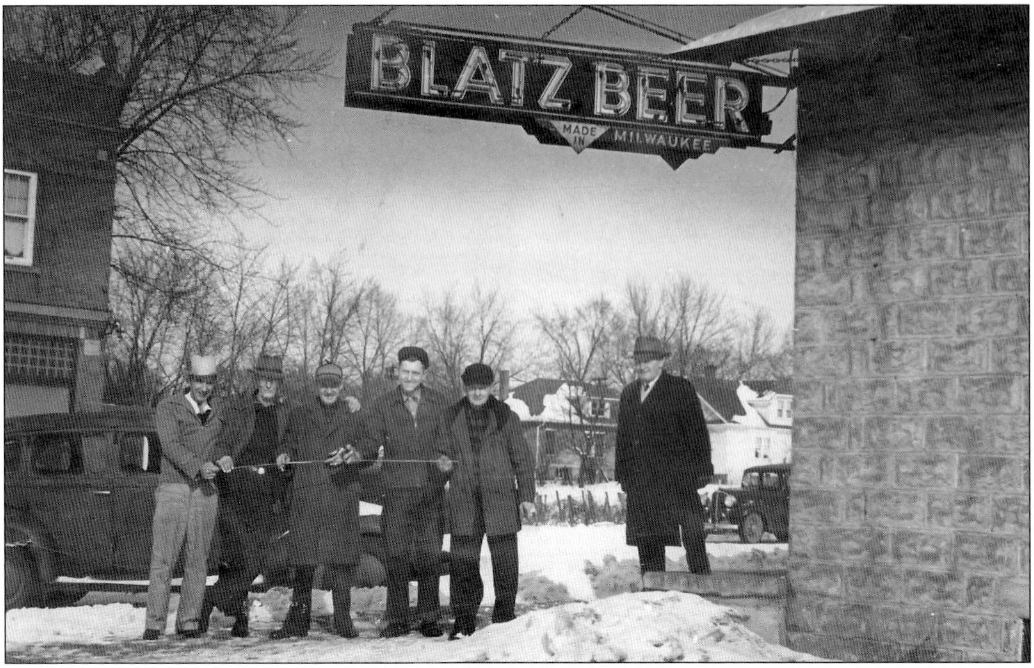

A boys' gathering is seen in both photographs. Identifications and years for both images are not known, but a good time is sure being had. The above image looks to have been taken in winter outside of a local bar in the center of town. The photograph below features five men seated outside enjoying some beverages. Quite possibly, this could have been taking place close to the DuPage River. (Both, courtesy of David and Patricia Enders, Rose Marie Enders, and the Winfield Historical Society.)

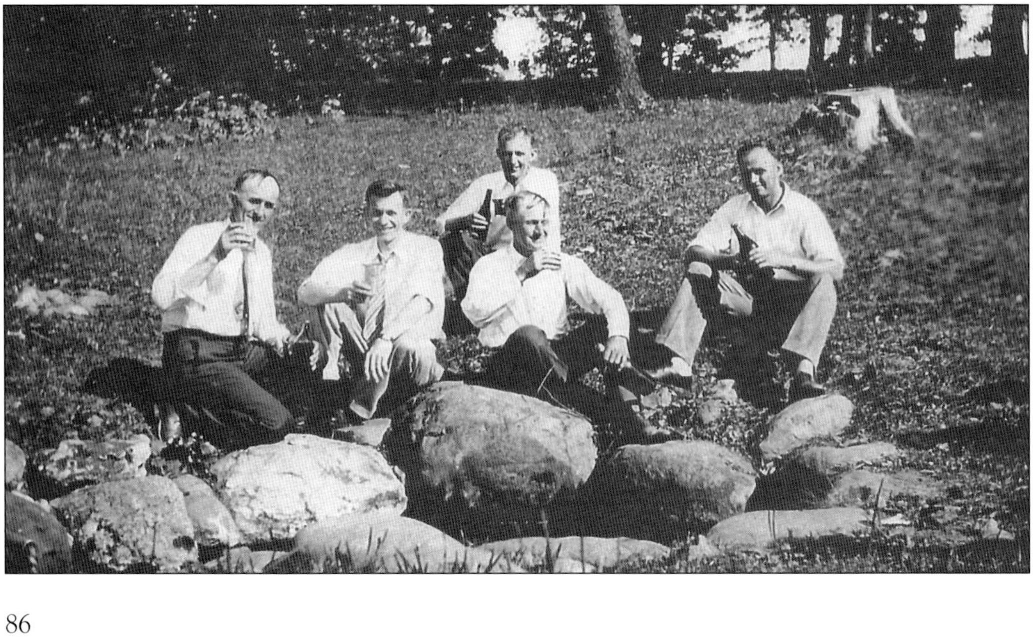

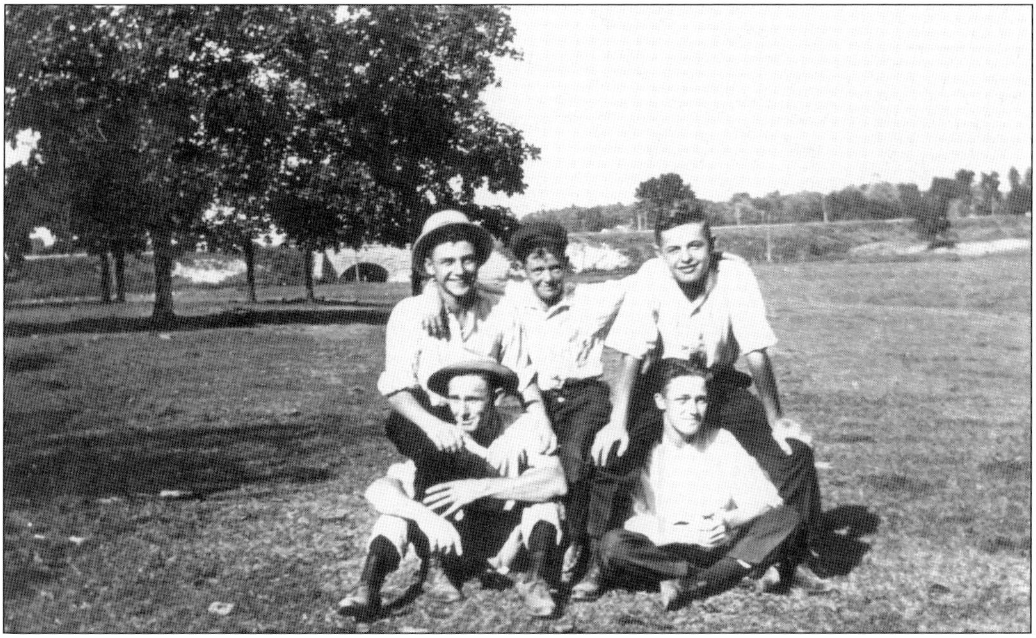

The DuPage River in Winfield was quite popular for recreational activities, both in summer and winter. Louise Spanke shares many stories in her book from many early residents of the community. Marie McCabe shares that picnics were popular along the river, with crayfish and frog legs being quite popular. Skinny-dipping was also quite popular. Turtles were often dug up along the riverbank for turtle stew. During the winter, the frozen river was quite popular with ice-skaters. The two photographs shown here feature a boys' gathering along the river, though no identifications of those pictured are known. Helen Enders noted the river in the background, and there were no homes nearby at this time. The image below features some open trails along the river. (Both, courtesy of Helen Enders and the Winfield Historical Society.)

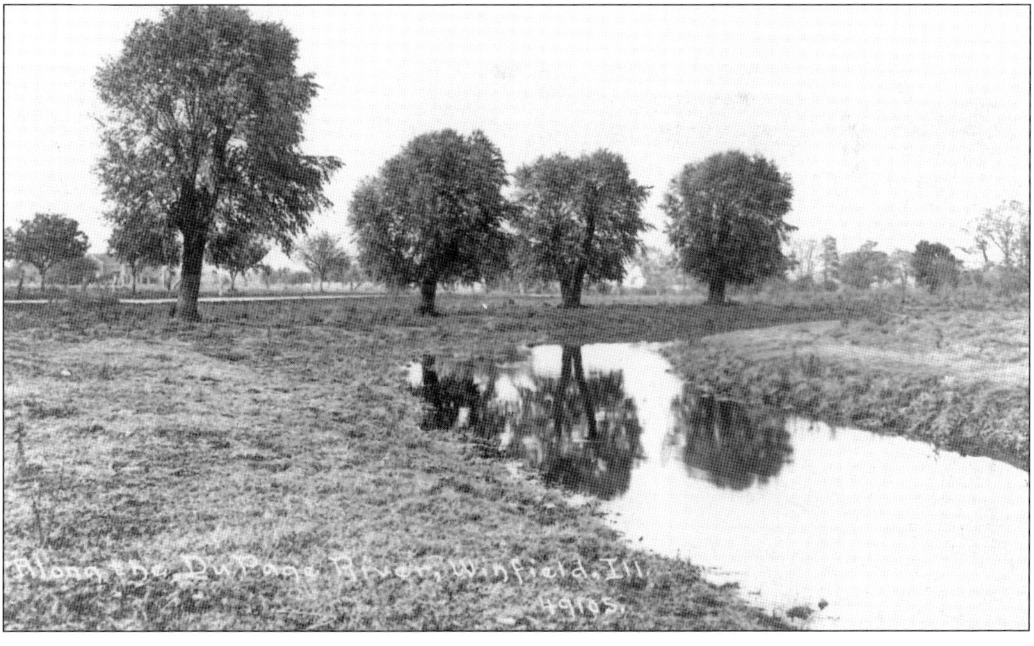

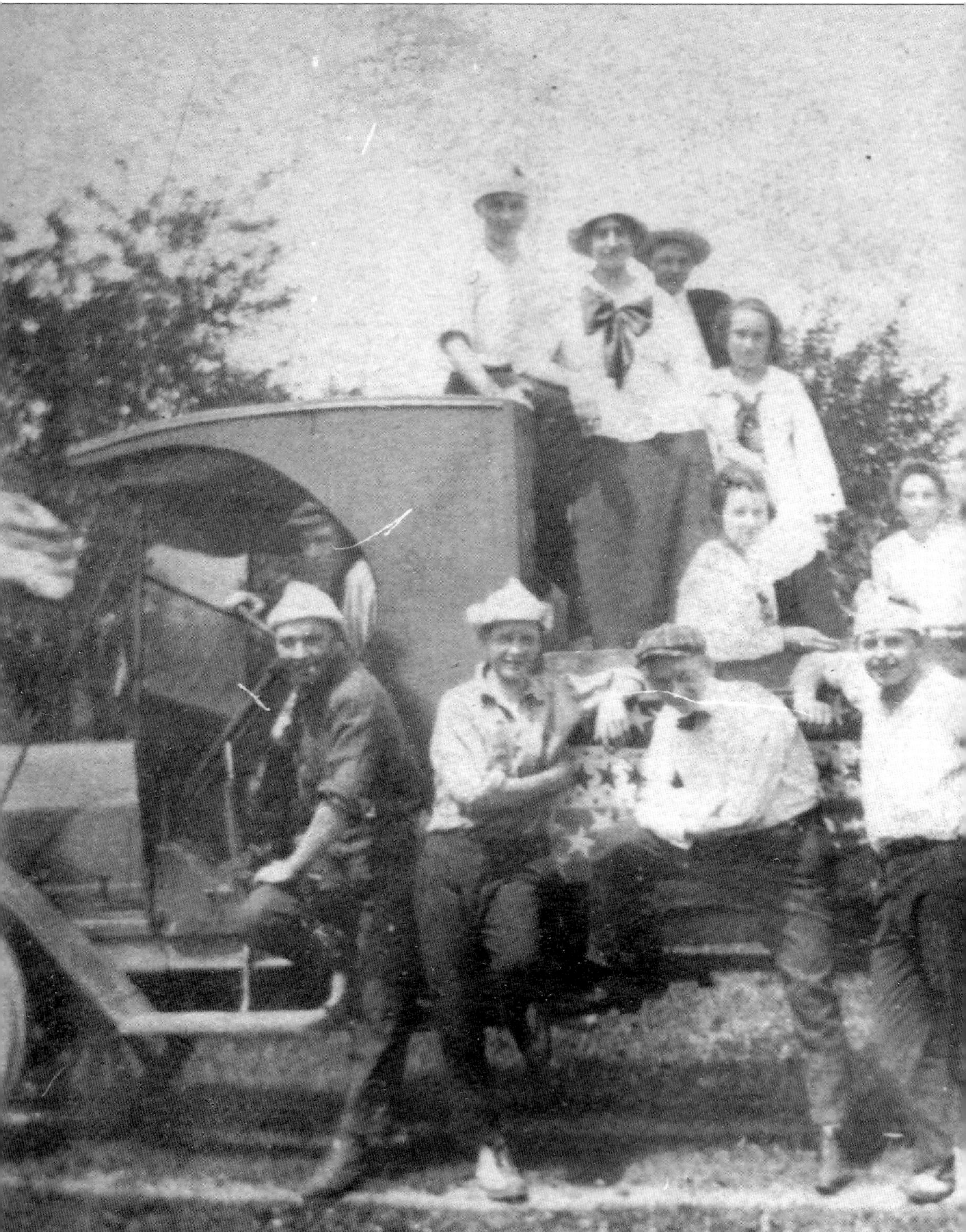

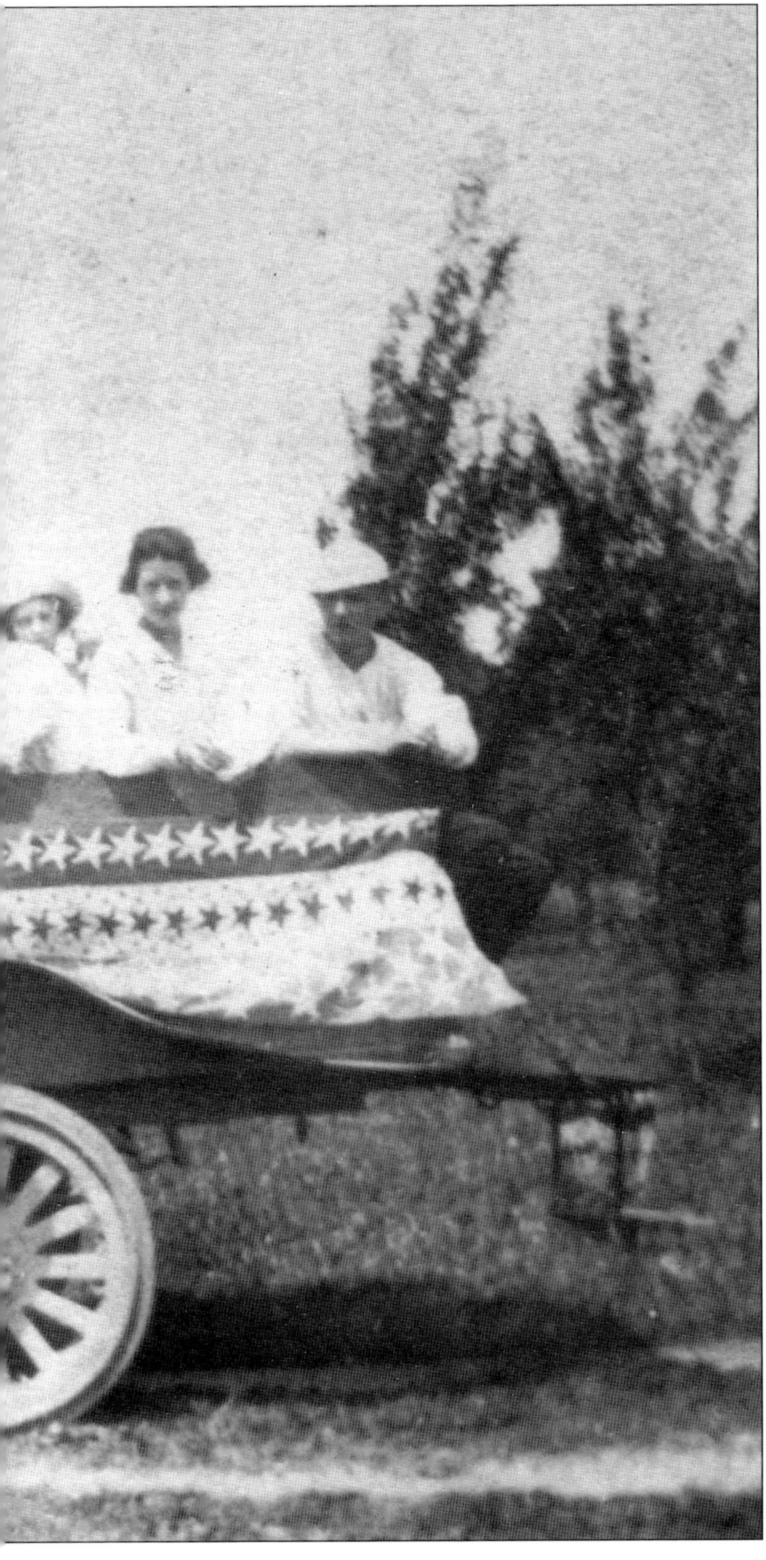

Picnickers are on their way to the lime kiln for some friendly fun. According to Tillie Schramer, J.V. Schramer is at the wheel of the truck. From left to right are (standing in front the truck) Jake Zeier, Henry Higgins, Paul N. Sehnem, and Larry Enders; (standing in the truck) Anthony Besch, Mary Schmidt Zeier, Jacob Mueller, and Tillie Schramer; (seated in the truck) Helen Rutchman, Angela Schramer, Ella Gauger, Jake Baum, Cornelia Higgins Besch, Marie Higgins McCabe, and Bernard Besch. The exact year of this photograph is not known, though it could possibly be around an Independence Day holiday, due to the patriotic décor that adorns the truck. (Courtesy of Jas. McCabe and Winfield Historical Society.)

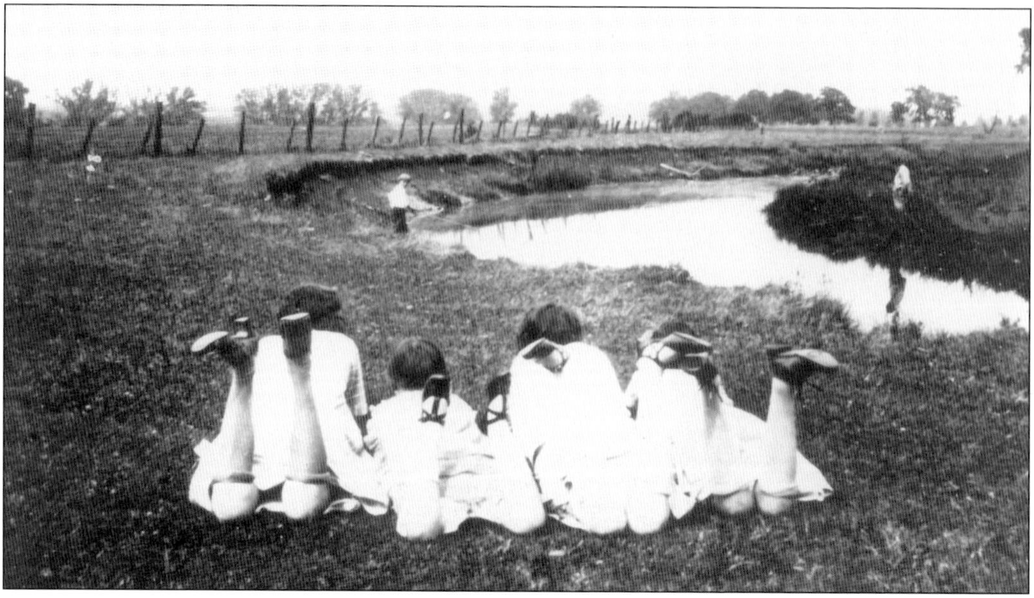

The lime kiln was a popular picnicking spot in Winfield was located just north of Gary's Mill Road, in what is now the Elsen Forest Preserve. The kiln featured a spring that sent its streams to the nearby DuPage River. Louise Spanke notes stories of picnics being held at this locale. These two images feature activities going on at the lime kiln. Above is a girls' "leg show," though the girls are not identified. The image below features a recreational gathering at the lime kiln's spring. Again, those pictured are not identified. (Both, courtesy of the Winfield Historical Society.)

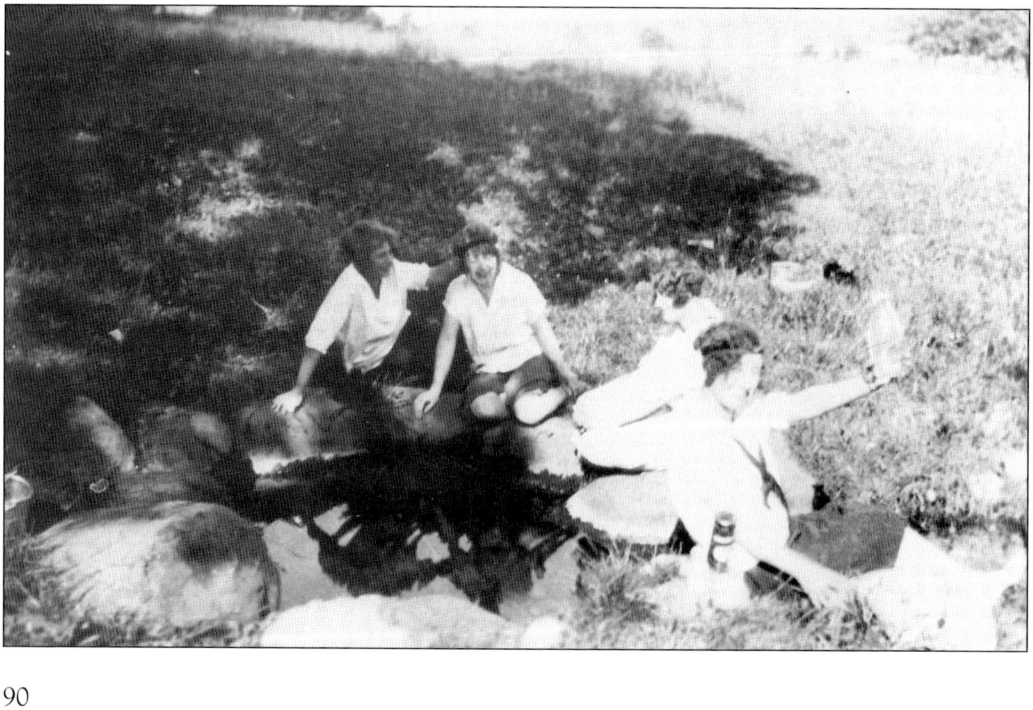

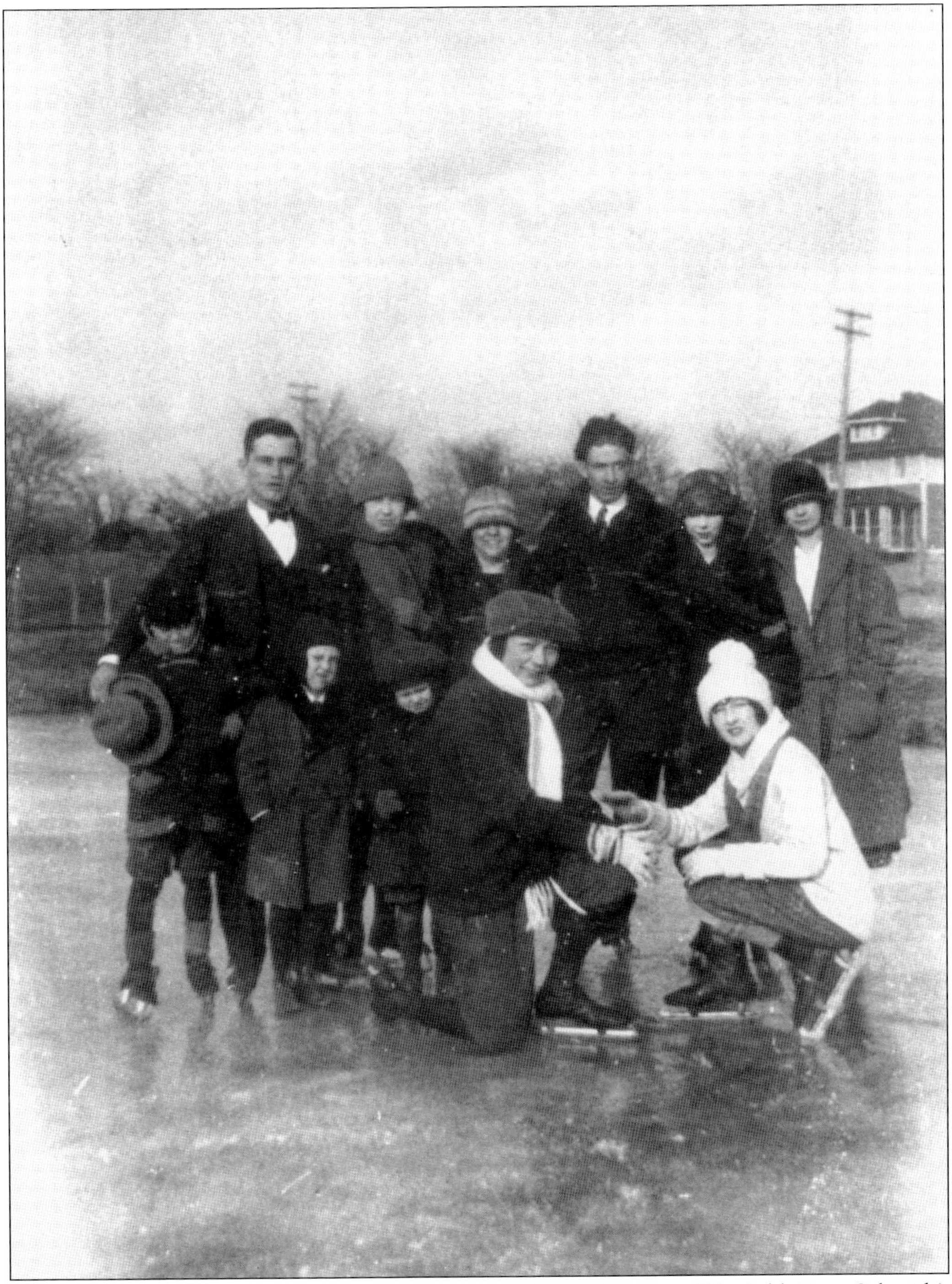

The DuPage River was not the only popular locale for ice-skating in Winfield. Peter Schmidt's man-made pond was also quite popular in the wintertime with the locals. This photograph shows a gathering of 11 unidentified individuals for a late-afternoon skate. The exact year is not known, but this gathering is symbolic of the pond's popularity. (Courtesy of the Winfield Historical Society.)

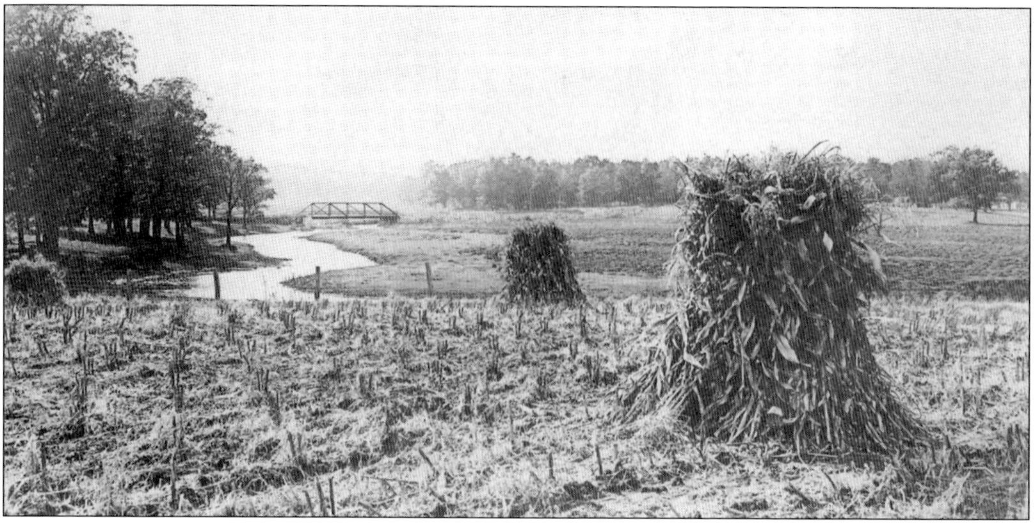

The DuPage River was more than just for play and hosting social activities. It did provide some special scenery. The photograph above shows a harvest scene along the river in 1910. Louise Spanke includes this photograph in her book and states that the view is looking north along the river from Matt Schramer's farm. The bridge that is visible in the background is the first Beecher Street Bridge. The image below seems to be from the same period around 1910, though the locale is quite different and slightly denser. It is still fine scenery nonetheless. (Both, courtesy of the Winfield Historical Society.)

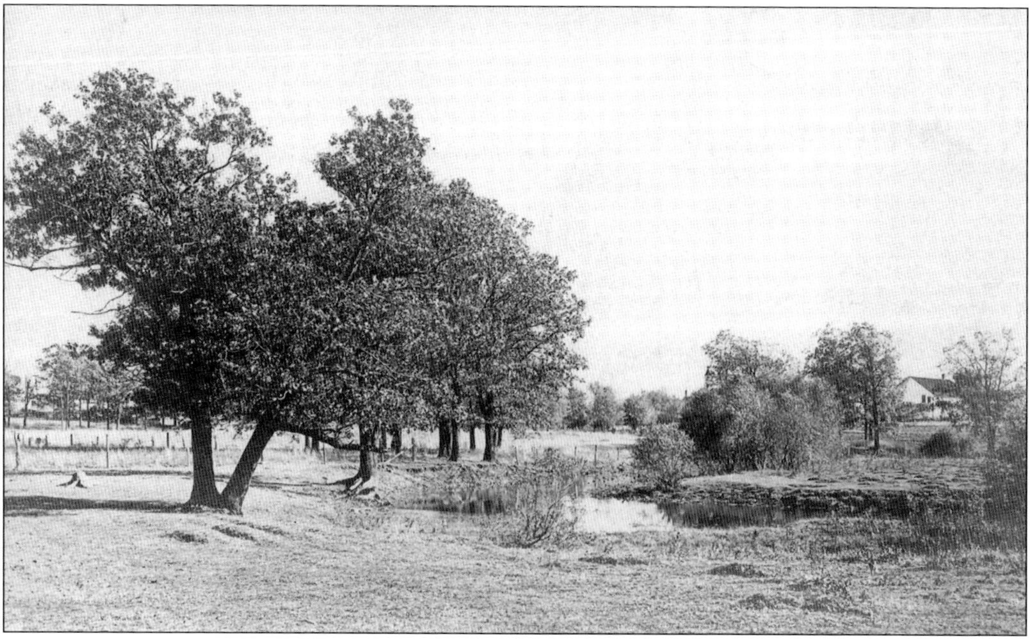

Four

FORESTER HALL

Yourself and Lady

are invited to attend a Joint Installation of officers of

St. Aloysius Court No. 148 C. O. F.

and

Madonna Court No. 786, W. C. O. F.

at Forester Hall, at 8 O'clock

Tuesday Evening, January 14, '13

Dancing and Supper Free — Music by Stoos

Foresters Only — Present This Card at the Door

This is an invitation that went out to Joseph Kline for a social gathering and joint installation of officers at Forester Hall on Tuesday evening, January 14, 1913. The invite was for all the male members of the St. Aloysius Court No. 148 of the Catholic Order of Foresters and the female members of the Madonna Court No. 786 of the Women Catholic Order of Foresters. (Courtesy of the Winfield Historical Society.)

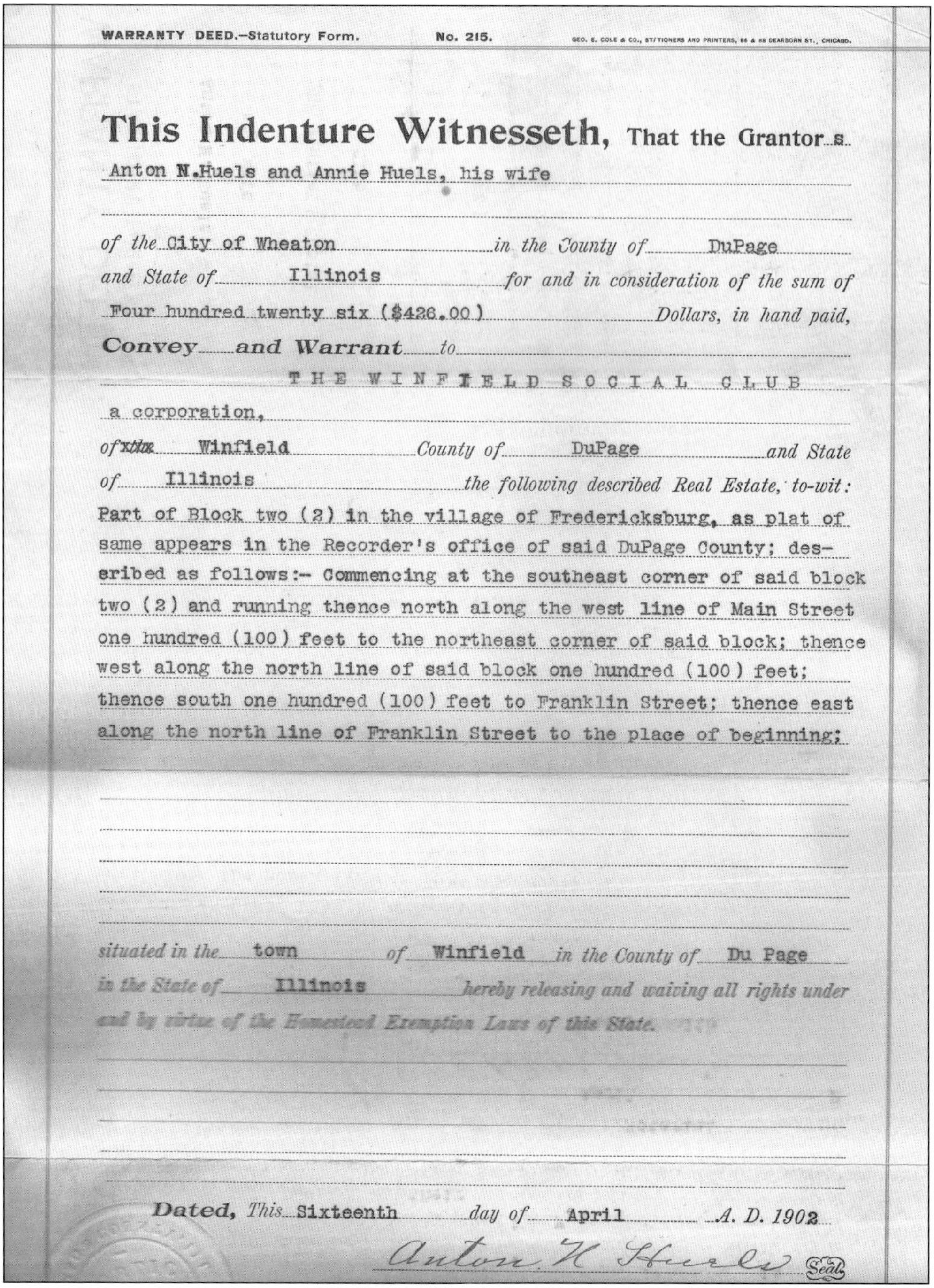
WARRANTY DEED.—Statutory Form. No. 215. GEO. E. COLE & CO., STATIONERS AND PRINTERS, 86 & 88 DEARBORN ST., CHICAGO.

This Indenture Witnesseth, That the Grantor s

Anton N. Huels and Annie Huels, his wife

of the City of Wheaton *in the County of* DuPage

and State of Illinois *for and in consideration of the sum of*

Four hundred twenty six ($426.00) *Dollars, in hand paid,*

Convey *and* **Warrant** *to*

THE WINFIELD SOCIAL CLUB

a corporation,

of Winfield *County of* DuPage *and State*

of Illinois *the following described Real Estate, to-wit:*

Part of Block two (2) in the village of Fredericksburg, as plat of same appears in the Recorder's office of said DuPage County; described as follows:- Commencing at the southeast corner of said block two (2) and running thence north along the west line of Main Street one hundred (100) feet to the northeast corner of said block; thence west along the north line of said block one hundred (100) feet; thence south one hundred (100) feet to Franklin Street; thence east along the north line of Franklin Street to the place of beginning;

situated in the town *of* Winfield *in the County of* Du Page

in the State of Illinois *hereby releasing and waiving all rights under and by virtue of the Homestead Exemption Laws of this State.*

Dated, *This* Sixteenth *day of* April *A. D. 1902*

Anton N Huels (Seal)

Seen here is a warranty deed, a statutory form that conveyed and warranted specified land to the Winfield Social Club from Anton Huels and his wife. The land in question specified in this deed eventually became home to Winfield's Forester Hall. The Winfield Social Club had the exact same membership as that of the St. Aloysius Court No. 148, Catholic Order of Foresters. Prior to meeting at Forester Hall, members of the Foresters met first in the basement of St. John the Baptist Church and then later at Hamm's tavern. (Courtesy of the Winfield Historical Society.)

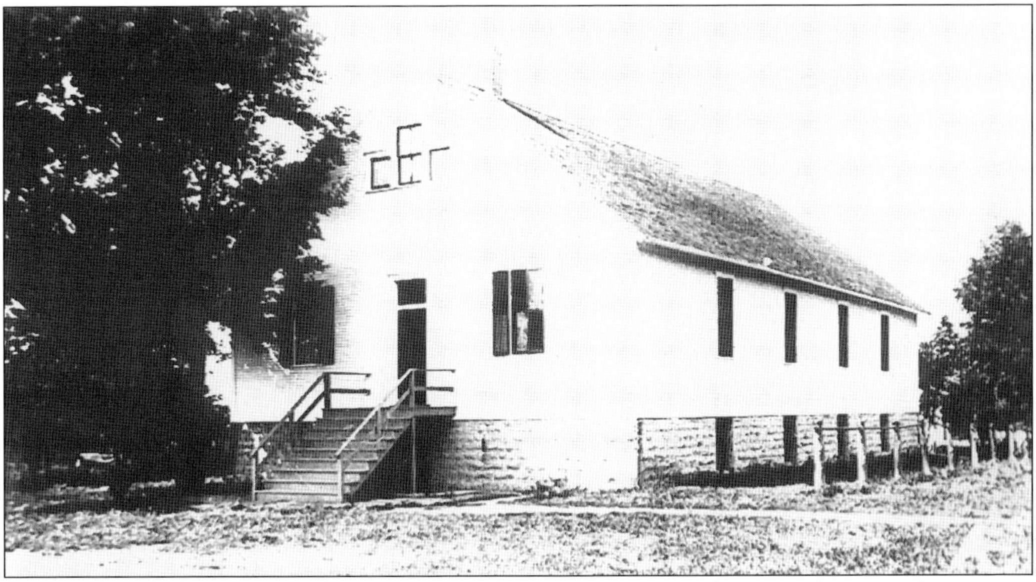

The image above shows the exterior of Forester Hall as it appeared in its early years of existence. For many years, this was the social gathering spot for the community. It was later remodeled and converted into a fire station for the Winfield Fire Department. The image below features a 1905 gathering of the St. Aloysius Court No. 148, Catholic Order of Foresters. Among the members pictured are, from left to right, (first row) Christ Miller (1), Michael Besch (2), Anthony Huels (5), Matthias Mueller (7), and John Enders (9). In the second row, John Welland is second from the right, and in the third row, flanking the banner, are Christopher Enders (left) and John Foxen, while Jacob Mueller is to the right of Enders. (Both, courtesy of the Winfield Historical Society.)

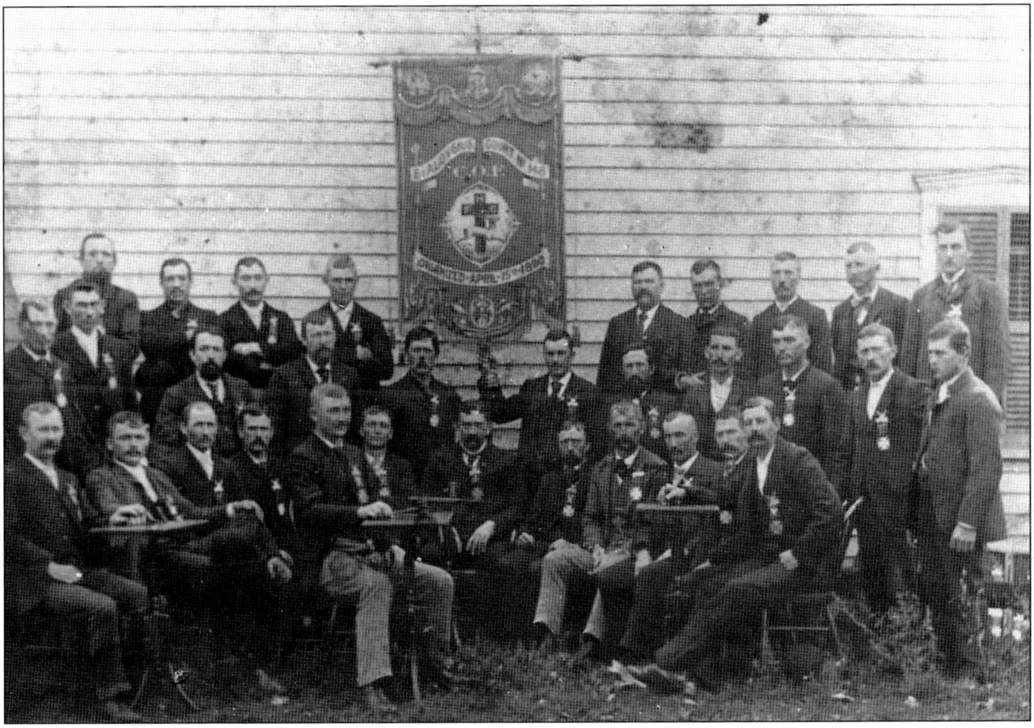

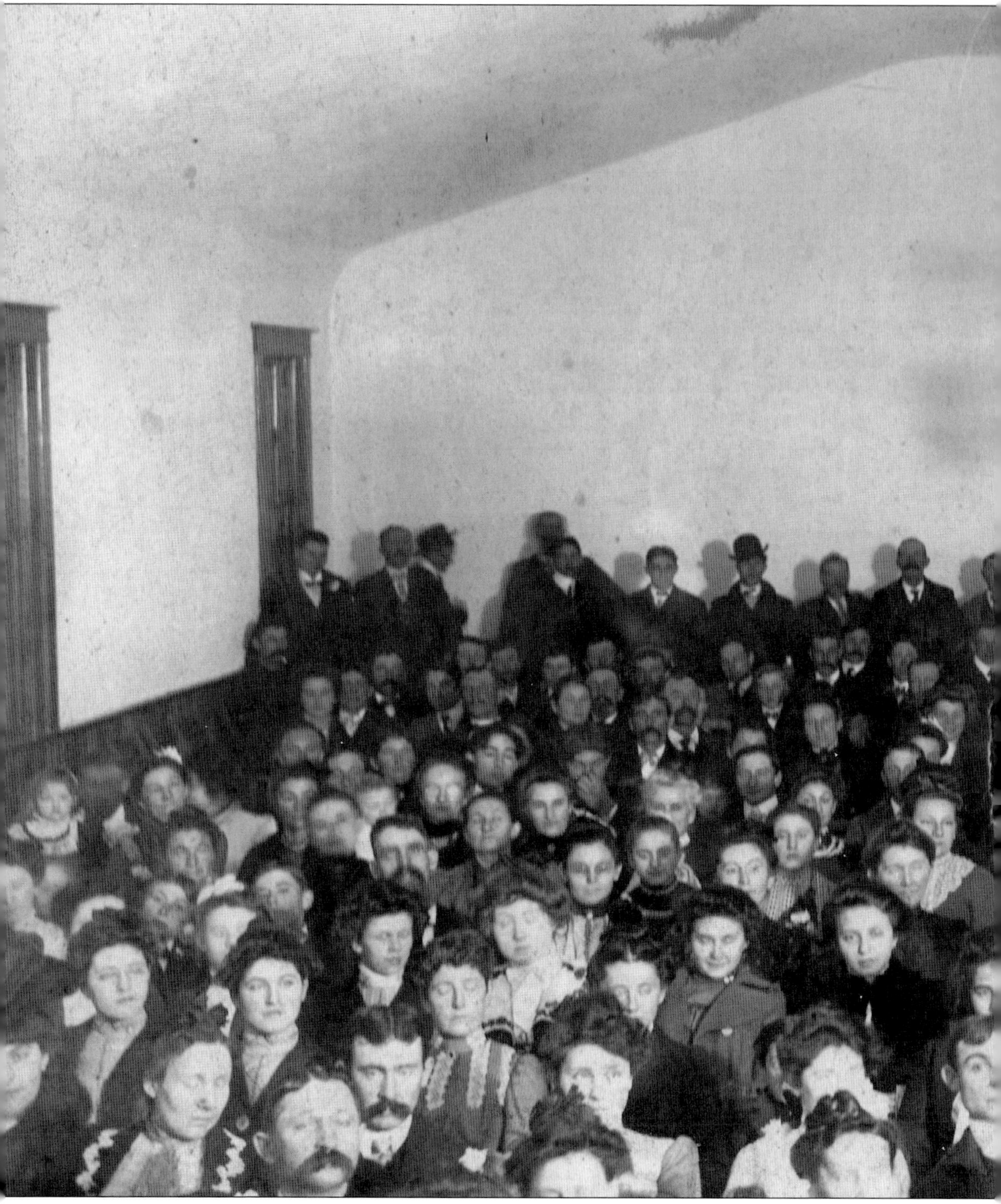

The grand opening of Forester Hall was on November 19, 1902. The structure itself was built earlier in the year. Activities were held in town in order to raise funds for the construction of this building. According to the *Wheaton Illinoian*, which covered the grand opening, "a program will be rendered consisting of German and English addresses; music by an orchestra and vocal

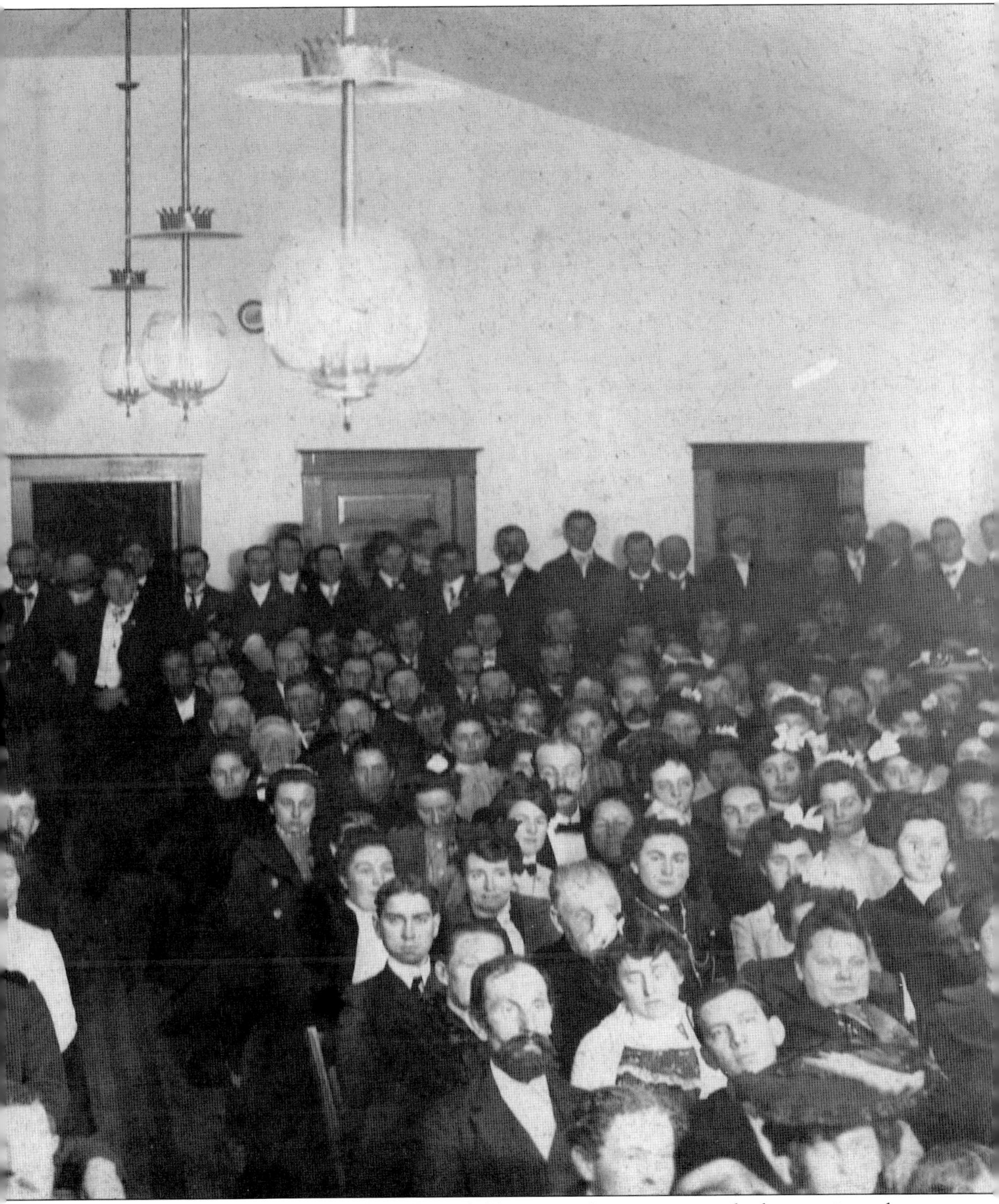

selections by the Caecilia Mannerchor of Winfield, a musical organization of a dozen voices who are first class. A social will follow the program after which a dance will be indulged in to settle the new building." This photograph shows the gathering of members inside the new building. (Courtesy of the Winfield Historical Society.)

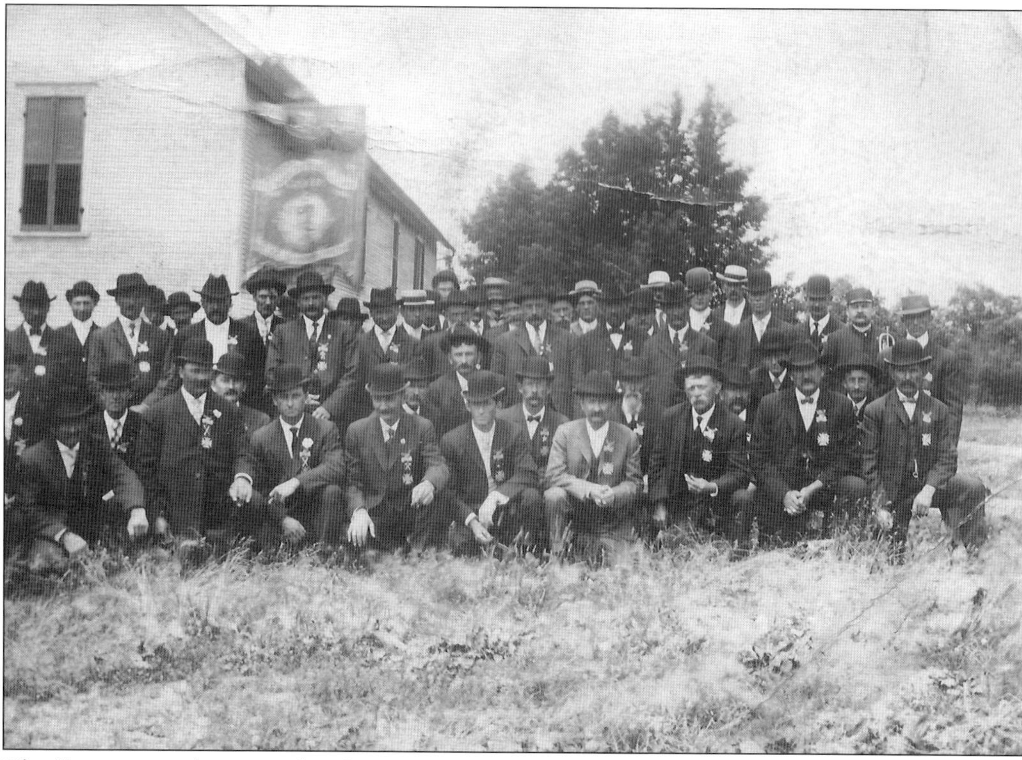

The Foresters gather outside of Forester Hall, though the exact year of both photographs is unknown. The image above features the Foresters kneeling and donning hats, while the one below shows the group sitting. Among Winfield men that belonged to the Foresters were Nick Fuchsen, Matthias Mueller, Peter Jungels, Valentine Klein, John Enders, Paul Sehnem, Frank Miller, Matt Tinnes, Michael Besch, Al Schmidt, John Meyer, Mike Tinnes, Nicholas Schramer, John Besch, Chris Miller, John Schramer, Nick Schramer, John Weiland Jr., Nicholas Enders, John Berkes, and John Heinz. (Both, courtesy of the Winfield Historical Society.)

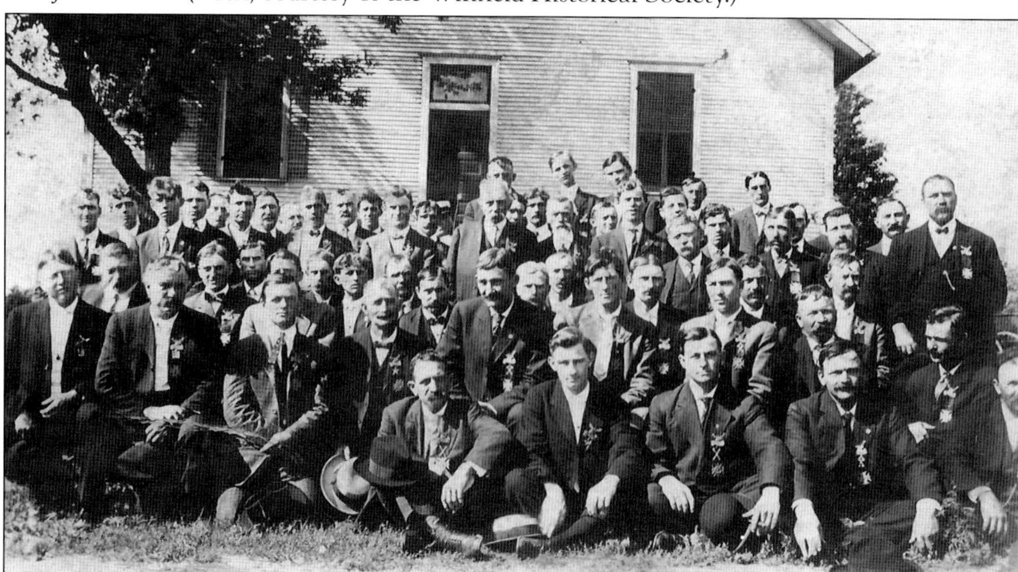

Five

St. John the Baptist Church and School

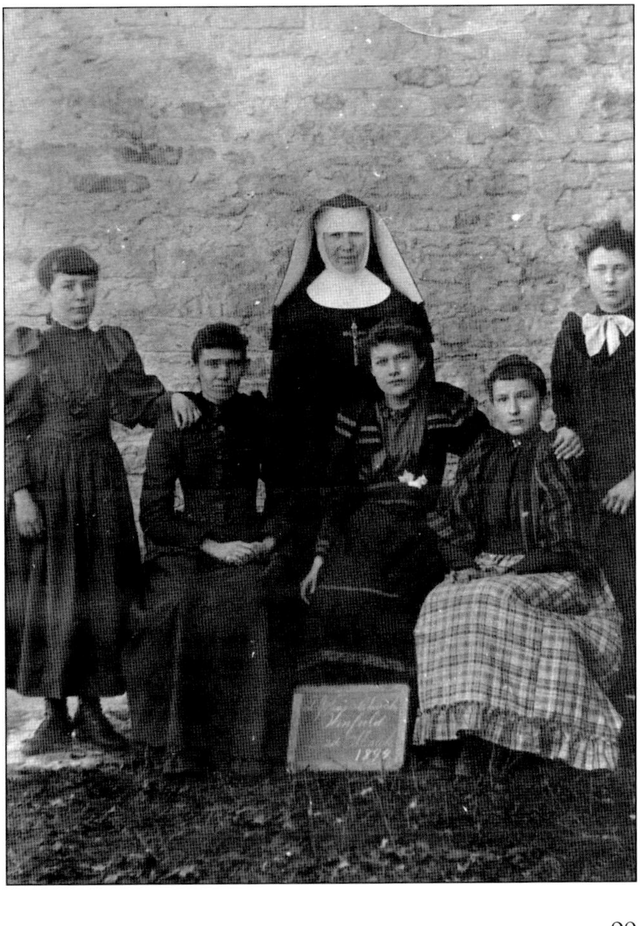

Sister Hildegarde is pictured with members of St. John the Baptist Church and school in 1898. Sister Hildegarde is the only identified person in this photograph, with possible members of the Daleiden and Fuchsen families flanking her. (Courtesy of the Winfield Historical Society.)

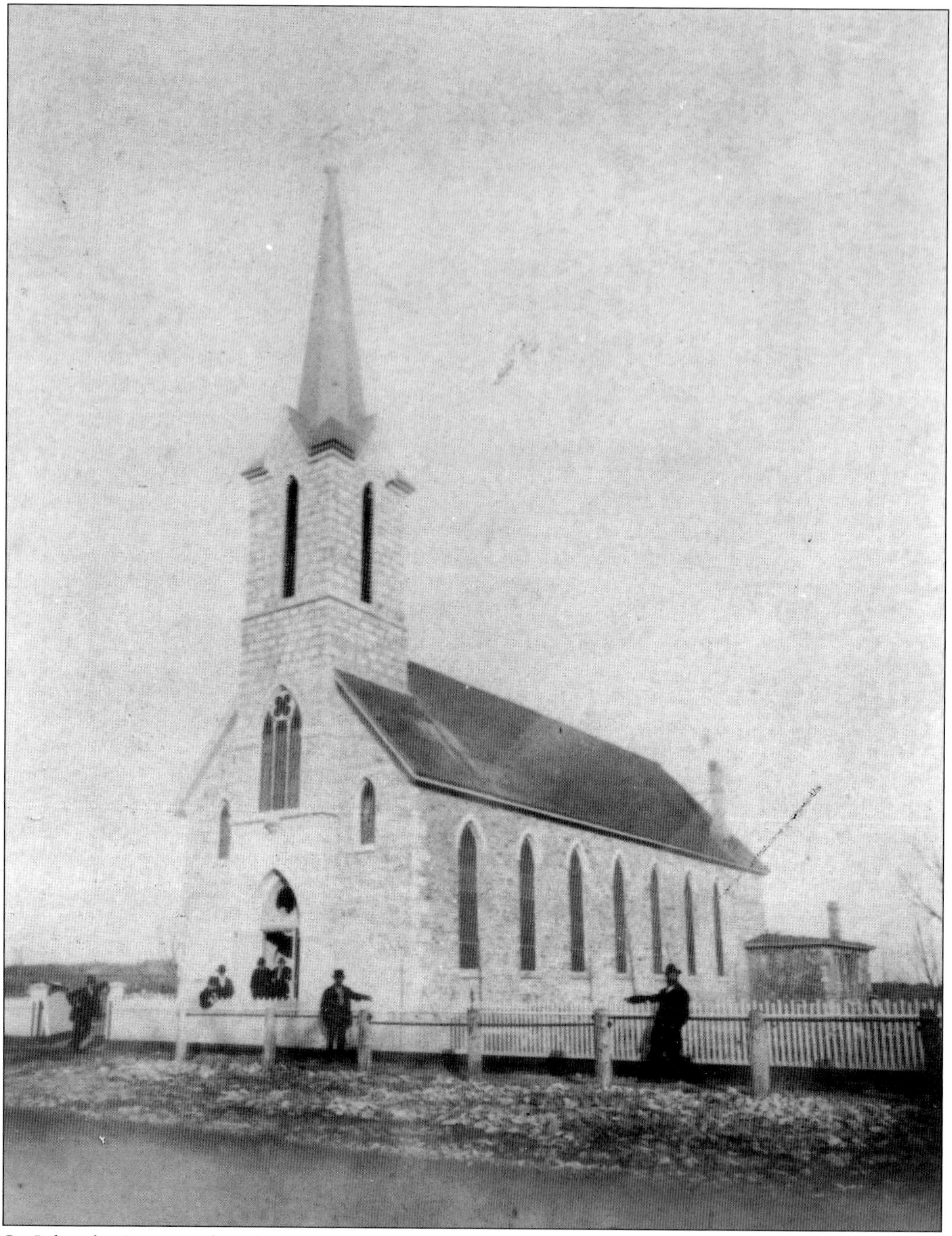

St. John the Baptist Church is in this c. 1879 photograph shortly after it was enlarged. On February 21, 1867, a warranty deed that was dated five days earlier conveyed a one-acre plot of land for a payment of $1 from Julius M. Warren to Rt. Rev. James Duggan, DD, Bishop of the Diocese of Chicago, that was to be used for the Catholic Church and Winfield. That one-acre plot became home to St. John the Baptist Church. Information regarding the warranty deed, Document 8277 as it was entered into the records of DuPage County, appears in Louise Spanke's *Winfield's Good Old Days: A History*. (Courtesy of the Winfield Historical Society.)

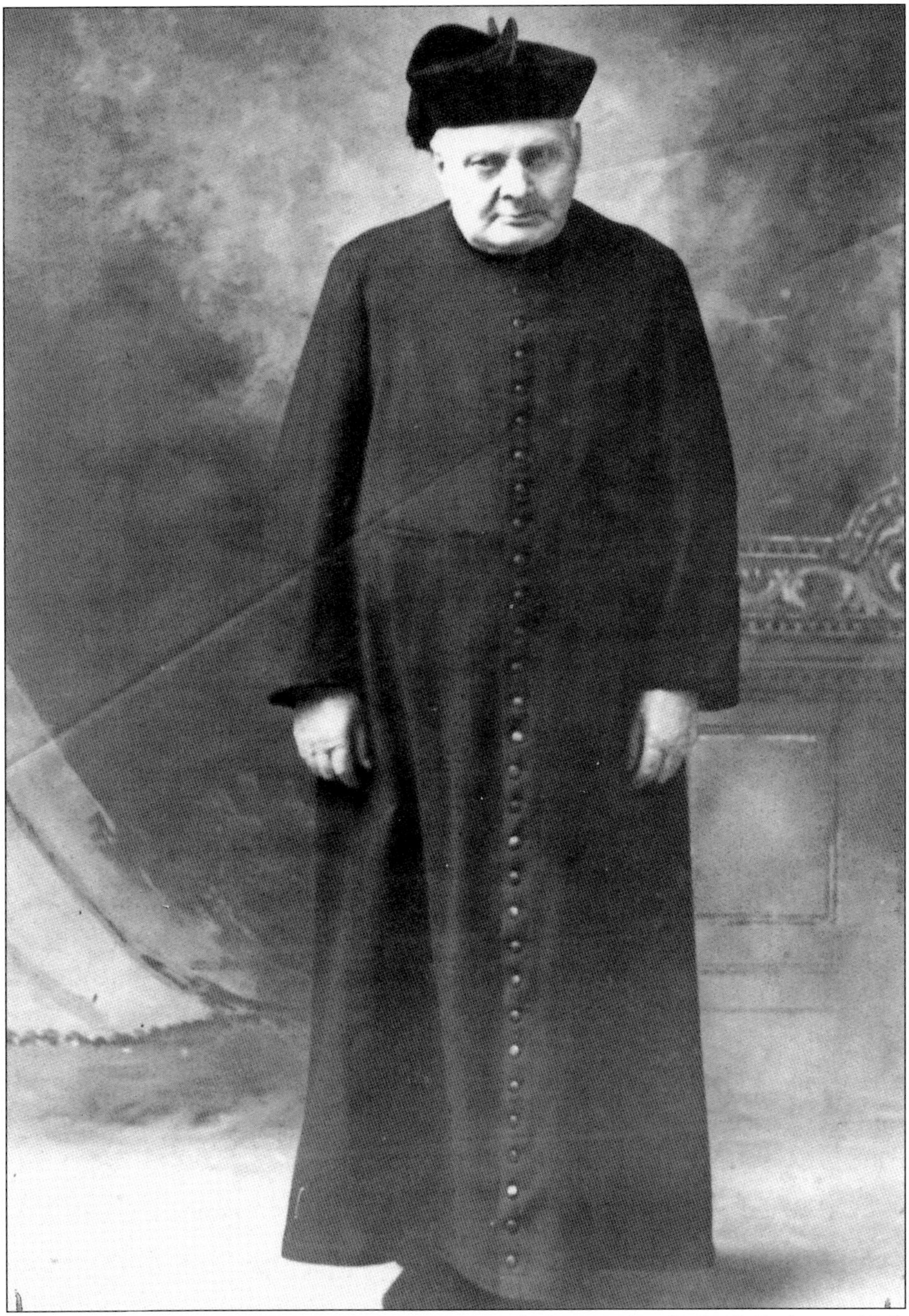

Fr. John Wiederhold was born in Neuenheerse, Westphalia, on April 13, 1841. At age 12, he left home to start his preparation for the priesthood. He came to the United States in 1864. Wiederhold attended the University of St. Mary on the Lake in Chicago for four years, followed by a year at St. Francis Seminary in Milwaukee. He was ordained by Bishop John Martin Henri in January 1869 and was sent to St. John the Baptist parish in Winfield, where he would serve until his death in February 1921. Louise Spanke includes Father Wiederhold's biographical information in her book *Winfield's Good Old Days: A History*. (Courtesy of the Winfield Historical Society.)

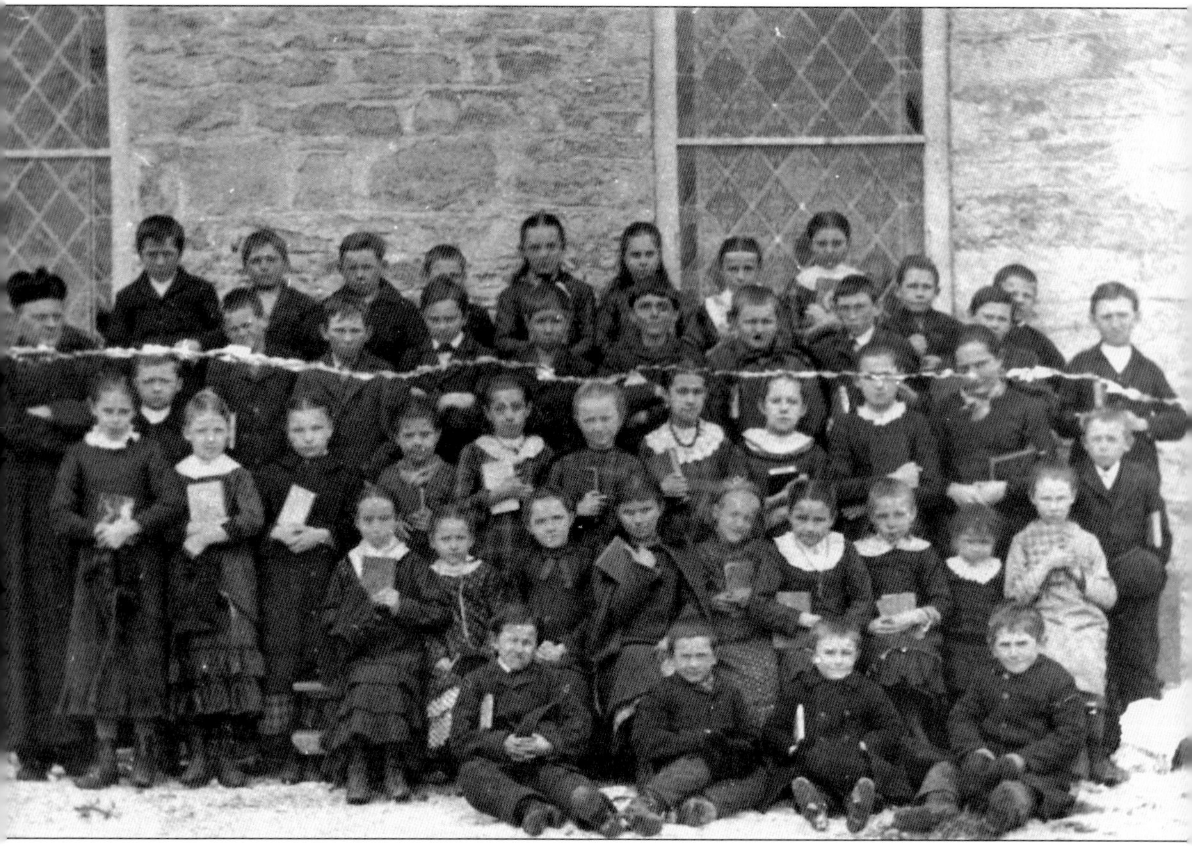

Father Wiederhold is pictured with pupils at St. John the Baptist School in 1879. There is no identification for most of the students in the 1879 class, though Father Wiederhold can be seen at the far left at the start of about the fourth row and Therese Enders is fourth from the right in the third row. (Courtesy of the Winfield Historical Society.)

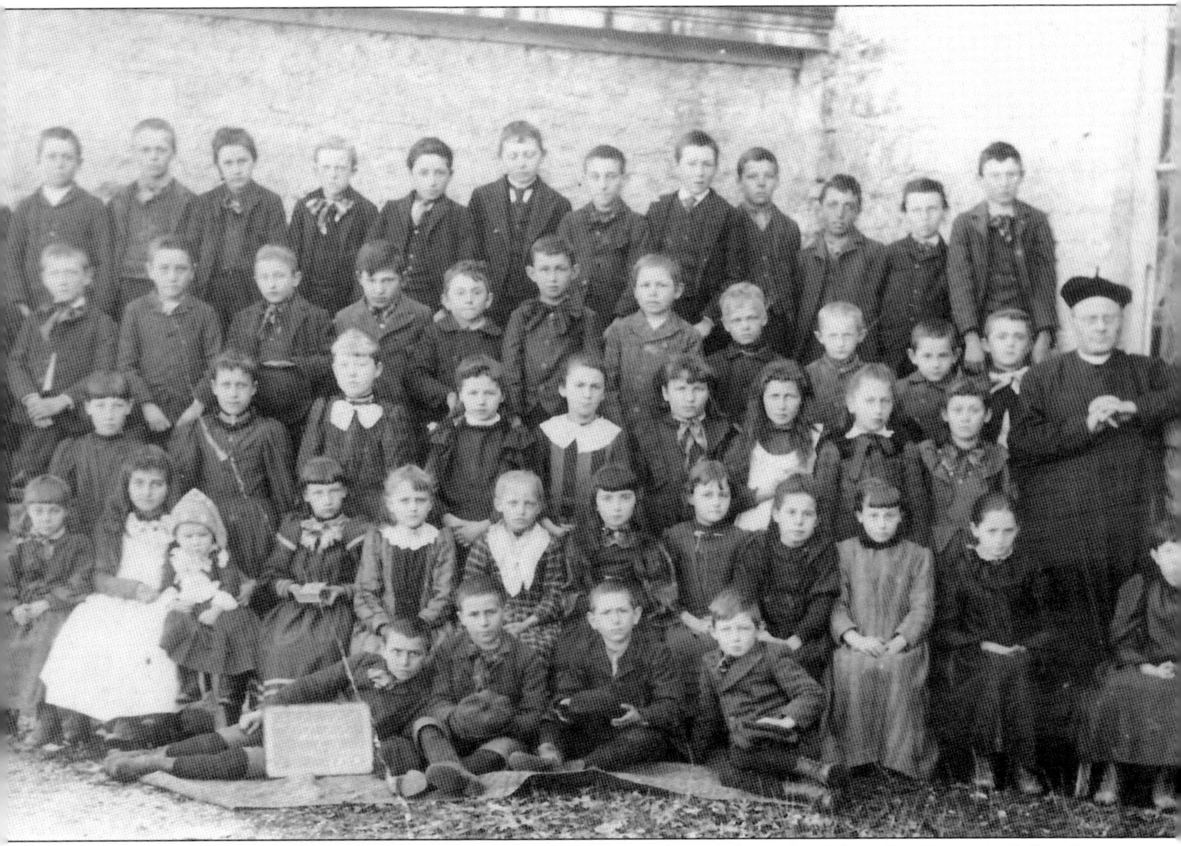

In this 1898 photograph, Father Wiederhold is seen with pupils at St. John the Baptist School. For this photograph, identifications are again limited, though Louise Spanke does note that Father Wiederhold is on the far right at the end of second and third rows. To his left is Lulu Zeier. Anthony Hamm is in the first row, third from the left, while Lena Foxen is behind him. Andrew Stark is identified in the back row, second from the left. (Courtesy of Helen Enders and the Winfield Historical Society.)

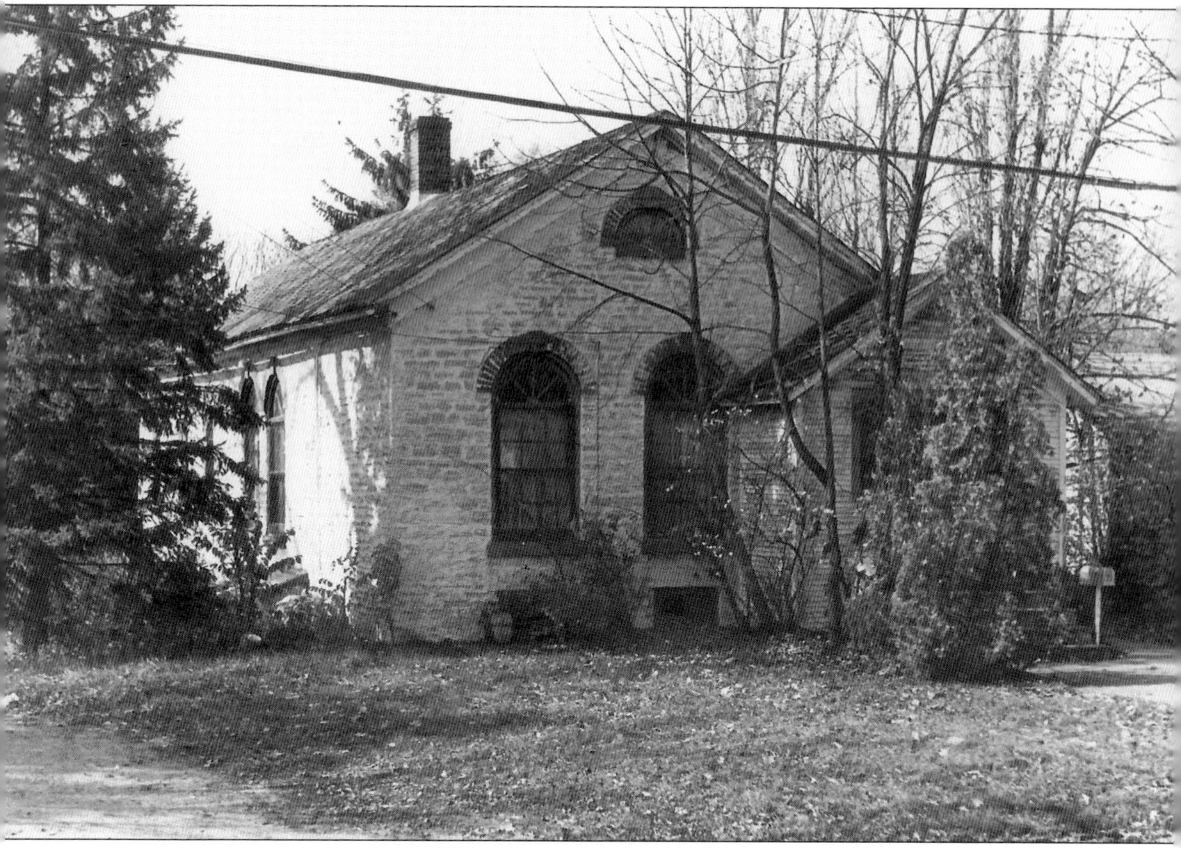

Prior to 1882, families sent their children to Catholic instruction in an upstairs room in a store building that was run by Henry Germann on Church Street. As membership in the parish increased and the church was enlarged, Sisters Paula, Euphemia, and Michaela of the Order of School Sisters of St. Francis arrived to start the new Catholic school. The school was located across the street from St. John the Baptist Church, and it fulfilled this role, as well as being the first rectory, from 1882 to 1940. Louise Spanke remarks that it is astounding to note that, from 1899 to 1922, St. John the Baptist School only had two principals: Sister Hildegarde (1899 to 1914) and Sister Laurentia (1914 to 1922). Instruction was in both English and German up until the United States entered World War I in 1917. (Courtesy of the Winfield Historical Society.)

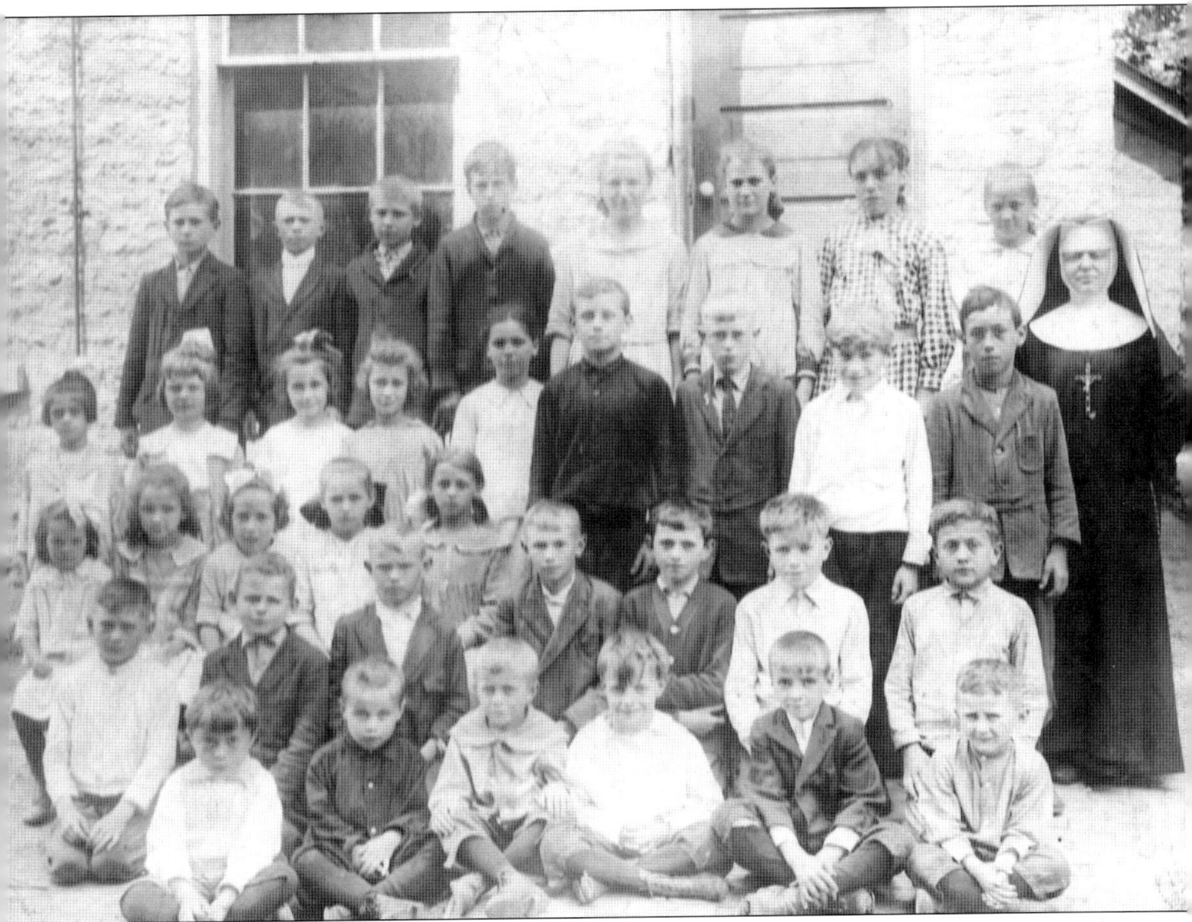

Students are seen at St. John the Baptist School in this undated photograph. Among those seated in the first row are Raymond Weiland, Joseph Enders, George Daleiden, Francis Zeier, who are the first four from left to right in the row. Kneeling in the second row is William Enders (far left). In the third row, Helen Besch is second from the left, while Gertrude Nagle and Tillie Klein are the last two on the right. In the fourth row are, from left to right, Mary Daleiden, Marcia Predergast, Clara Higgins, Clara Baum, Gertrude Besch, Peter Baum, Victor Lies, Joseph Zeier, and Mike Kammes. In the fifth row is Jake Schramer (far left). (Courtesy of David and Patricia Enders and the Winfield Historical Society.)

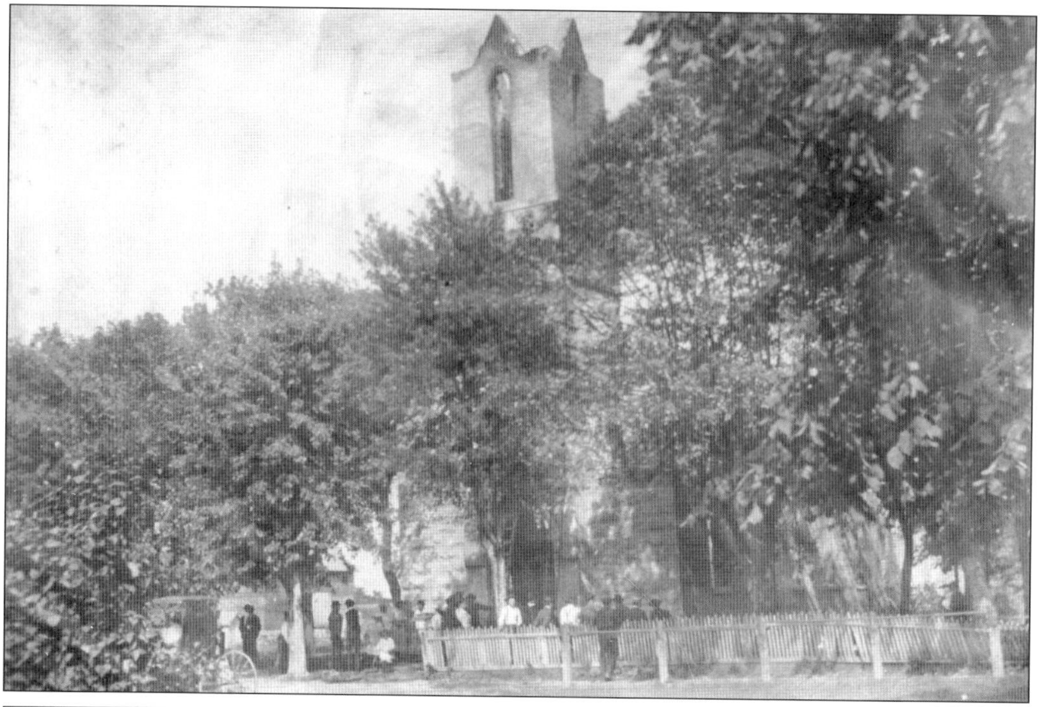

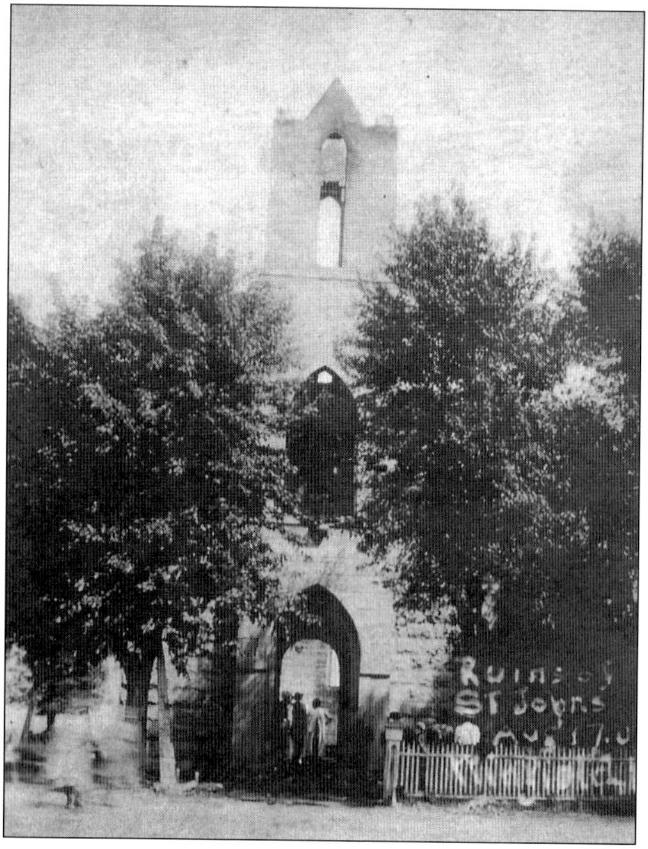

On the afternoon of August 17, 1906, a thunderstorm hit Winfield and a single bolt of lightning hit the wooden steeple of St. John the Baptist Church. The strike set the church ablaze, and it quickly burned within a half hour. Villagers reacted quickly to the tragedy to try and do what they could to help. A story circulated that Father Wiederhold had to call Christ Daleiden and William Zeier down from the burning roof. When the fire was finally extinguished, only the altars, pews, stations of the cross, and communion rail could be saved. (Above, courtesy of the Frank and Mae C. Schlick estate; left, courtesy of the Winfield Historical Society.)

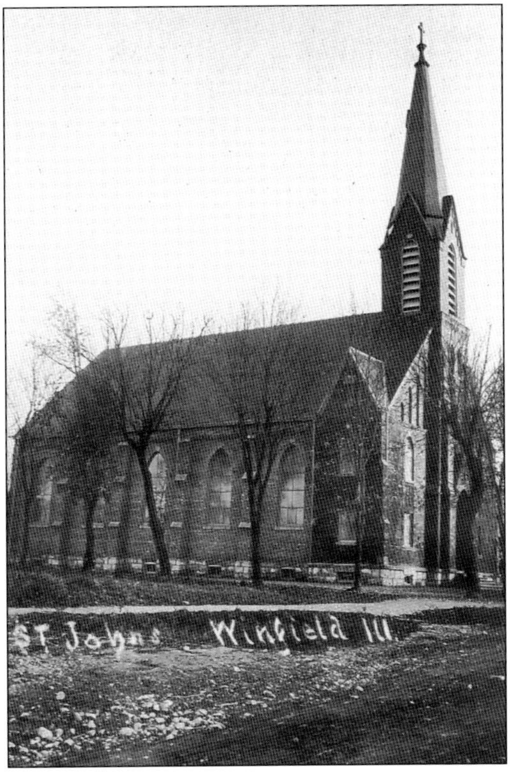

Indeed, the church was immediately rebuilt. According to the *Wheaton Illinoian* on October 13, "Men have begun tearing away the damaged parts of the walls." The paper also reports that it was expected that the foundation for the new church would be laid before the settling in of winter 1906–1907. Archbishop Quigley laid the cornerstone for the new foundation on November 25, 1906, and the new St. John the Baptist Church was dedicated on August 18, 1907, one year after the disastrous blaze. The view in the image below looks north along Church Street toward St. John the Baptist Church, which is on the right, and the school and rectory on the left. (Both, courtesy of the Winfield Historical Society and St. John the Baptist Church.)

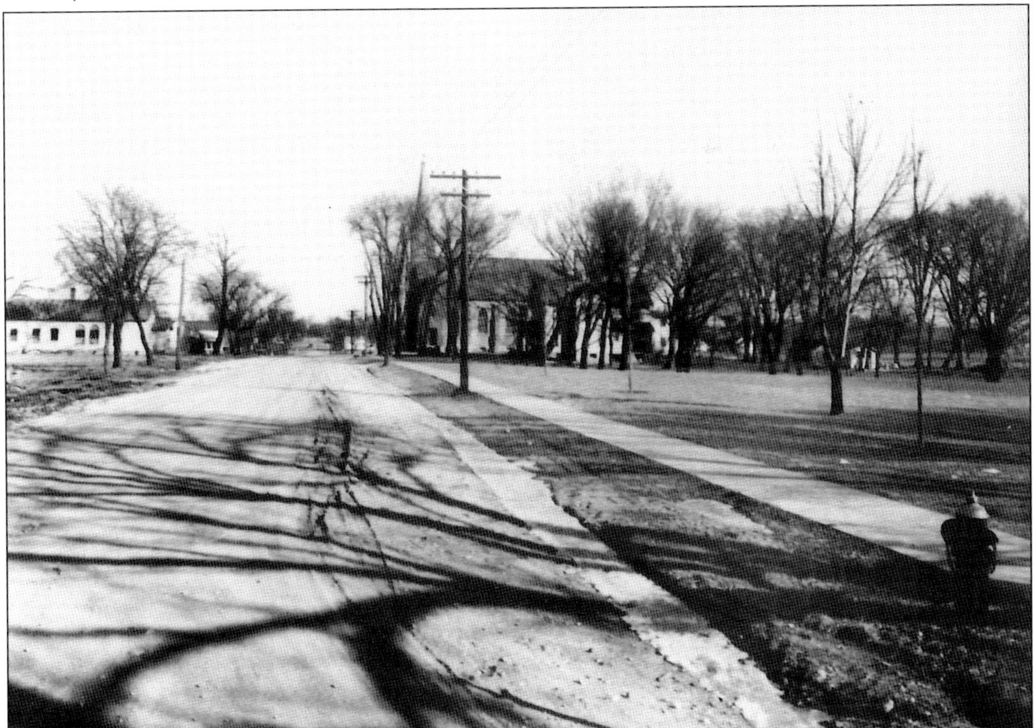

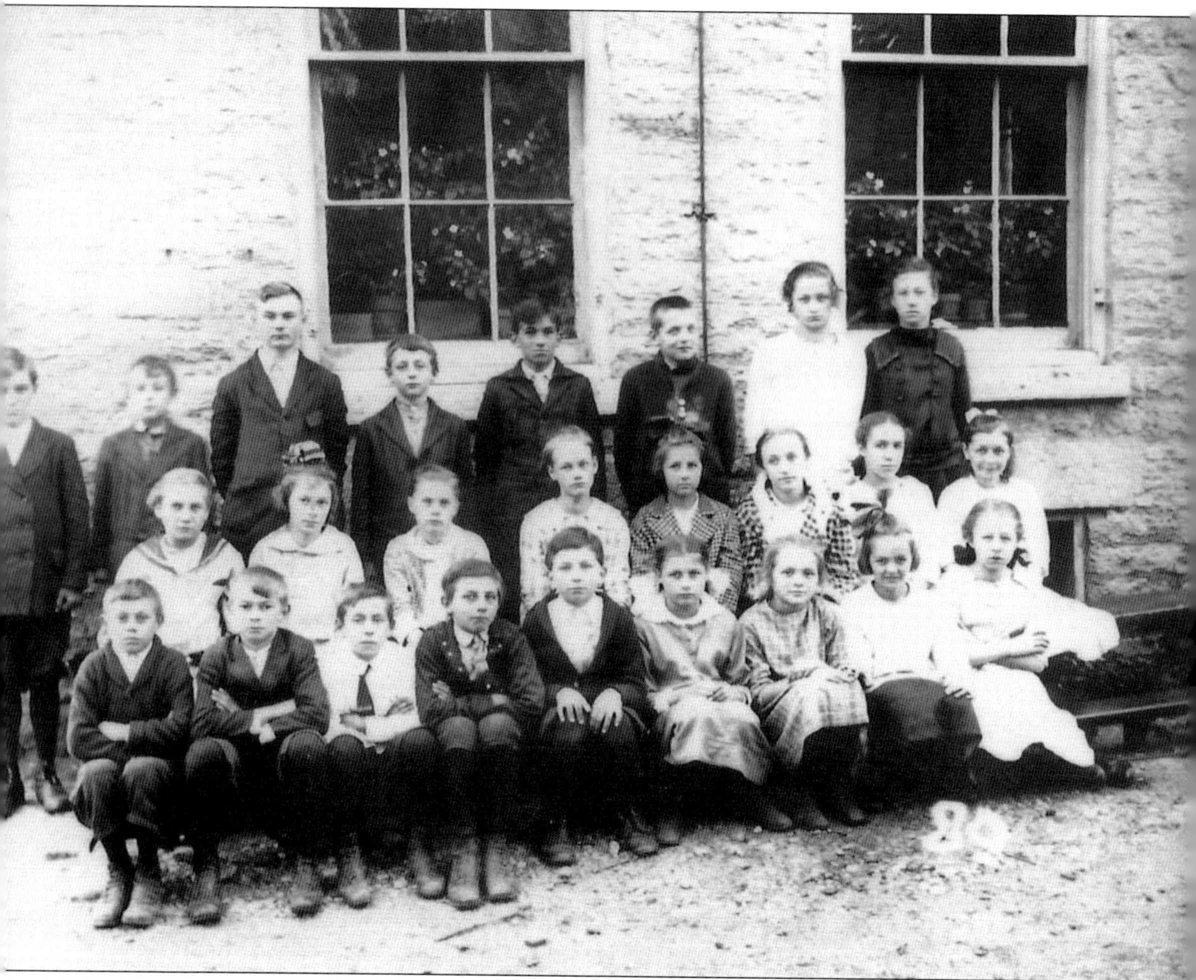

Seen here are the students enrolled at St. John the Baptist School in 1914 and 1915. From left to right are (first row) Anthony Daleiden, Joe Kosusnik, unidentified, Edwin Dieter, Al Besch, Elizabeth Dieter, Lucy Klein, Edna Hopkins, and Helen Enders; (second row) Marie Mittman, Frances Wageman, Catherine Daleiden, Helen Baum, Alice Higgins, Gertrude Heinz, Anna Kammes, and unidentified; (third row) Bill Hager, Leo Berkes, John Baum, Emile Thieme, George Dieter, Peter Enders, Anna Besch, and Hilda Roth. (Courtesy of Helen Enders and the Winfield Historical Society.)

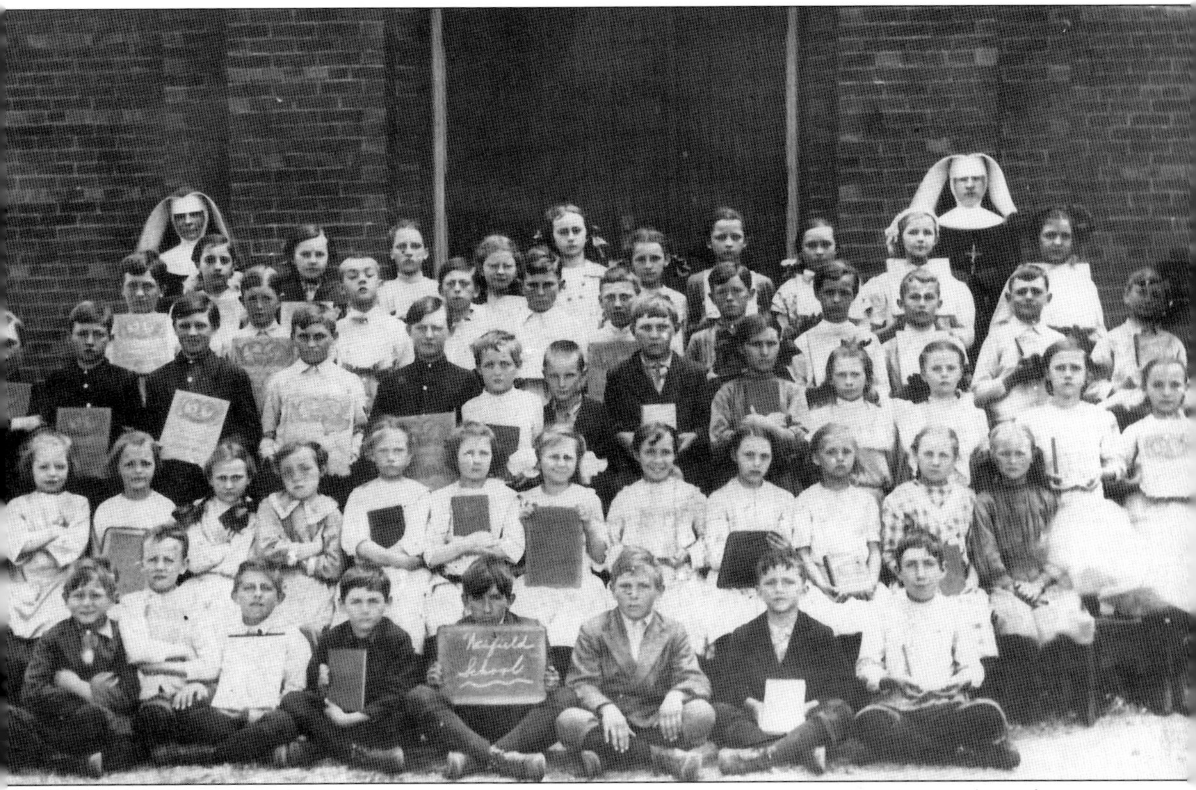

Students enrolled at St. John the Baptist School in 1912 are, from left to right, (first row) Anthony Daleiden, Jacob Schramer, Leo Berkes, Edwin Dieter, Christ Armbrust, George Dieter, Edward Schramer, Al Besch, and Theodore Kammes; (second row) Elizabeth Dieter, Helen Enders, Lucy Klein, Elizabeth Mittman, Lena Kammes, Helen Baum, Alice Higgins, Matilda Schramer, Anna Kammes, Alma Armbrust, Theresa Klein, and Mare Mittman; (third row) Leo Lies, George Roth, John Kosusnik, Nicholas Dieter, Jacob Baum, Peter Enders, William Hager, Edward Rau, Agnes Rau, Hattie Kosusnik, Catherine Daleiden, Hilda Roth, and Gertrude Heinz; (fourth row) Edward Besch, Henry Higgins, Edward Foxen, William Daleiden, John Schramer, Michael Mittman, Richard Higgins, William Klein, Edward Enders, Frank Wolsfeld, and John Baum; (fifth row) Henrietta Wolsfeld, Elizabeth Bauler, Theresa Hager, Eleanor Kline, Katherine Wolff, Frances Wageman, Anna Besch, Tillie Schramer, Alice Enders, and Amanda Armbrust. (Courtesy of the Winfield Historical Society.)

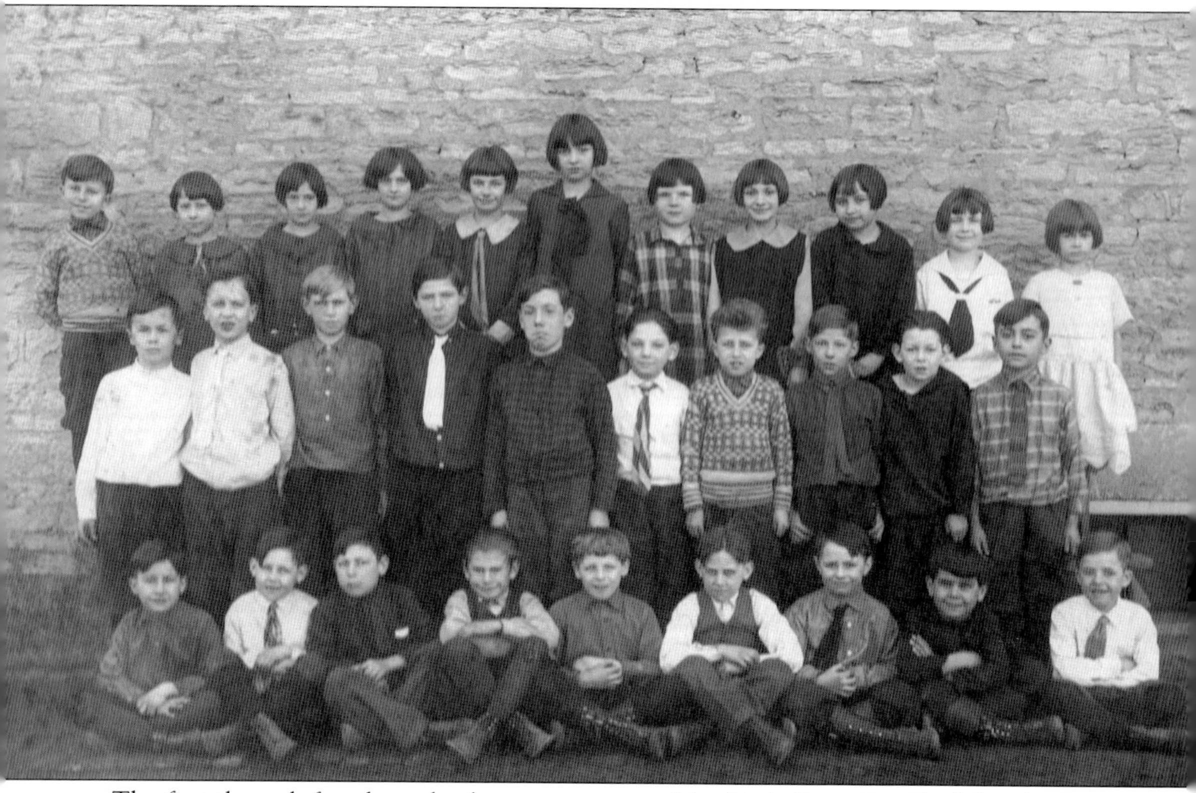

The first-through-fourth-grade classes convene at "the Little Room" at St. John the Baptist Church in 1926. From left to right (first row) are James Berkes, Marion Karwoski, unidentified, John Kosusnik, unidentified, Chester Karwoski, Pat Collins, John P. Jungels, and Richard Tinnes; (second row) Arthur Enders, Francis Herdell, two unidentified, William Kammes, John Heinz, Joseph Meyers, Clarence Schramer, Donald Zur, and Raymond Schramer; (third row) Otto Meyers, Rita Schramer, two unidentified, Olive Schwartz, Paulina Holbach, Laurine Higgins, Louise Schramer, and Mary Kosusnik. (Courtesy of Alice Besch and the Winfield Historical Society.)

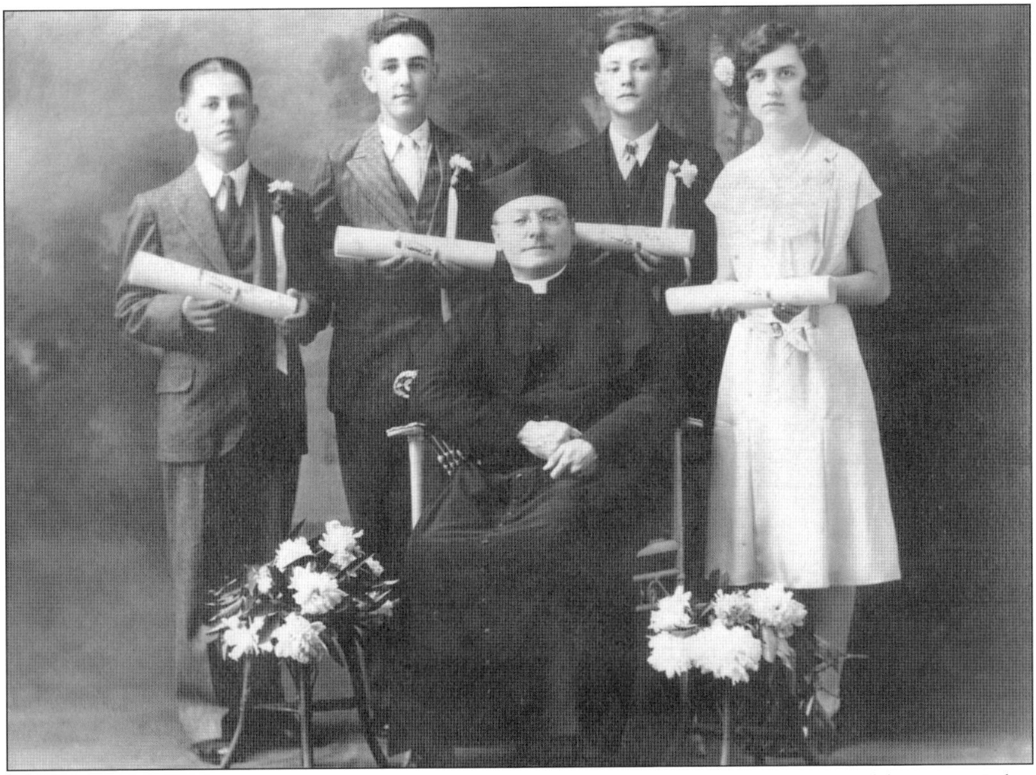

Fr. Henry M. Franz and students from St. John the Baptist School are pictured here. Fr. John Wiederhold was the longest-serving pastor at the church, having been there from 1869 to his death in February 1921. Father Franz succeeded Father Wiederhold, and he served as pastor for the next 15 years until ill health forced him to retire in 1936. The popular August Homecoming Festivals for St. John the Baptist Church were initiated under Father Franz, and they were a yearly staple until giving way to more popular programs, such as the DuPage County Fair. (Both, courtesy of the Winfield Historical Society.)

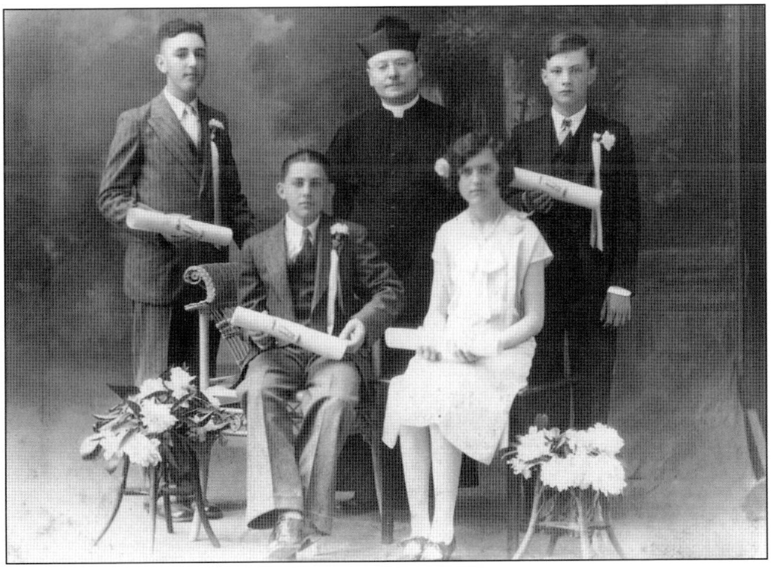

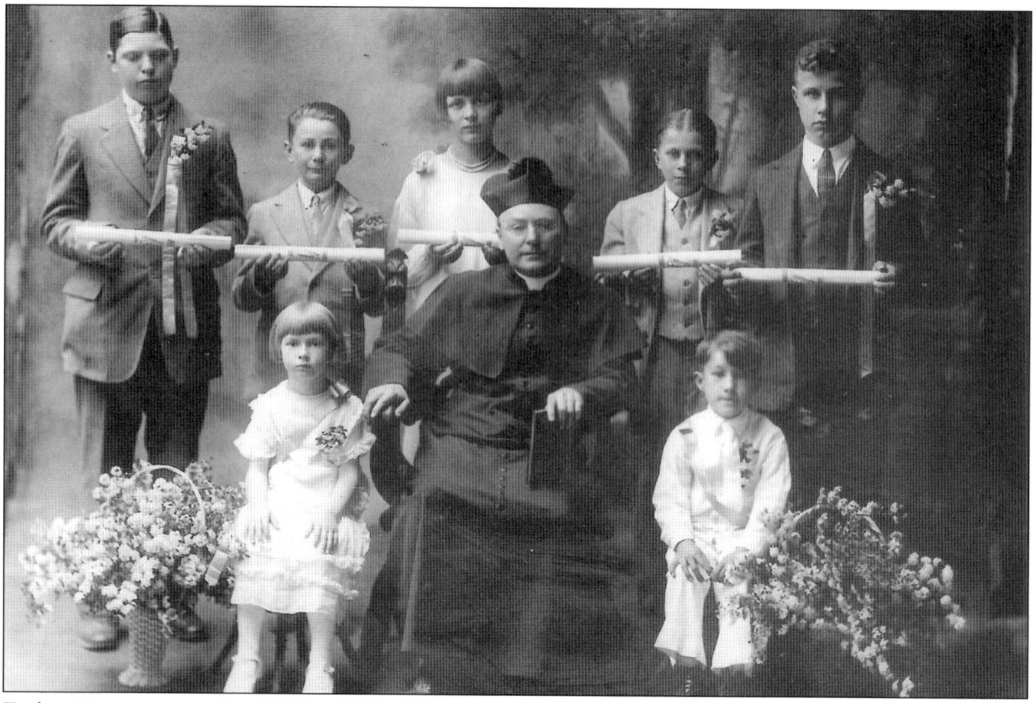

Father Franz is seated with a graduation class from St. John the Baptist School sometime during the 1920s. Frank Schlick is identified on the far left in the row behind Father Franz, but the rest are unidentified. The image below features Father Puetz outside of St. John the Baptist Church in 1942. Standing with him are, from left to right, Jake Zeier, John Heinz, John Schramer, Frank Klein, and Ed Nagle. (Above, courtesy of Kevin Davis; below, courtesy of the Winfield Historical Society.)

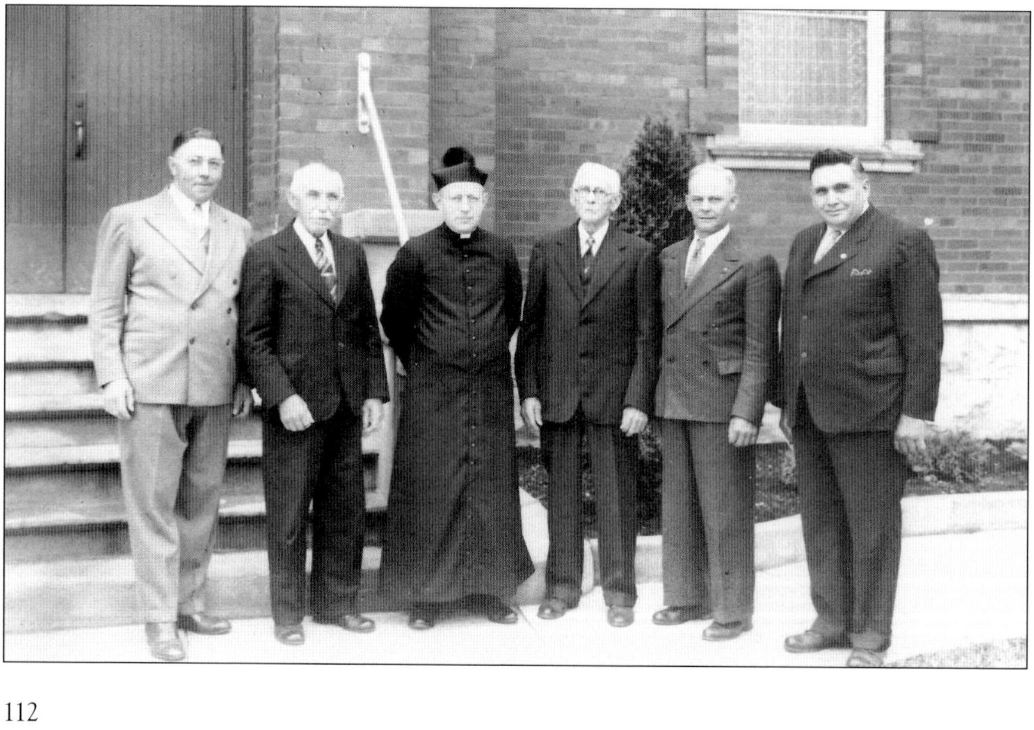

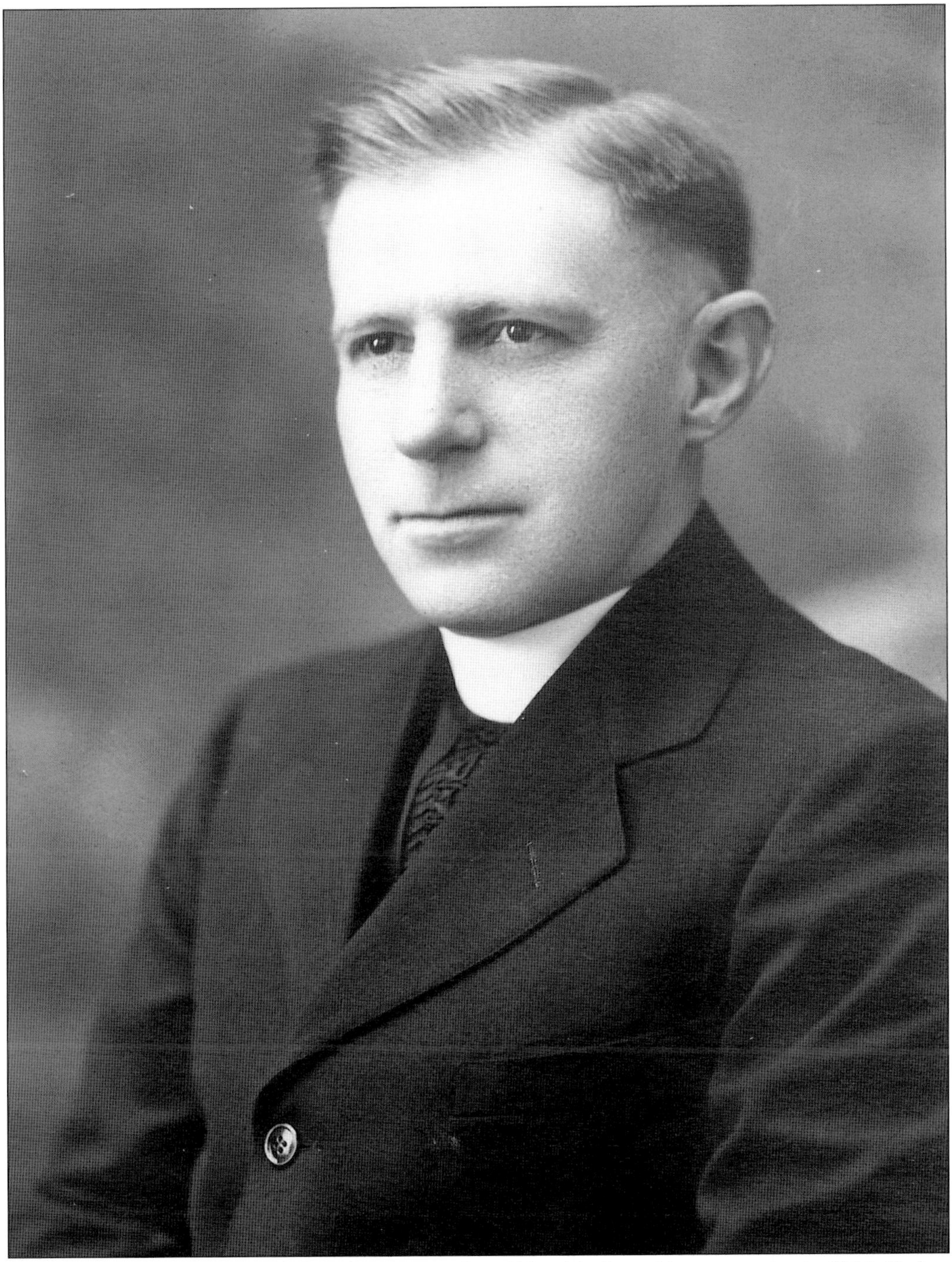

Father Henry Puetz succeeded Father Franz after ill health forced him to retire in 1936. Father Puetz was instrumental in welcoming post–World War II newcomers to the parish. Louise Spanke notes that Father Puetz was instrumental in overseeing the construction of a new St. John the Baptist School, which brought students from the former school across the street in an old stone building. Father Puetz served at St. John the Baptist Church until his death in 1952. (Courtesy of the Winfield Historical Society.)

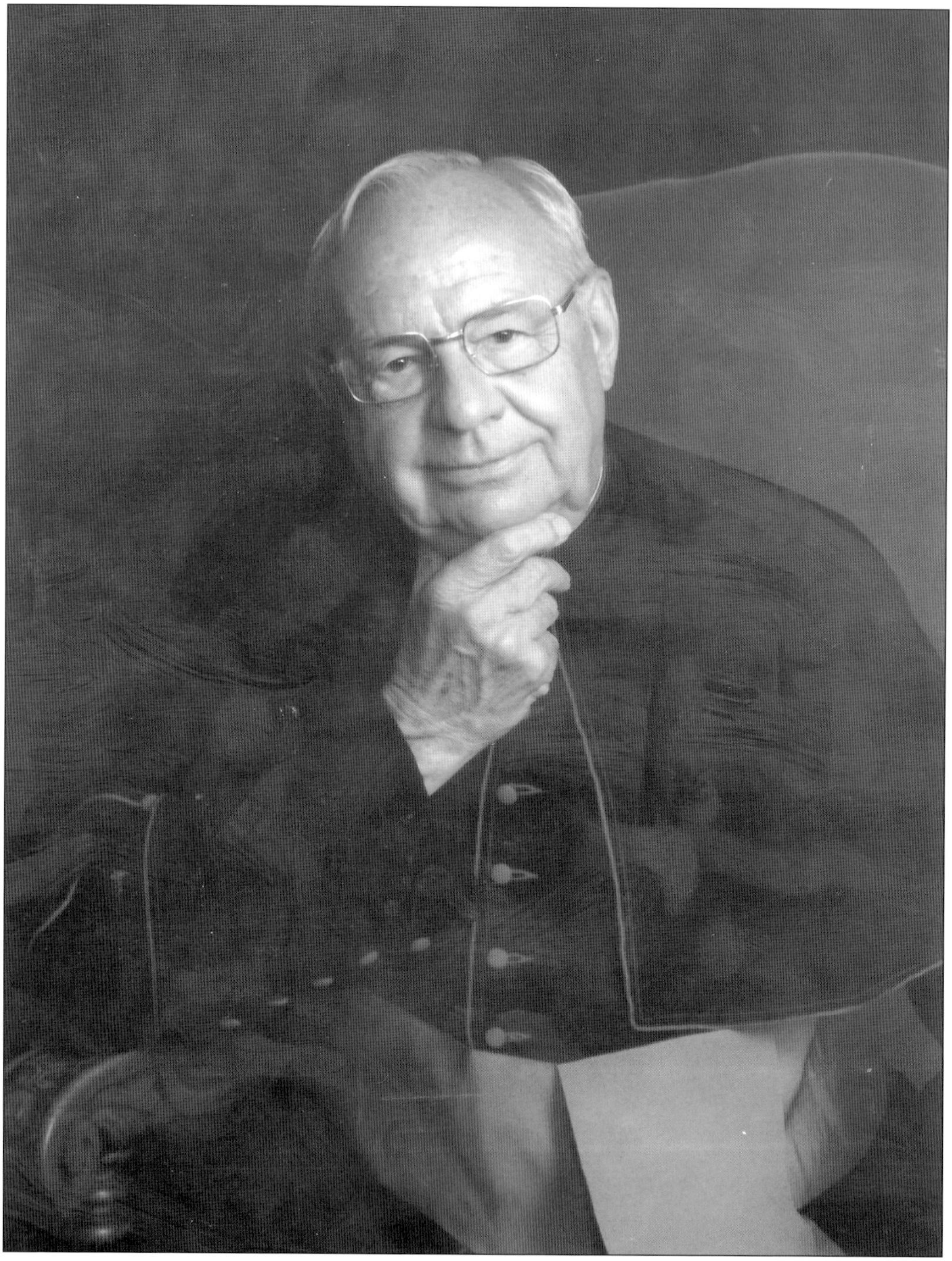

Msgr. Vincent J. Cloos was fourth pastor at St. John the Baptist Church. He was a native Chicagoan. His grandparents, originally from Luxembourg, came to Chicago from Wisconsin. Monsignor Cloos studied at St. Mary's of the Lake Seminary in Chicago. Under Cloos, there was the construction of a new home for the nuns, the Casa Sancta, in 1953; the construction of a new baptistery in 1963 (as a gift of the Elsen family); and construction of a new complex of rectory, office space, and meeting rooms in 1966. (Courtesy of the Winfield Historical Society.)

Six

Winfield Public School

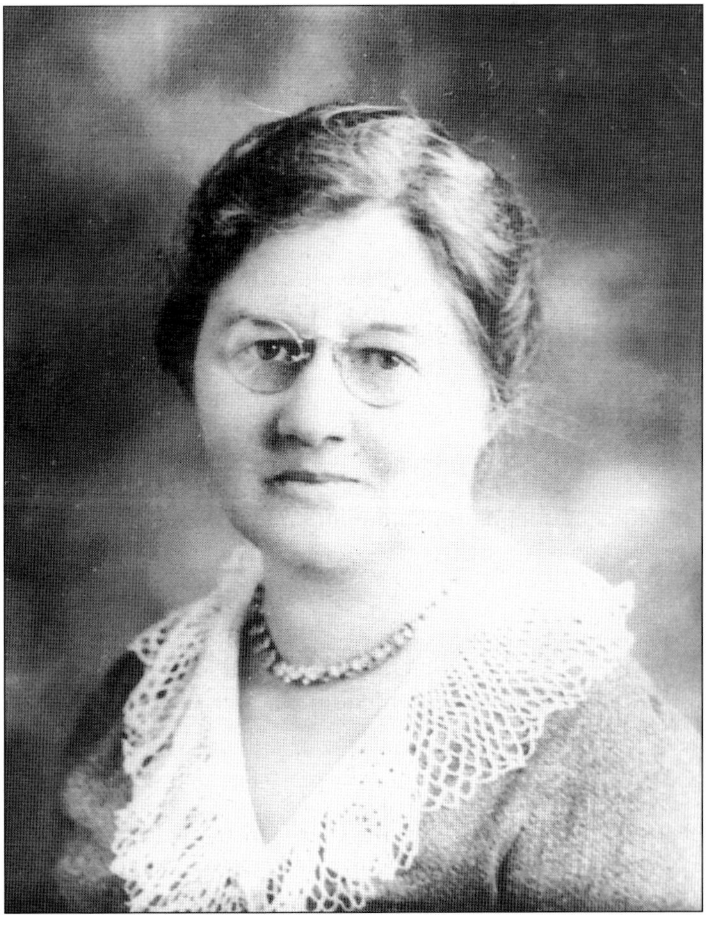

Verena Miller was a teacher at Winfield Public School in the early years of the community. Louise Spanke shares a story from Anna Klein, recalling her having to go to public school for instruction by Miller after attending St. John the Baptist School. There is also a Verena Miller listed in Spanke's book who served as postmistress in Winfield for nearly 12 years, from 1946 to 1926. It is not known if they are the same person. (Courtesy of the Winfield Historical Society.)

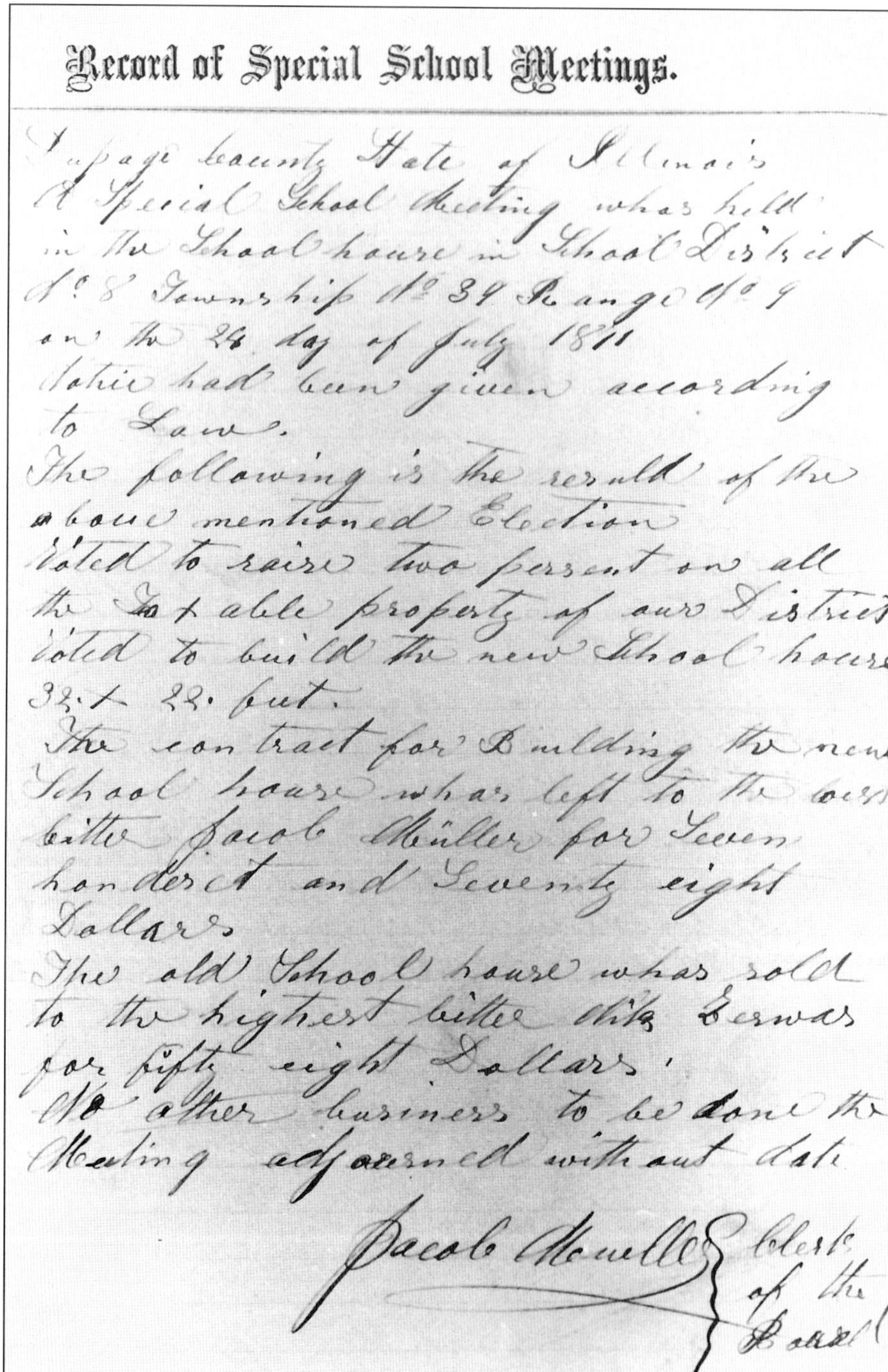
Record of Special School Meetings.

Dupage County State of Illinois
A Special School Meeting whas held
in the School house in School District
No 8 Township No 39 Range No 9
on the 24 day of July 1871
Notice had been given according
to Law.
The following is the result of the
above mentioned Election
Voted to raise two persent on all
the Taxable property of our District
Voted to build the new School house
32 x 22. feet.
The contract for Building the new
School house whas left to the lowest
bitter Jacob Müller for Seven
hunderd and Seventy eight
Dollars
The old School house whas sold
to the highest bitter Mike Gerwas
for fifty eight Dollars.
No other business to be done the
Meeting adjourned with out date

Jacob Mueller Clerk of the Board

Seen here is a copy of minutes as recorded by Jacob Mueller for School District No. 8. The minutes cover the voting to build a new schoolhouse in the community, while the old schoolhouse was sold to the "highest bidder." Jacob Mueller served on the school district board for 14 years. Other area residents to serve included Gilbert Higgins, Jacob Kline, Mathias Huels, Nicholas Enders, Michael Besch, John Enders, and Paul C. Sehnem. (Courtesy of the Winfield Historical Society.)

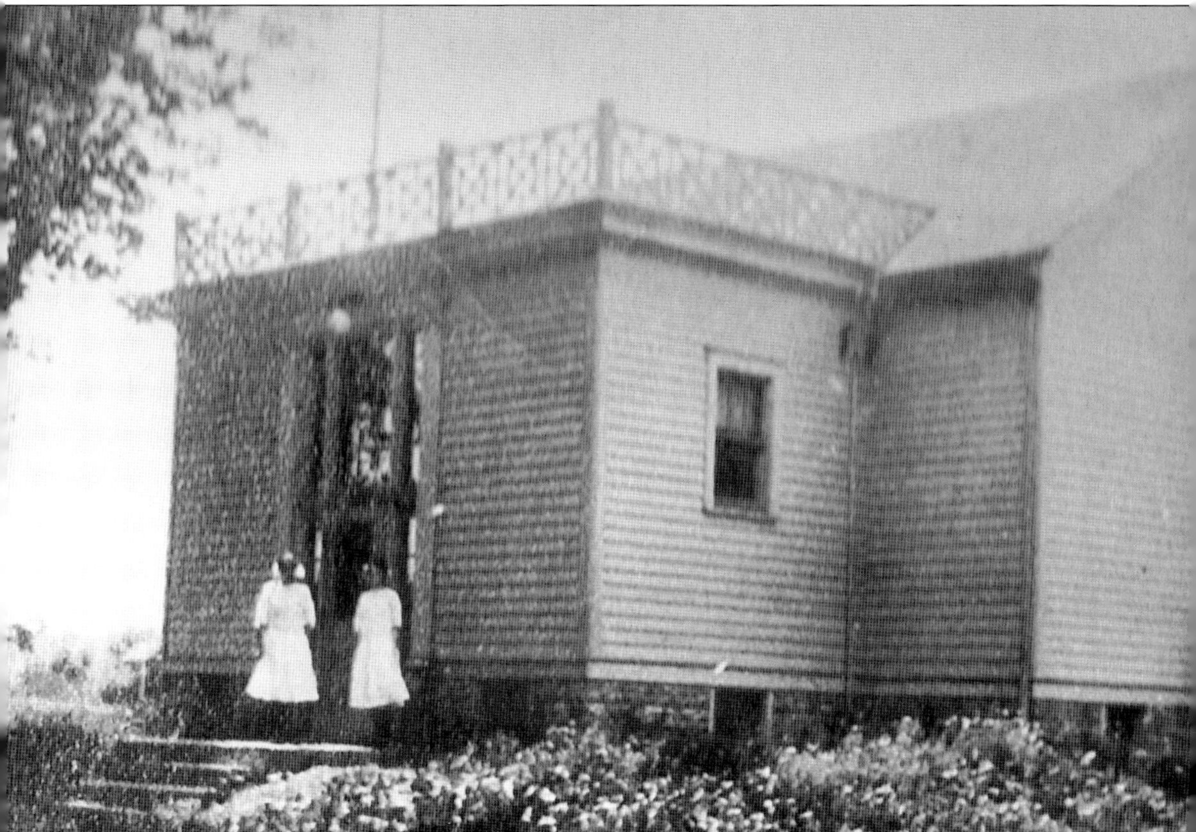

The Winfield Public School is seen here newly remodeled in 1918. A new schoolhouse was opened in 1871, and it consisted of one room complete with a platform up front for the teacher and a potbelly stove. In this particular photograph, Bertha Atkinson (left) and her sister Marie stand on the steps of the school. The Winfield Public operated on a one-teacher system until 1939. Louise Spanke shares a recollection from Bertha Atkinson that, of the ten that graduated in 1918, five were from her own family. (Courtesy of the Winfield Historical Society.)

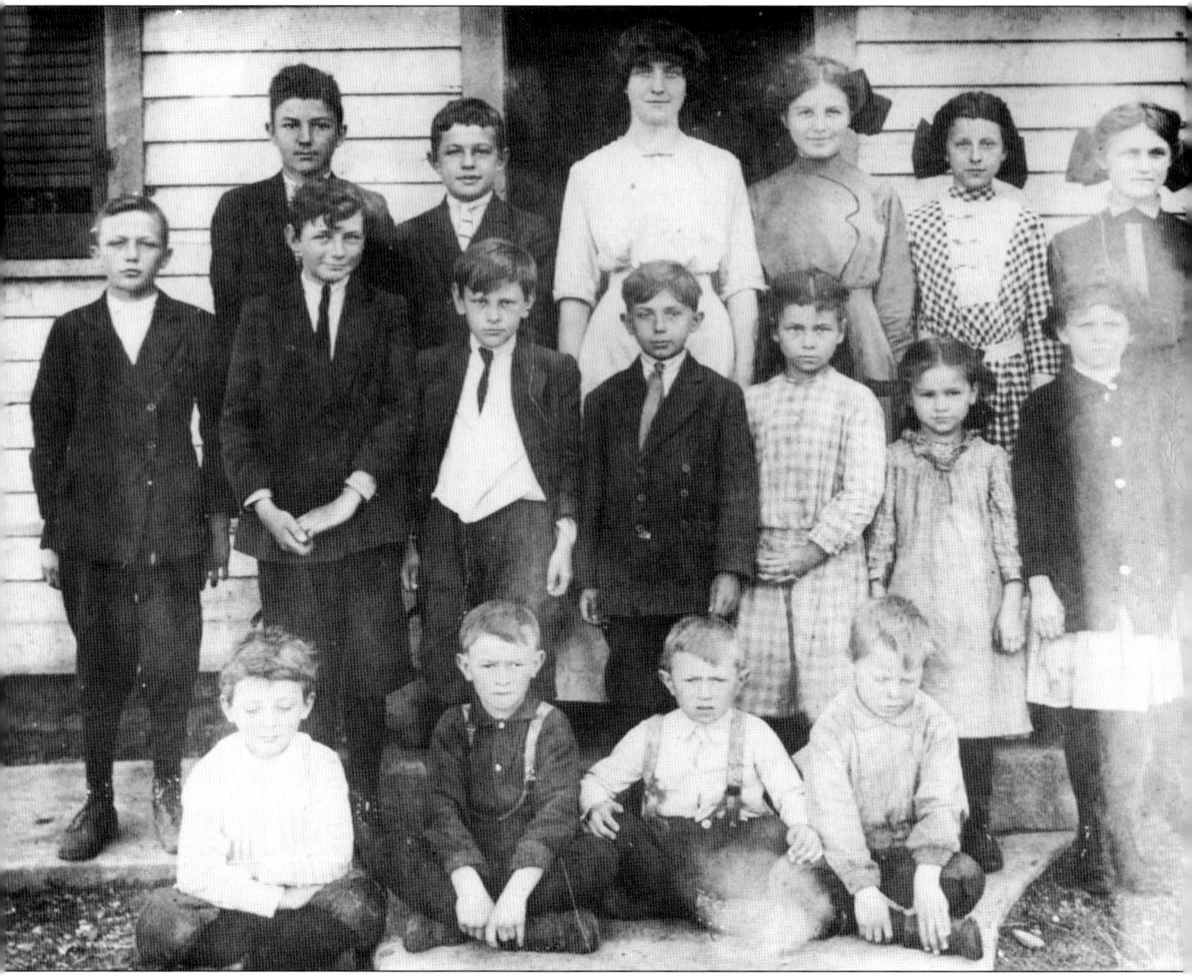

A class convenes for a photograph at the Winfield Public School in 1912–1913. From left to right are (first row) Emile Thieme, Joseph Kosusnik, Anthony Kosusnik, and Raymond Rutchman; (second row) Bernard Besch, Jacob Mueller, Lawrence Vogt, Gilbert Boie, Marie Atkinson, Gertrude Besch, and Bertha Atkinson; (third row) Anthony Besch, Lawrence Enders, Florence Theis (teacher), Marie Foxen, Helen Rutchman, and Emma Enders. (Courtesy of the Winfield Historical Society.)

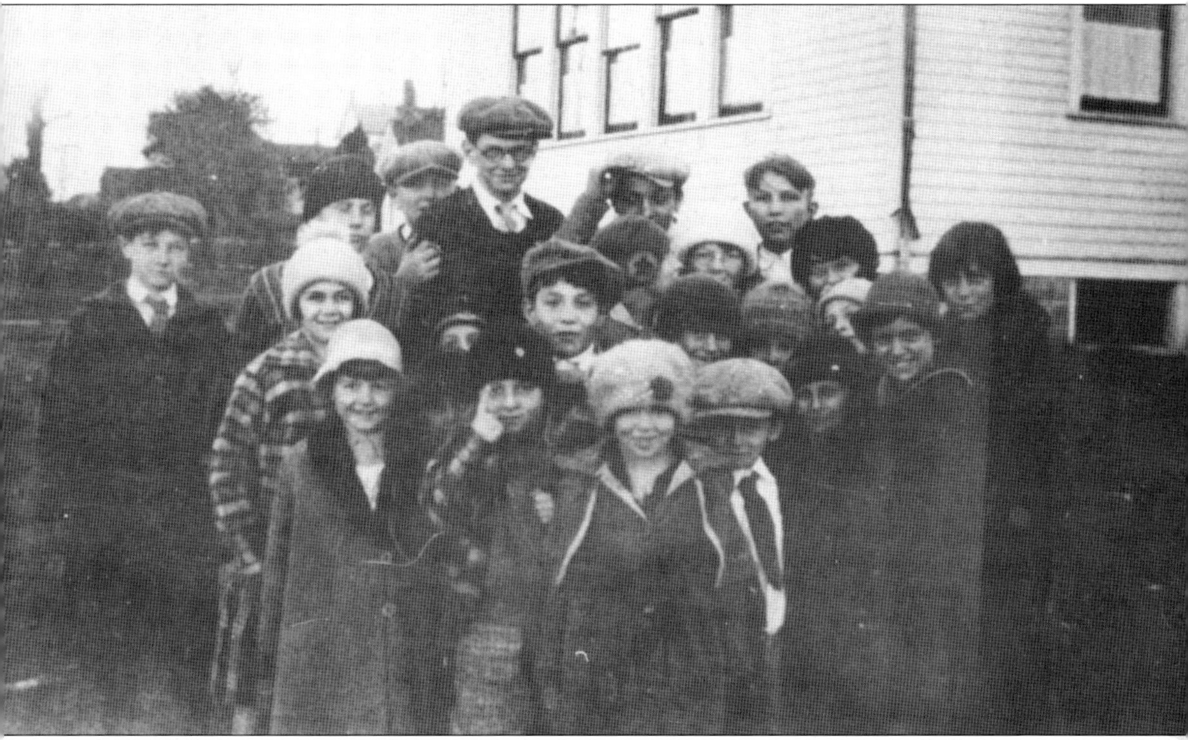

Students at the Winfield Public School gather for a photograph in 1927. Identification of those in the image is limited, but in the first row far left is Virginia Hopkins. In the center with his cap askew is Waldeman Hirt. In the back row, standing tall and wearing glasses is Frank Hartray, while Rudolph Neubauer Jr. is the boy not wearing a hat at right in the back row. Jerome Hartray is at the far left in the back row. (Courtesy of Rose Marie Enders and the Winfield Historical Society.)

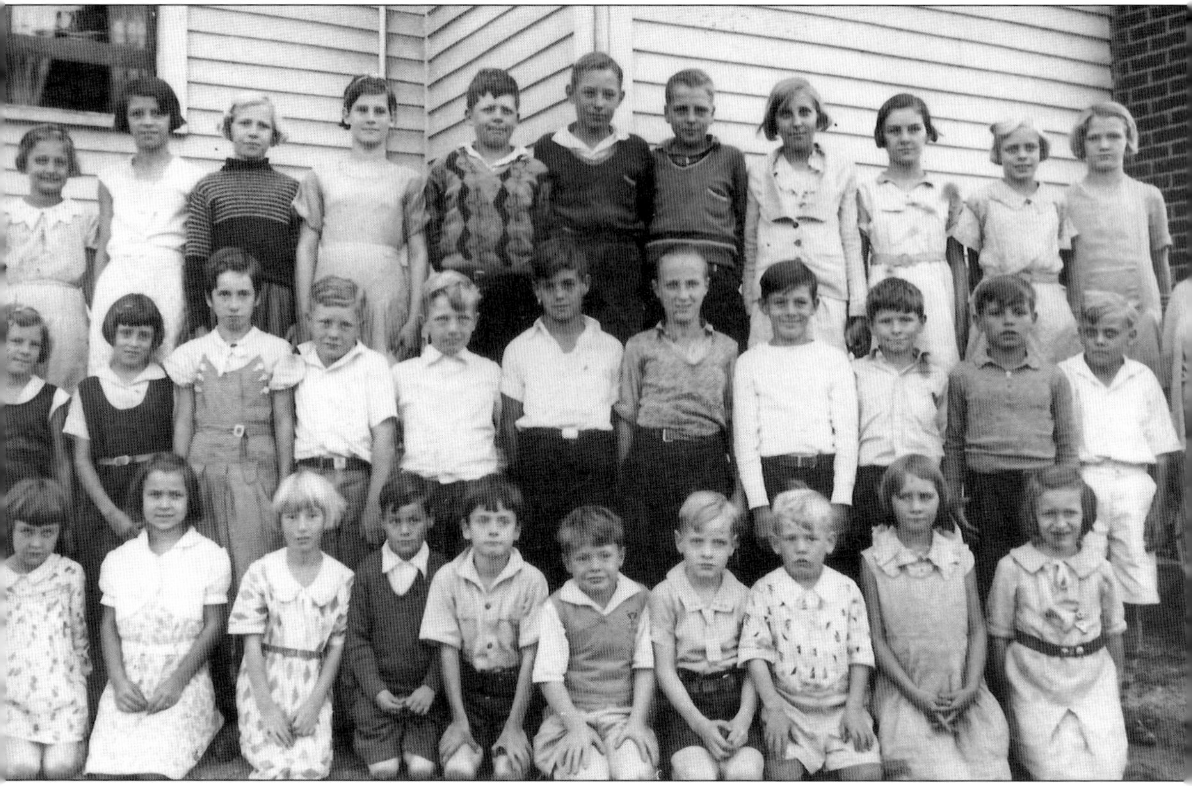

Students and their teacher at the Winfield Public School in 1934 gather for a class photograph. From left to right are (first row) Eleanor Miller, Arlene Poltrock, Harriet Brehm, Jack Penniall, Haig Naylor, unidentified, Leonard Allanson, Robert Brehm, Sheila Penniall, and Evelyn Jacobs; (second row) Theresa Kailer, Agnes Mummert, Nancy Naylor, Walter Orwall, unidentified, Ralph Penniall, Lamont Hanley, William Cox, Harry Fisher, Heinz Dresch, Harold Vogt, and Mabelle Cavanaugh (teacher); (third row) Eileen Orwall, Helen Cox, Shirley Neubauer, Dorothy Kailer, James Getz, Rudolph Neubauer Jr., Frank Gould, Christine Vogt, June Oneson, Winnie Allanson, and unidentified. (Courtesy of the Winfield Historical Society.)

Seven

THE REST FARM AND SANITARIUM

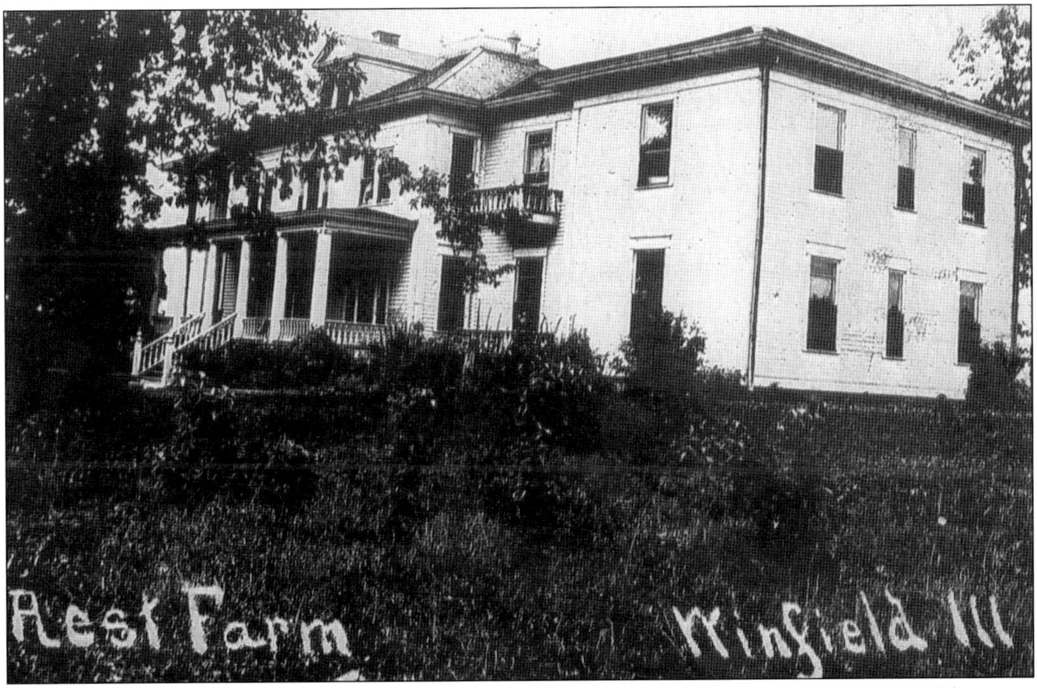

Jessie Forsythe selected Winfield to be the site of a new rest home that she and her sister Christine would be operating in November 1897. The rest home that is pictured is a two-story frame building (no longer standing) set upon a wooded hillside that is near what is now the entrance to Central DuPage Hospital. The rest home was actually a rest-cure center that specialized in rest and massage for its patients. Its attendants were referred to as nurses. The rest farm was in existence until 1908, when following the death of her sister, Jessie sold the establishment to Mrs. Emanuel Mandel. Jessie died a year later in a traffic accident. (Courtesy of the Winfield Historical Society.)

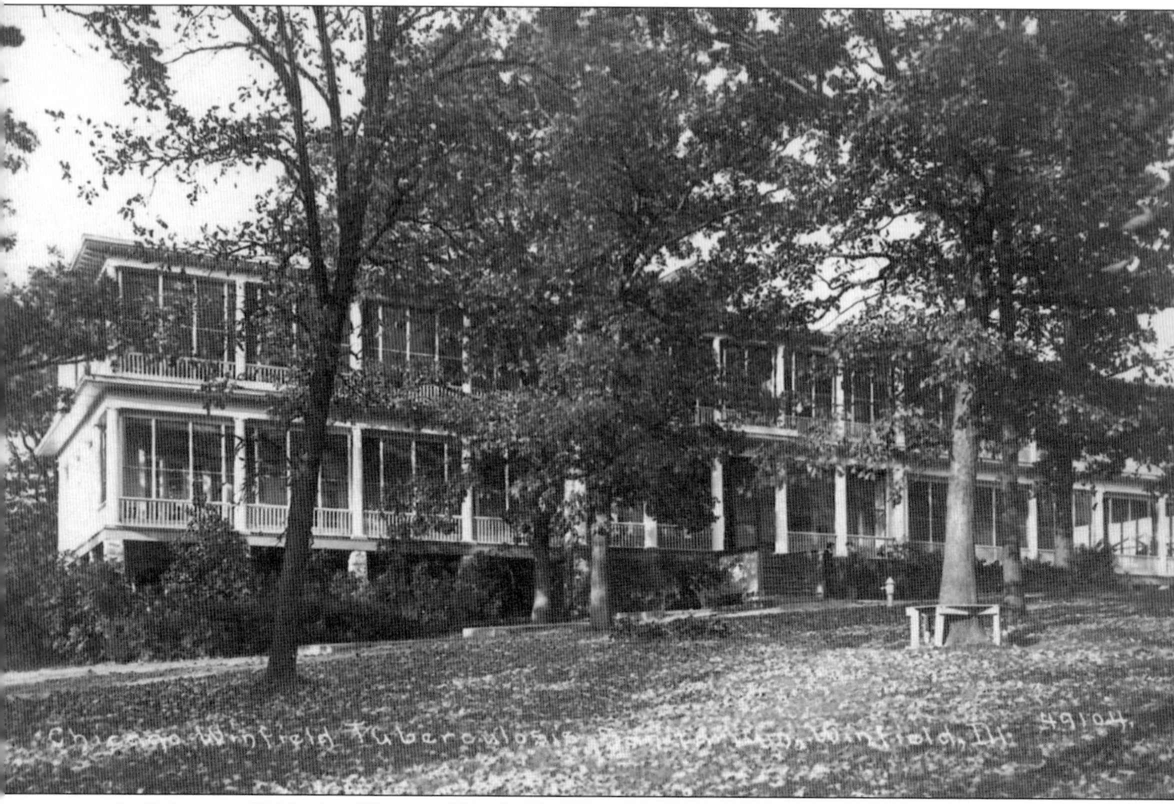

In February 1909, the Chicago-Winfield Tuberculosis Sanitarium opened on the grounds of the old rest farm. The sanitarium was a new facility for tuberculosis patients. In its February 5 issue, the *Wheaton Illinoian* reports that "Charles A. Stonehill, president of the Chicago Mercantile Company, has given the building and grounds to three Chicago charitable organizations—the Baron Hirsch Woman's Club, the Jewish Consumption Relief Society, and the Willing Workers. The institution will be run by these societies, but will be nonsectarian." In this photograph is how the first sanitarium building looked upon its opening. (Courtesy of the Winfield Historical Society.)

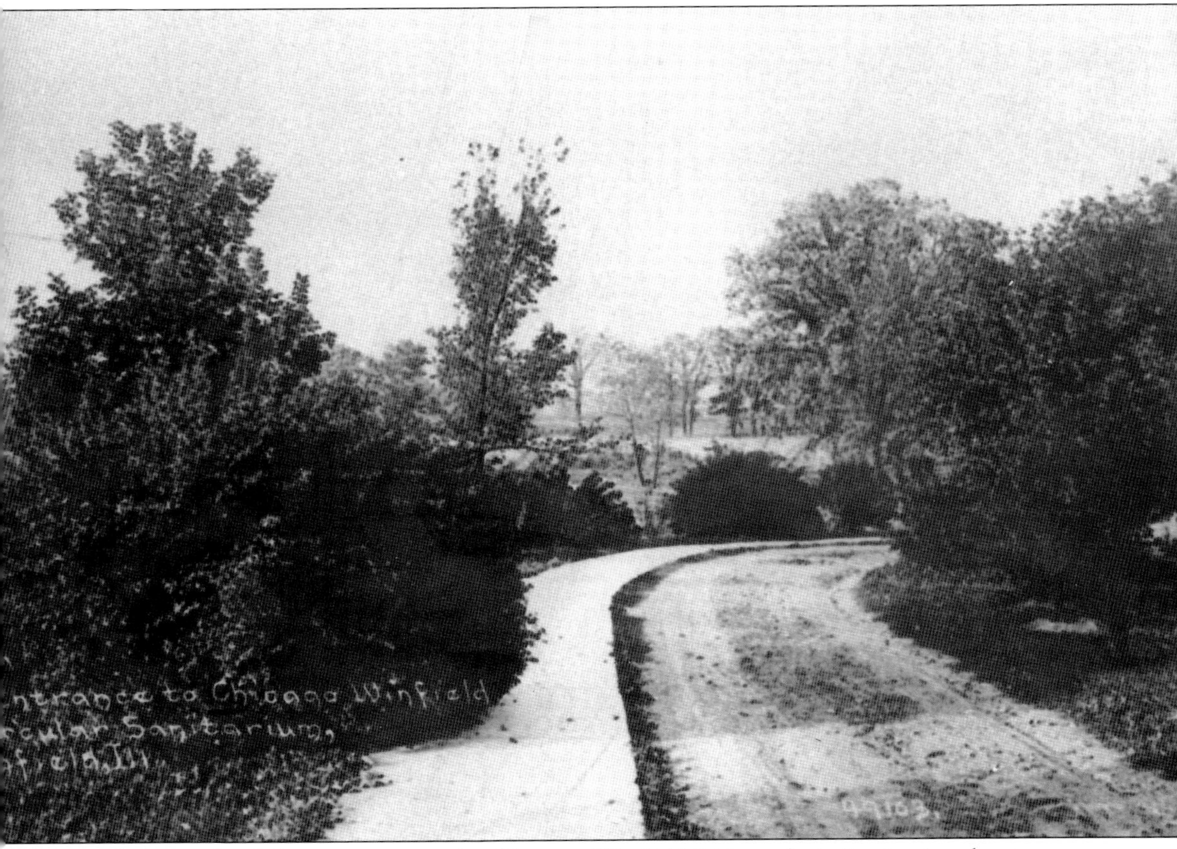

This photograph of the entrance to the Chicago-Winfield Tuberculosis Sanitarium begins to give an idea of the size of the institution's land. The sanitarium was stated to have 100 feet of frontage, and 20 acres of the sanitarium's grounds were to be set aside for poultry and fruit farming. Dr. Theodore V. Sachs was the chief of staff for the sanitarium. (Courtesy of the Winfield Historical Society.)

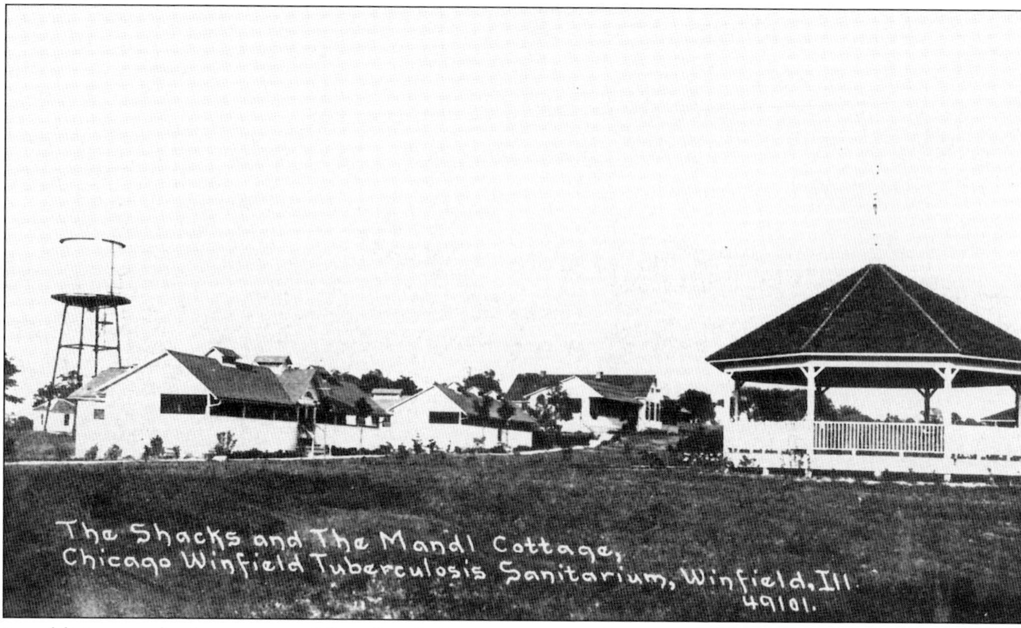

In addition to the frontage and farmland, the sanitarium also consisted of seven cottages that could accommodate up to 10 people at a time. The photograph above focuses on the sanitarium's open-air shacks, Mandel Cottage, and gazebo in 1910. The one below gives an additional view of these cottages. Additionally, the sanitarium was fitted with French doors rather than windows. This was done with the intention that beds could be rolled out on the veranda. An article in the *Wheaton Illinoian* notes the improved management of the sanitarium and the new walks that had been built on the grounds. (Above, courtesy of the DuPage County History Museum; below, courtesy of the Winfield Historical Society.)

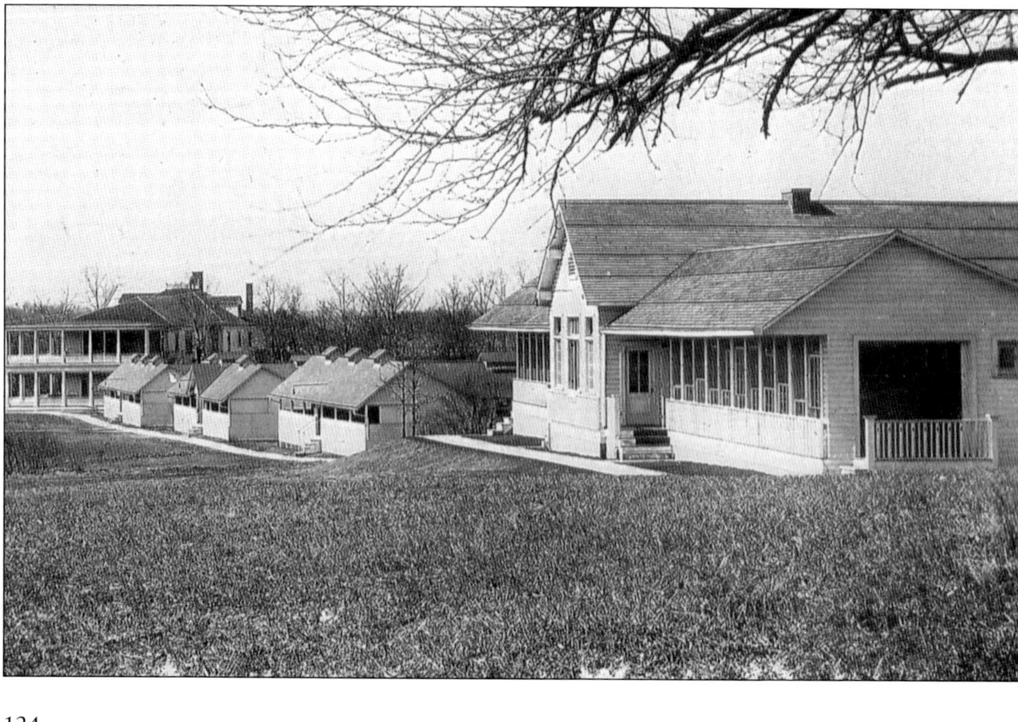

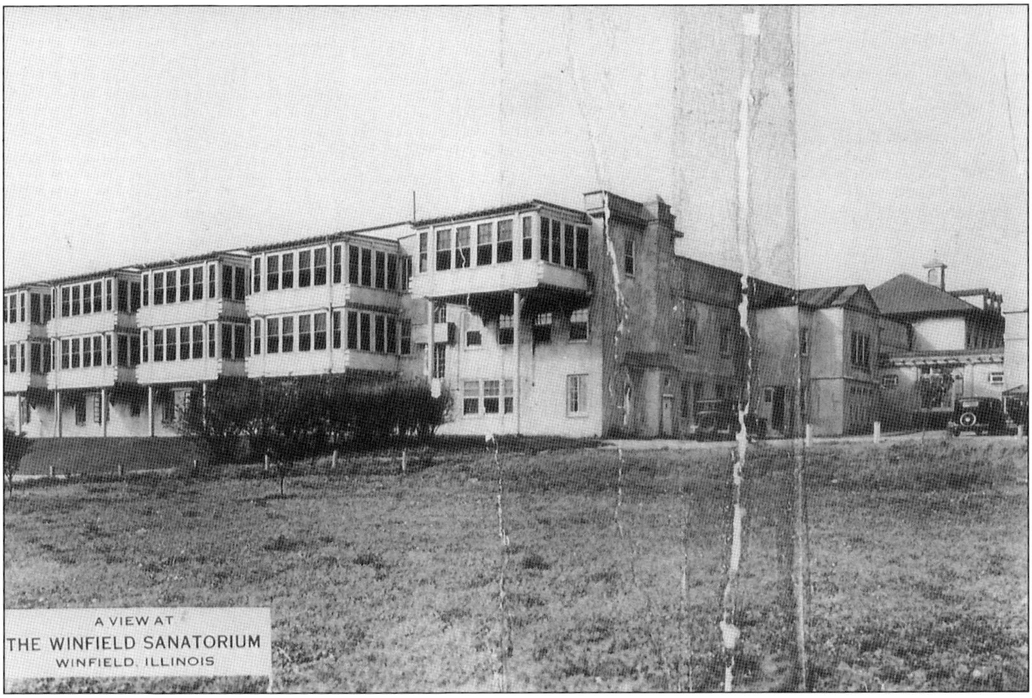

The young village and sanitarium had a close relationship. The sanitarium employed many local residents of early Winfield. Additional land would soon be acquired to the east of the sanitarium, which would prove to be rather handy. This was because the original sanitarium building burned in a fire. A new sanitarium was built on the new land, and this second building is the focus of these two photographs. The lifespan for this second building, though, was rather short, as it too would be destroyed in a fire in the early 1940s. (Both, courtesy of the Winfield Historical Society.)

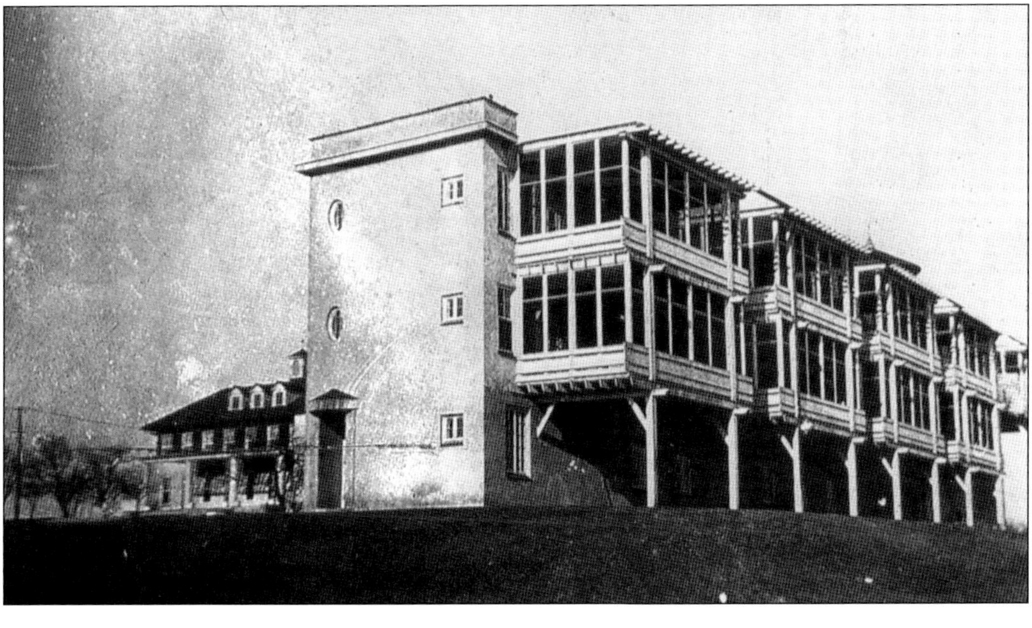

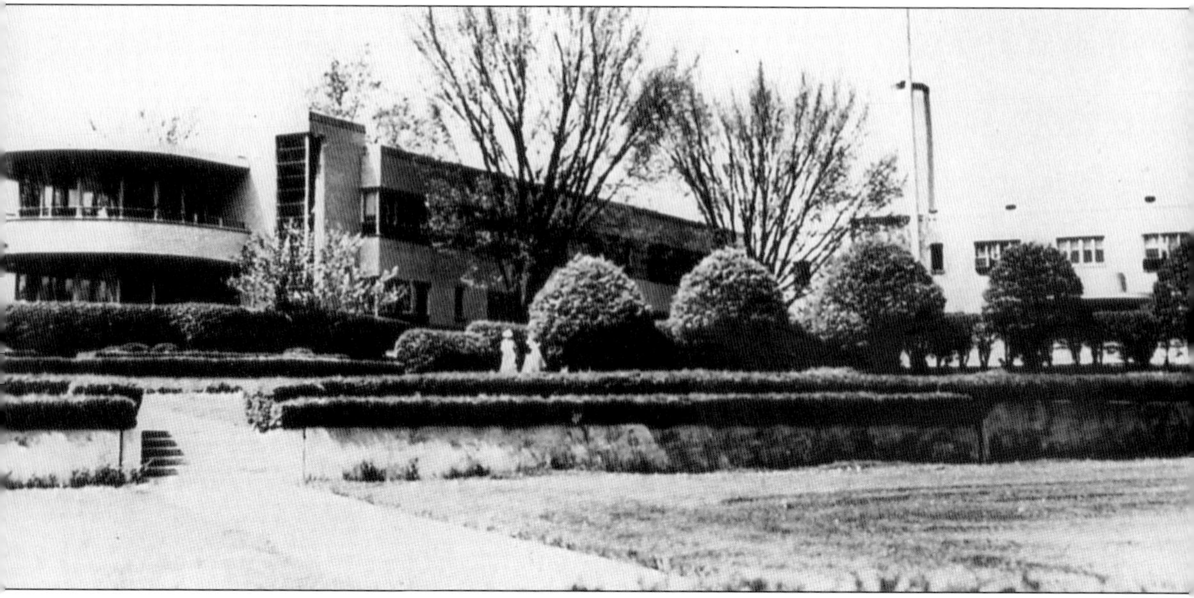

After the burning of the second sanitarium building, a third building was constructed. However, the advancement in medical practices in treating tuberculosis began to wear on the sanitarium. Those being treated for tuberculosis were declining each year, with 158 listed patients there in 1957. In 1962, the sanitarium passed from the Jewish Federation of Chicago to the Central DuPage Hospital (CDH) Association. The building that is pictured here was incorporated into the new CDH Association complex. (Courtesy of the Winfield Historical Society.)

About the Winfield Historical Society

It is the mission of the Winfield Historical Society to present and educate the community about the history of Winfield and its surroundings. To that end, the historical society has renovated Hedges Station, the oldest building in Winfield as well as the oldest standing rail depot in Illinois, to house a local history museum. There, the historical society will collect and preserve photographs, papers, and artifacts in its collection while presenting exhibits and programs designed to engage and educate visitors. For more information about the Winfield Historical Society, Hedges Station, and upcoming programs and events, please visit its website, www.winfieldhistory.org.

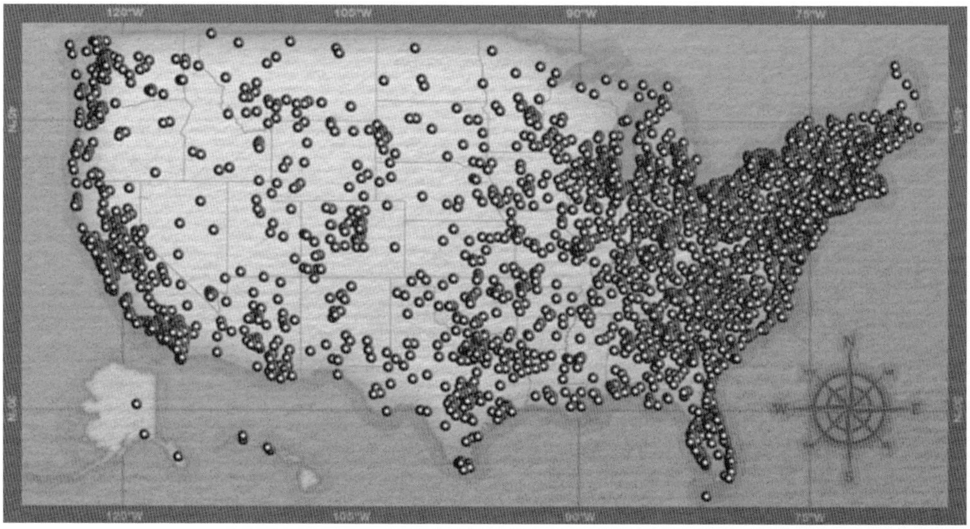